HISTORICAL DICTIONARIES OF RELIGIONS, PHILOSOPHIES, AND MOVEMENTS
Edited by Jon Woronoff

Historical Dictionary of the Gay Liberation Movement

Gay Men and the Quest for Social Justice

Ronald J. Hunt

*Historical Dictionaries of Religions,
Philosophies, and Movements, No. 22*

NON CIRCULATING

The Scarecrow Press, Inc.
Lanham, Maryland, and London
1999

SCARECROW PRESS, INC.

Published in the United States of America
by Scarecrow Press, Inc.
4720 Boston Way
Lanham, Maryland 20706

4 Pleydell Gardens, Folkestone
Kent CT20 2DN, England

British Library Cataloguing in Publication Information Available

Library of Congress Cataloging-in-Publication Data

Hunt, Ronald J., 1940–
   Historical dictionary of the gay liberation movement: gay men
and the quest for social justice / Ronald J. Hunt.
     p. cm. — (Historical dictionaries of religions,
philosophies, and movements : no. 22)
    Includes bibliographical references.
    ISBN 0-8108-3587-8 (alk. paper)
    I. Gay liberation movement—Historical dictionaries. I. Title.
II. Series.
HQ76.5.H86   1999
305.9′0664—dc21
                                       98-39383
                                        CIP

To

W. S. Gorup

Contents

Acknowledgments

In 1978, I was approached by a group of gay men at Ohio University who asked me to sponsor a readings course on gay politics. Despite the fact that I was openly gay at the time and was a Ph.D. in Political Science, I was woefully unprepared for the task. This readings course was my first exposure to the literature on gay politics, with many of the readings selected by the students. It was this experience that became the catalyst for the development of "Gay and Lesbian Politics," a course that I initially taught as an Arts and Sciences experimental course and that I have subsequently offered since 1984 as a regularly scheduled course in the Department of Political Science. I am indebted to these individuals as well as to the hundreds of students that I have susequently encountered who have taught me much of what I know about the subject. Many of these students were associated with the university's gay, lesbian, bisexual, transgendered student association (variously known as the Gay Peoples Alliance, GALA, and Open Doors).

I am also grateful to the Department of Political Science, which afforded me the opportunity to schedule "Gay and Lesbian Politics" at a moment in time when such course offerings were exceedingly rare and fraught with controversy. The College of Arts and Sciences has also been instrumental in the development of this course through the aforementioned opportunity to offer the course on an experimental basis, and by allowing a faculty development leave in 1996 that afforded me the opportunity to begin work on this volume in earnest.

I am indebted as well to a number of individuals. Bill Gorup and I have discussed many of the issues presented in this volume so extensively that I am unsure where his ideas leave off and my own begin. I'm grateful to the Reverend Jan Griesinger, Tony Rominsky, and David Rayside for providing me with information that proved instrumental in the completion of this volume. Alden Waitt read an initial draft of the manuscript, and her suggestions and editorial help improved the final version enormously. And, finally, I'm indebted to Jon Woronoff, the series editor, for his careful review of the text and for his patience with my idiosyncrasies. His keen eye helped refine many of the details in this historical dictionary.

It goes without saying that I alone am responsible for the final version of this volume, a volume that focuses on the contributions of gay and bisexual men. In no way should it be inferred that the role of lesbians has been any less extensive. I hope that readers will find the book helpful in gaining a greater understanding of the gay liberation movement from its inception to the present day.

Editor's Foreword

Of the various movements in this series, none is so young as gay liberation. But it is also one of the most vigorous, with new groups and organizations continually emerging. Starting with the efforts of only a handful of individuals and languishing for years with organizational memberships in the hundreds, gay rights organizations now boast thousands of members, whereas the movement as a whole involves millions. Beginning with a few causes, the agenda has grown into new areas, and new strategies have been adopted to achieve the goals. Meanwhile, the movement has spread geographically. Once limited to Europe and North America, it now covers most of the world. During the past century, the gay liberation movement has made enormous progress. But it still has much farther to go and future progress promises to be as hard won as that achieved by previous generations.

This evolution is described in the *Historical Dictionary of the Gay Liberation Movement*. It describes many of the key organizations and their leaders, many of the essential issues and the range of strategies, and the situation in numerous countries. This last aspect is notable, because gay liberation is no longer a "Western" phenomenon, and it is important to know what is happening elsewhere. Most of the information is provided through extensive entries in the dictionary; the introduction sums up the overall situation and the chronology traces the progression of the movement. There is also a comprehensive bibliography that reflects the burgeoning literature. This volume focuses on the impact of gay and bisexual men (and their allies) on the gay liberation movement. A subsequent volume will trace the role of lesbians in the movement.

This volume was written by Ronald J. Hunt. Dr. Hunt studied economics and politics at Ohio State University where he received his Ph.D. in Political Science. He is currently associate professor of Political Science at Ohio University in Athens, Ohio where he teaches "Gay and Lesbian Politics." He has been involved in a wide range of political as well as professional activities devoted to increasing the public's awareness of gay and lesbian issues and to advancing the cause of gay and lesbian rights.

Jon Woronoff
Series Editor

Acronyms

AC	Action Committee (Aktionsausschuss)
ACT-UP	Aids Coalition to Unleash Power
AGLESC	Action Group for the Liberty of Expression of Sexual Choice (Grupo de Acción por la Libertad de Expresión de la Elección Sexual)
AIDS	Acquired immune deficiency syndrome
ALI	American Law Institute
AMO	Azanian Men's Organization
ANC	African National Congress
APA	American Psychiatric Association
APPGA	All-Party Parliamentary Group on AIDS
ASK	Association for Social Knowledge
AT	Albany Trust
BSSP	British Society for the Study of Sex Psychology
CAMP	Campaign Against Moral Persecution
CGRO	Coalition for Gay Rights in Ontario
CHE	Committee (later Campaign) for Homosexual Equality
COS	Community of the Special (Gemeinschaft der Eigenen)
CPUSA	Communist Party of the United States of America
CRC	Culture and Recreational Center (Cultuur-en-Ontspannings Centrum)
CRH	Council on Religion and the Homosexual
DOB	Daughters of Bilitis
DOMA	Defense of Marriage Act
DS	Dorian Society
DSHC	Dutch Scientific-Humanitarian Committee (Nederlandsch Wetenschappelijk-Humanitair Komitee)
EC	European Community
ECARH	Emergency Committee Against the Repression of Homosexuals (Comité d'Urgence Anti-Répression Homosexuelle)
ECHO	East Coast Homophile Organizations
ENDA	Employment Non-Discrimination Act
ERCHO	Eastern Regional Conference of Homophile Organizations

EU	European Union
FRG	Federal Republic of Germany
GAA	Gay Activists Alliance
GAIDE	Gay Aid Identification Development and Enrichment
GALZ	Gays and Lesbians in Zimbabwe
GASA	Gay Association of South Africa
GDR	German Democratic Republic
GFA	German Friendship Association (Deutscher Freundschaftsverband)
GLAC	Gay and Lesbian Association of Cuba
GLF	Gay Liberation Front
GLOW	Gay and Lesbian Organization of the Witwatersrand
GPHL	Group Pride for Homosexual Liberation (Grupo de Orgullo Homosexual de Liberación)
GRNL	Gay Rights National Lobby
HIB	Homosexual Interest Group Berlin (Homosexuelle Interessen-Gemeinschaft Berlin)
HIV	Human immunodeficiency virus
HL	Homeros Lambda
HLFM	Homosexual Liberation Front of Mexico (Frente de Liberación Homosexual de Mexico)
HLG	Homosexual Liberation Group (Groupe de Libération Homosexuelle)
HLG–PEL	Homosexual Liberation Group–Politics and Everyday Life (Groupe de Libération Homosexuelle–Politique et Quotidien)
HLRF	Homosexual Law Reform Fund
HLRS	Homosexual Law Reform Society
HOSI	Homosexual Initiative (Homosexuelle Initiative)
HRC	Human Rights Campaign
HRCF	Human Rights Campaign Fund
HUAC	House Un-American Activities Committee
HV	HOSI Vienna (HOSI Wien)
ICCPR	International Covenant on Civil and Political Rights
ICSE	International Committee for Sexual Equality
IGA	International Gay Association
IGLHRC	International Gay and Lesbian Human Rights Commission
ILGA	International Lesbian and Gay Association
ILGA–J	International Lesbian and Gay Association–Japan
ILGA–P	International Lesbian and Gay Association–Portugal
INLGO	International Network of Lesbian and Gay Officials
ISS	Institute for Sexual Science (Institut für Sexualwissenschaft)

JCHON	Joint Council for Homophile Organizations in Norway (Fellesraadet for Homofile Organisasjoner i Norge)
LAGO	Lesbians and Gays against Oppression
LASE	Latvian Association for Sexual Equality
LCE	League for Civil Education
LCHR	Leadership Council on Human Rights
LGAP	Lambda Groups Association of Poland
LHLG	Lambda Homosexual Liberation Group (Grupo Lambda de Liberación Homosexual)
LLDEF	Lambda Legal Defense and Education Fund
LP	Lambda Prague (Lambda Praha)
MCC	Metropolitan Community Church
MR	*Mattachine Review*
MS	Mattachine Society
MSNY	Mattachine Society of New York
MSW	Mattachine Society of Washington, D.C.
MULH	Moscow Union of Lesbians and Homosexuals
NA/1948	The Norwegian Alliance of 1948 (Det Norske Forbundet Av 1948)
NACHO	North American Conference of Homophile Organizations
NAIH COC	Netherlands Association for the Integration of Homosexuality COC (Nederlandse Vereniging tot Integratie van Homoseksualiteit COC)
NASER	National Alliance for Sexual Equal Rights (Riksförbundet för Sexuellt Likaberättigande)
NFHO	National Federation of Homophile Organizations
NGLTF	National Gay and Lesbian Task Force
NGT	National Gay Task Force
NOGL	National Organization of Gays and Lesbians (Landsforeningen for Bøsser og Lesbiske)
NYDOB	New York Daughters of Bilitis
NZHLRS	New Zealand Homosexual Law Reform Society
OLGA	Organization of Lesbian and Gay Activists
OSCE	Organization for Security and Cooperation in Europe
PAF	Phone-A-Friend
PAL	Paedophile Action for Liberation
PFLAG	Parents and Friends of Lesbians and Gays
PIE	Paedophile Information Exchange
PRC	People's Republic of China
PRT	Revolutionary Workers' Party (Partido Revolucionario de los Trabajadores)
PWA	Person with AIDS
RF	Radical Faeries

RHAF–F	Revolutionary Homosexual Action Front–France (Front Homosexuel d'Action Révolutionnaire)
RHAF–M	Revolutionary Homosexual Action Front–Mexico (Frente Homosexual de Acción Revolucionaria)
SA	Storm Troops (Sturmabteilung)
SER	Sexual Equal Rights (Sexuaalinen Tasavertaisuus R.Y.)
SGL	Sydney Gay Liberation
SHC	Scientific-Humanitarian Committee (Wissenschaftlich-humanitäres Komitee)
SHL	Student Homophile League
SHR	Society for Human Rights
SHWG	Swiss Homosexual Work(ing) Groups (Homosexuelle Arbeitsgruppen der Schweiz)
SIR	Society for Individual Rights
SLRS	Sexual Law Reform Society
SMG	Scottish Minorities Group
SOH	Swiss Organization of Homophiles (Schweizerische Organisation der Homophilen)
SS	Elite Guard (Schutzstaffel)
STAR	Street Transvestite Action Revolutionaries
TAO	Transvestite Transexual Action Organization
TAT	Transsexuals and Transvestites
TOGS	Transvaal Organization for Gay Sport
TWGR	Third World Gay Revolution
UN	United Nations
USFI	Union for Sexual Freedom in Ireland
VBA	Veterans Benevolent Association
WLSR	World League for Sexual Reform

Chronology

1864   Birth of the early homosexual rights movement: The publication of the first of 12 volumes on the subject of same-sex love by Karl Heinrich Ulrichs, under the pseudonym Numa Numantius. In this collection of essays, Ulrichs advances the notion that sexual orientation is inborn and protests the inhumane treatment of urnings.

1865–1867   Ulrichs speaks publicly at two legal congresses—at Graz in 1865 and at Munich in 1867—in opposition to articles in the Prussian legal code that criminalize male sexual intercourse. These are the first recorded instances of public utterances protesting the oppression of same-sex love.

1868   The first use of the terms *heterosexuality/homosexuality* by Karl Maria Kertbeny in a letter to Ulrichs.

1869   Kertbeny protests the criminalization of male homosexuality in two pamphlets critical of the Prussian legal code. This marks the first printed use of the terms *homosexuality/heterosexuality.*

1871   The consolidation of modern Germany. The adoption of Paragraph 175 of the German Imperial Code of Laws that criminalized homosexual relations. The repeal of Paragraph 175 became the principal focus of the early homosexual rights movement in Germany.

1886   Adoption of the "Outrages on Public Decency" amendment (the Labouchère amendment) to the Criminal Law Amendment Act of 1885 in Great Britain. This British sodomy statute supplemented the Act of 25 Henry VIII, c.6, the original British sodomy law enacted in 1533. Both laws became the target of repeal efforts in Britain after World War II.

1895   The arrest and conviction of the prominent playwright and writer Oscar Wilde in London, for violation of the

"Outrages on Public Decency" statute. His imprisonment became a rallying cry for those committed to the emancipation of homosexuals.

1897   Founding, in Berlin, of the first homosexual rights organization in the world, the Wissenschaftlich-humanitäres Komitee (Scientific-Humanitarian Committee [SHC]), by the noted German sexologist Magnus Hirschfeld and others. Hirschfeld initiates petition to repeal Paragraph 175.

1902   Founding of the Gemeinschaft der Eigenen (Community of the Special [COS]), a second German homosexual rights organization, by former members of the Scientific-Humanitarian Committee. Although ideological foes, the Community of the Special cooperates with the Scientific-Humanitarian Committee in the effort to repeal Paragraph 175.

1910   Draft penal code extending the provisions of Paragraph 175 to women introduced into the Reichstag. Extension of 175 to women subsequently defeated in parliament.

1914   Foundation of the British Society for the Study of Sex Psychology (BSSP), a scholarly society devoted to the dissemination of the scientific understanding of sexuality. Between its founding and World War II, the society advances the cause of homosexual liberation through scholarly studies of sexual orientation.

1914–1918   World War I.

1918   USSR abolishes the Czarist legal code and with it Article 995 (the Russian sodomy statute).

1919   Creation of the Institut für Sexualwissenschaft (Institute for Sexual Science) by Magnus Hirschfeld. Housed in the same building in Berlin as the Scientific-Humanitarian Committee, the institute sponsors studies of sexuality and acts as a repository for information on human sexuality.

1920   Formation of a coalition of German gay groups by Kurt Hiller, the Aktionsausschuss (Action Committee [AC]) to renew the effort to repeal Paragraph 175 after World War I. The AC was composed of the Scientific-Humanitarian Committee, the Community of the Special, as well as the Deutscher Freundschaftsverband (German Friendship Association [GFA]), a third homosexual rights organization founded in 1919. The AC disintegrated in 1923 after the withdrawal of the GFA.

1921   The World League for Sexual Reform (WLSR), an international scholarly society devoted to the scientific study of human sexuality, is founded by individuals associated with the ISS and the BSSP. Among other projects, the WLSR promotes the cause of homosexual rights through its studies of sexual behavior and its appeals to decriminalize consensual adult same-sex relations. The WLSR disbands after its 1932 meeting in Brno.

1924   The first homosexual rights organization in the Americas, the Society for Human Rights, is founded in Chicago. This short-lived group was inspired by the Bund für Menschenrecht (League for Human Rights), originally known as the GFA.

1925   The Kartell für Reform des Sexualstrafrechts (Coalition for the Reform of the Sexual Crimes Code) fills the void left by the collapse of the AC. This coalition included the SHC, and six other organizations, including women's rights groups. Its 1927 draft penal code, which called for the decriminalization of male homosexual relations, was never enacted.

1933   The building that housed the SHC and ISS in Berlin is ransacked by Nazi youth on 6 May; most of the contents were burned on 10 May as part of a nationwide mass book burning.

1934   USSR recriminalizes sodomy between men in the form of Article 154a.

1935   Paragraph 175a, a statute that broadened the definition of sodomy to include, among other things, sexual foreplay between men, is enacted in Germany. 175a leads to a great increase in the number of convictions and the incarceration of thousands of gay men in civilian prisons.

Gay rights groups banned in Germany.

1939–1945   World War II. Thousands of gay men (forced to wear pink triangles) incarcerated in German concentration camps.

1945–1946   Origins of the modern homosexual rights movement. After the war, reemergence in Europe of homosexual rights organizations, such as the "Shakespeare Club," the forerunner of the Cultuur-en-Ontspannings Centrum (Cultural and Recreational Center), in the Netherlands.

The beginning of the homosexual rights movement in North America with the creation of the Veterans Benevolent Association in New York City.

1951   The Mattachine Society (MS) is founded in Los Angeles by Harry Hay. The MS, together with One and the first lesbian organization, the Daughters of Bilitis (1955), were the mainstays of the gay rights movement in the United States prior to Stonewall.

1953   The first French gay rights organization, Arcadie, is developed out of the circulation lists of André Baudry's journal *Arcadie*. Arcadie fights the institution of the Pétain-de Gaulle law, which established unequal ages of consent for homosexual versus heterosexual intercourse, and becomes the primary gay rights organization in France until the emergence of more radical organizations in the early 1970s.

1957   Publication of the "Report of the Committee on Homosexual Offenses and Prostitution" (the Wolfenden report) in Great Britain. The report recommends the decriminalization of homosexual sodomy.

1958   Formation, in Britain, of the Homosexual Law Reform Society (HLRS), to push for the legal reforms advocated by the Wolfenden report. The HLRS becomes Britain's first gay rights organization.

U.S. Supreme Court rules that impoundment of *One Magazine* by the Los Angeles postmaster constituted a violation of freedom of the press.

1961   The state of Illinois becomes the first U.S. state to rescind a sodomy statute. At the time, all states in the union criminalized sodomy.

1964   The Association for Social Knowledge (ASK) founded in Canada. One of Canada's first gay and lesbian rights organizations, ASK campaigns for the elimination of Canada's sodomy laws, derivatives of British statutes, the Act of 25 Henry VIII, c.6, and the Labouchère Amendment.

The Society for Individual Rights (SIR) is founded in San Francisco.

The first gay and lesbian rights organization in New Zealand, the Dorian Society (subsequently renamed the New Zealand Homosexual Law Reform Society) is founded. It led a successful 22-year battle to rescind New Zealand's sodomy statutes, a legacy of British colonialism.

1967   The Sexual Offenses Act decriminalizes sodomy in England and Wales between consenting adults. Provisions of the 1967 statute extended to Scotland in 1980 and to Northern Ireland in 1982.

1968   The German Democratic Republic abolishes Paragraph 175, decriminalizing homosexual sodomy in East Germany for the first time since its original enactment in 1871.

The Homosexual Law Reform Fund, the first of many gay and lesbian rights organizations in South Africa, is founded in Johannesburg. It successfully fought the enactment of a sodomy statute.

1969   Following the lead of East Germany, the Federal Republic of Germany (West Germany) abolishes provisions of Paragraph 175 pertaining to consensual adult homosexual sodomy.

Canadian Criminal Code reform, similar to the Sexual Offenses Act in Britain, decriminalizes consensual adult homosexual relations.

Stonewall riots in New York City from June 27–29. Origins of the contemporary gay and lesbian rights movement.

The Gay Liberation Front (GLF) is founded on 31 July in New York City. A more overtly political group than either the MS or the DOB, the GLF expands the gay and lesbian rights agenda to include other left-wing causes and attempts to build coalitions with other minority groups. Although short-lived, GLF groups quickly spring up around the United States and around the world, transforming the style and content of the gay and lesbian rights movement.

Gay Activist Alliance (GAA) formed by dissident members of the GLF unhappy with the direction of the GLF. The more structured and mainstream GAA focuses on civil rights initiatives, electing gays and lesbians to office, as well as to fighting for the recision of sodomy laws. The GAA becomes the prototype of contemporary gay and lesbian civil rights groups such as the National Gay Task Force and the Human Rights Campaign Fund.

1970   The international impact of the GLF was felt as far away as Australia, with the formation of the Campaign against Moral Persecution (CAMP). Based in Sydney, CAMP initiated a long, but ultimately successful, drive to repeal Australian sodomy statutes, a process only recently completed.

1973–1974   The American Psychiatric Association (APA) rescinds its classification of homosexuality as a mental illness after several years of debate, a process initiated by the assault on the 1970 convention of the APA by activists associated with the GLF, GAA, and MS.

Foundation of the National Gay Task Force (now the National Gay and Lesbian Task Force) in New York City, now the oldest gay, lesbian, and bisexual rights organization in the United States.

The first federal civil rights legislation designed to protect the rights of lesbians and gays is introduced into the U.S. Congress by Representatives Bella Abzug and Edward Koch. Although neither it nor any similar civil rights legislation has ever been enacted at the federal level in the United States, it is the forerunner of the Employment Non-Discrimination Act, currently pending action in Congress.

The first gay and lesbian rights group in the GDR to seek official recognition from the government was the Homosexuelle Interessen-Gemeinschaft Berlin (Homosexual Interest Group Berlin). Although their petition was rejected, this organization set the stage for emergence of gay and lesbian activism in East Germany and may have been the first politically active gay and lesbian rights group in Eastern Europe.

1977   Among the first gay and lesbian civil rights bills enacted in the Americas were those in the province of Quebec, Canada, and Dade County, Florida.

Election of the first openly gay male candidate for public office in the United States, Harvey Milk, to the San Francisco Board of Supervisors (City Council).

1978   One of the first public demonstrations advocating gay and lesbian rights in Mexico, on 26 July, is staged by the Frente Homosexual de Acción Revolucionaria (Revolutionary Homosexual Action Front) at a Mexico City march commemorating the Cuban Revolution. This organization presaged the emergence of other politically active gay and lesbian organizations throughout Mexico as well as Central and South America.

Harvey Milk and Mayor George Moscone are assassinated on 27 November, shortly after the enactment of a gay and lesbian civil rights bill in San Francisco.

The International Gay Association (now the International Lesbian and Gay Association) is founded in Coventry, England, by the Campaign for Homosexual Equality, a British organization, and the CRC from the Netherlands. This is the first international organization devoted to gay and lesbian civil rights.

1981   Norway enacts civil rights legislation protecting the rights of gays and lesbians, thus becoming the first country in the world to enact a nationwide law. The Norwegian legislation establishes a trend emulated by other Scandinavian countries as well as France and other countries, such as the Netherlands.

1982   Wisconsin becomes the first U.S. state to enact a gay and lesbian civil rights bill. Ten other states have followed the Wisconsin example (Maine rescinded its statute in 1998).

1986   *Bowers v. Hardwick.* Countering a trend toward the decriminalization of sodomy in Europe and Canada, the U.S. Supreme Court upholds the constitutionality of U.S. states to prohibit sodomy in their criminal codes.

New Zealand decriminalizes adult homosexual relations.

1989   The enactment of the Danish Registered Partnership Act on 26 May establishes the precedent of the legal recognition of gay and lesbian marriages. Other Scandinavian countries, as well as such countries as the Netherlands, have emulated the Danish example, and gay and lesbian partnerships are currently under negotiation in the ongoing unification processes of the European Union.

1993   On 5 May, in *Baehr v. Lewin,* the Hawaii Supreme Court ruled that the state's refusal to grant marriage licenses to gay and lesbian couples constituted an apparent violation of the state constitution's "equal protection of the laws" provision. The high court orders the State of Hawaii to appear in a Hawaii trial court to defend its contention that "compelling state interests" justified its discrimination against same-sex marriages.

1994 Adoption of the interim constitution of South Africa. Reflecting the influence of gay rights activists, such as Simon Nkoli, the interim constitution includes sexual orientation as a constitutionally protected right. South Africa thus became one of only three countries in the world that accords gay and lesbian rights constitutional protection (along with the Netherlands and Canada).

1996 *Romer v. Evans.* Widely regarded to be the first significant victory for gays and lesbians in the U.S. Supreme Court. In this historic decision, the Supreme Court ruled that U.S. states may not prohibit the enactment of civil rights legislation protecting the rights of gays and lesbians, thus defeating a political strategy of conservative religious groups such as Colorado for Family Values.

Baehr v. Miike (formerly *Baehr v. Lewin*). Hawaii state trial court judge rules against the State of Hawaii and orders the issuance of marriage licenses to gay and lesbian couples. The court stays the order pending appeal of the decision to the Hawaii Supreme Court.

1997 The state of Tasmania repeals two criminal sodomy statutes, eliminating the last of such laws prohibiting homosexual intercourse in Australia.

1998 Twenty-fifth anniversary of the National Gay and Lesbian Task Force, the oldest existing U.S. gay and lesbian rights organization.

South Africa's high court declares apartheid-era sodomy laws unconstitutional, eliminating the last vestiges of prohibitions against homosexual intercourse in the common law of South Africa.

1999 June 27–29 marks the 30th aniversary of the Stonewall riots in New York City, the event that sparked the contemporary gay and lesbian rights movement.

Introduction

The gay liberation movement is most easily conceived as comprising three distinct periods. The first period, known as the early homosexual rights movement, 1864–1935, originated on the eve of the formation of modern Germany and culminated with the overthrow of the Weimar Constitution and the consolidation of one-party rule by the Nazi Party.[1] As it was predominantly a German phenomenon, the history of the early homosexual rights movement is coterminous with the history of modern Germany prior to World War II.

The second period, 1945–1968, the modern homosexual rights movement, originated after World War II. In contrast to the early homosexual rights movement, the modern movement was characterized by an increase in the number and vitality of homosexual rights organizations, principally in Britain, France, the Netherlands, and North America, and the emergence of lesbian organizations distinct from their gay male counterparts.

A third period, the contemporary gay and lesbian rights movement, is most often dated from 1969, the year of the Stonewall riots and the formation of the Gay Liberation Front in New York City. Although short-lived, the Gay Liberation Front inaugurated a new era in gay and lesbian political organizing, a more public and militant era.

The contemporary movement has also been characterized by a wide geographical dispersion of gay and lesbian organizations. Aside from Western Europe and North America, where the modern gay rights movement had become a permanent feature of the political landscape, there are now gay and lesbian rights organizations in Africa, Asia, Australia/New Zealand, Eastern Europe, and Latin America.

Finally, because of the impact of AIDS on gay men, gays, and lesbians initiated the development of organizations devoted to representing the interests of people with AIDS. Although not gay rights organizations per se, AIDS organizations have addressed a major international health crisis that affects gay men, a function ill-suited to gay and lesbian rights organizations.

The geographical dispersion of the gay and lesbian rights movement in recent years represents a significant opportunity and a great challenge. Gay and lesbian rights are now discussed in legislatures

1

throughout the world as well as in international organizations such as the European Union and the United Nations. Major legal victories have been achieved. And, never before has the opportunity to forge an international movement been as imminent as it is today. The first international organization of gays and lesbians was created shortly after Stonewall, and it has continued to grow in membership and influence.

Nevertheless, serious obstacles to gay and lesbian liberation persist, as do obstacles to the formation of an international movement. Gays and lesbians have yet to achieve full legal equality with heterosexuals anywhere in the world, and many countries, particularly in the Middle East and Africa, continue to punish homosexual intercourse with severe penalties. Similarly, cultural, linguistic, racial, and gender differences continue to frustrate the achievement of an international movement. Not only are there unresolved differences between gay men and lesbians, but there are also equally divisive racial tensions that undermine the solidarity of the movement. Also, the emergence of gay and lesbian organizations in Latin America, Africa, and Asia have raised issues related to the relevance of the Western European/North American conception of homosexuality to such cultures, and thus the relevance of the Western European/North American gay and lesbian rights movement to other regions of the world.

The Early Homosexual Rights Movement (1869–1935)

The early homosexual rights movement emerged on the eve of the consolidation of modern Germany in 1871 and was sparked by proposals to include criminal penalties for homosexual intercourse between men in the new German legal code. Sodomy, as well as adultery and fornication, had long been proscribed by the Christian religion, and these proscriptions became the basis of both Christian penitential literature as well as Christian canon law. European secular law also bore the imprint of Christian sexual taboos since the promulgation of the *Codex Justinianus* in Byzantium in the sixth century A.D.

Sodomy statutes were of particular concern to homosexuals as they, in effect, prohibited all forms of homosexual intercourse, often with severe penalties. Recent scholarship has documented the link between Roman law, Christian canon law, and the origins of medieval and early-modern secular legislation criminalizing sodomy.[2]

At the dawn of the early homosexual rights movement, criminal statutes prohibiting sodomy were the rule in Europe and North America. Of particular relevance to the early homosexual rights movement was one such criminal statute, Paragraph 175 of the German legal code. Enacted in 1871, Paragraph 175 criminalized acts of oral and anal intercourse between men, and its significance lies in the response it elicited from the pioneers of the homosexual emancipation movement.

Thus, the early homosexual rights movement emerged as a movement devoted primarily to the reform of sodomy statutes. Because statutes penalizing sexual relations between women were comparatively rare, the focus of the early movement was on the legal imbroglios concerning homosexual men. The concerns of lesbians, which pertained primarily to the legal inequality of women, received relatively little attention.

Early Movement Leaders and Homosexual Rights Organizations: Conflict and Cooperation

Although the most prominent leaders and homosexual rights organizations were united around the necessity of repealing Paragraph 175 of the German legal code, they espoused vastly different ideologies. The chief ideological differences revolved around the significance of scientific etiologies of homosexuality; the relevance of the Classical Greek, Renaissance, and Germanic traditions of male eroticism; and the role of feminism in the homosexual emancipation movement.

The early homosexual rights movement bears the unmistakable stamp of the trend toward scientific etiologies of homosexuality. This is due in no small measure to the most influential early spokesperson of homosexual emancipation, Karl Heinrich Ulrichs. His contributions to the homosexual rights movement were many and varied. Ulrichs disclosed his sexual preference at a time when such public pronouncements were unheard of. He organized opposition to the enactment of Paragraph 175 and fought for its repeal after its enactment in 1871. Between 1864 and 1869 he published 12 volumes of research on same-sex love. Recently translated into English as *The Riddle of "Man-Manly" Love*,[3] its influence on the subsequent development of psychiatric conceptions of homosexuality and the homosexual rights movement was profound.

Ulrichs's principal theoretical contention was that sexual desire was inborn, an idea that he most likely derived from Johann Ludwig Casper, a German forensic medical doctor.[4] Ulrichs hypothesized the existence of a "third sex," individuals whose sexual desire was inverted from the norm. These individuals, whom Ulrichs labeled Urnings and Urningins (male and female homosexuals), displayed a sexual desire for individuals of the same sex, a condition he labeled uranism. He equated this inversion of sexual desire to left-handedness, arguing that Urnings and Urningins had no more control over their condition than persons born left-handed.

Although Ulrichs had no formal education in medicine, his influence on the psychiatric establishment was immense. Karl Wesphal, Albert Moll, and Richard von Krafft-Ebing, among others, were indebted to Ulrichs's contention that homosexuality was inborn. Karl Westphal was the author of the first clinical study of homosexuality in women, "Die Conträre Sexualempfindung" ("Contrary Sexual Feeling"). Albert Moll subsequently published an entire volume on homosexuality bearing the same title. The eminent Viennese psychiatrist and sexologist, Richard von Krafft-Ebing, became aware of Ulrichs as early as 1866 when Ulrichs sent him portions of his writings on the subject of inverted sexual desire. Krafft-Ebing acknowledged his indebtedness to Ulrichs, and his own theory of inversion in *Psychopathia Sexualis* influenced generations of students. However, whereas Ulrichs argued that inverted sexual desire was nothing more than a natural anomaly, Westphal, Moll, and Krafft-Ebing theorized inversion to be a mental illness. Thus, Ulrichs inadvertently gave impetus to the psychiatric classification of homosexuality as a mental illness.

And Ulrichs's work did not escape the attention of Magnus Hirschfeld. Hirschfeld was the cofounder of the first homosexual rights organization in the world, in 1897, the Wissenschaftlich-humanitäres Komitee (Scientific-Humanitarian Committee [SHC]). He was also the founder of the influential Institut für Sexualwissenschaft (Institute for Sexual Science [ISS]) in 1919. Hirschfeld too felt that homosexuality was an inborn condition and, like Ulrichs, argued that imprisonment was an irrational response to a biological predisposition. Basing his initial arguments on theories similar to those of Ulrichs, Hirschfeld led the SHC's 30-year effort to repeal Paragraph 175 of the German legal code.

Although scientific explanations of homosexuality attracted a wide following among early homosexual rights activists, they were not universally accepted. To the contrary, scientific etiologies were the objects of heated controversy. Karl Maria Kertbeny, a contemporary of Ulrichs, also spoke openly against the adoption of Paragraph 175 and is best remembered as the first person to use the term *homosexuality* in a published work. Kertbeny, however, was disdainful of Ulrichs's account of homosexual love. He scoffed at Ulrichs's suggestion that sexual attraction between men meant that they possessed a feminine disposition. Kertbeny rejected Ulrichs's third-sex theory, preferring to think of his own attraction to men as normal and healthy; and, he insisted, inversion was scientifically inexplicable.

Magnus Hirschfeld and the SHC were also not without opponents. Adolph Brand, Benedict Friedländer, and Wilhelm Jansen, founders of the Gemeinschaft der Eigenen (Community of the Special [COS]), in 1902, also publicly criticized Ulrichs's third-sex theory, and Hirschfeld for his endorsement of Ulrichs's theories. Although the SHC and the

COS cooperated intermittently over three decades to repeal Paragraph 175, they espoused very different views of homosexuality and were bitter opponents in the reform movement.

In contrast to scientific etiologies of homosexuality, the COS preferred to focus on the culture and aesthetics of male camaraderie. Drawing on the Classical Greek and Renaissance traditions of erotic relationships among youths and among adult men and boys as well as the German tradition of male friendship, the COS argued for the ethical superiority of male homoeroticism in comparison with the reproductive sexual union between men and women.

Related to this difference of opinion was another point of conflict between the SHC and the COS, the active promotion by the COS of sexual relations among boys and man-boy love, traditions which were on the wane throughout Europe at the turn of the century. The SHC focused its energies on establishing the legal right of adult men to engage in sexual relations with each other. The COS went further, claiming that sensuality between male youths was psychologically healthy and endorsing pedagogical eros, the spiritual and sexual union between adult men and boys.

There were other differences between the SHC and the COS. The SHC embraced the women's rights movement, viewing the struggle for the emancipation of women and homosexuals as counterparts in the effort to reform medieval ideas about sexuality. The research of the ISS also emphasized issues relevant to the physical and psychological health of women. But the COS was not open to women, focusing as it did on the importance of male bonding to the future of German civilization. The COS did not perceive women to be the spiritual or intellectual equals of men, and they assumed that the social role of women was naturally inferior to that of men.

The misogyny of the COS and its advocacy of man-boy love limited its appeal, as did its rejection of sexual science. Scientific explanations of human behavior were becoming increasingly respectable, and couching the advocacy of homosexual rights in the language of science had a far greater appeal than did appeals to cultural tradition. Although both the COS and the SHC remained active in the homosexual rights movement in Germany until the consolidation of power by the Nazi Party, the COS never rivaled the influence of the SHC.

The Campaign to Repeal Paragraph 175

The campaign to repeal Paragraph 175 is most closely associated with Magnus Hirschfeld and the SHC. Members of the COS, such as Benedict Friedländer and Adolph Brand, were also active in the repeal effort. Friedländer and Brand were originally members of the SHC, and there were initial signs of close cooperation between the COS and the SHC in the repeal drive. But the aforementioned differences between the COS and the SHC led to Friedländer's resignation and an attempt to attract members away from the SHC to the COS. The failure of this attempt led to a rupture between the two organizations. Although they continued to cooperate intermittently in the repeal effort, the efforts of the SHC were the most sustained and influential of the two groups.

The centerpiece of the SHC's repeal effort was a petition drive to garner the signatures of prominent physicians, scientists, lawyers, literary figures, and politicians in opposition to Paragraph 175. This, Hirschfeld hoped, would be enough to persuade the Reichstag to rescind the statute. Although the petition drive was very successful, the overall lobbying effort was not.

The names of many prominent individuals were among the more than 6,000 signatures ultimately garnered by the organizers. Perhaps the most significant was August Bebel, the influential Social Democratic Party leader. On more than one occasion, Bebel took the floor of the Reichstag to argue for the repeal of 175. Despite his influence, 175 was never brought to a vote on the floor of the Reichstag.

In 1911 an attempt to extend the provisions of 175 to women was defeated. For the first time, women's rights groups joined in the struggle to oppose the criminalization of homosexual sodomy. A coalition of women's groups and the SHC ultimately succeeded in preventing the draft penal code of 1910 from becoming law, and the proposal was never enacted.

World War I interrupted the activities of the SHC and the COS. The birth of the Weimar Republic, in 1919, however, rekindled hopes for the repeal of 175. In 1920, the SHC organized a coalition of three groups, the Aktionsausschuss (Action Committee [AC]), to rebuild the momentum for repeal. In addition to the SHC and the COS, the coalition consisted of the Deutscher Freundschaftsverband (German Friendship Association [GFA]). The coalition proved ineffectual due, in part, to the relatively apolitical nature of the GFA. After three years, the GFA withdrew from the coalition and it quickly fell apart.

Yet another coalition was formed in 1925, the Kartell für Reform des Sexualstrafrechts (Coalition for the Reform of the Sexual Crimes code). Organized by the SHC, it consisted of six other organizations interested in the reform of Germany's criminal code pertaining to sex crimes.[5] The coalition's draft penal code of 1927 appears to have had an impact on the deliberations of the Reichstag's Committee for Penal Code Reform. Although the Penal Code Reform Bill (which included a provision repealing 175) was reported out of the committee, the bill was tabled on the floor of the Reichstag, and supporters of repeal were

never again able to muster the votes to bring the issue to the floor. The Great Depression and the subsequent rise of the Nazi Party terminated efforts at sexual reform in Germany.

The International Impact of the German Reform Movement

Although the early homosexual rights movement was principally a German phenomenon, it had an impact far beyond the borders of Germany. Nowhere is this more evident than in Great Britain. Like Germany, Britain had a tradition of severe penalties for sodomy and for soliciting others of the same sex. Comparatively speaking, the British had an even lower tolerance for homosexuality than the Germans. Executions as well as life sentences for homosexual intercourse were not uncommon prior to the mid-19th century.

The conviction and subsequent imprisonment in 1895 of the famous playwright Oscar Wilde became an international symbol of the inhumane treatment of homosexuals in Britain. Convicted of gross indecency under the provisions of the Offenses on Public Decency Amendment of the British Criminal Law Amendment Act of 1885, Wilde was sentenced to two years at hard labor. The notoriety of his imprisonment and subsequent exile in Paris provided great impetus to the nascent protest movement in Great Britain as well as on the continent.

As in Germany, a tradition of protest literature also existed in Britain. Beginning in the 1880s, a number of well-known British intellectuals began to protest the irrational and inhumane treatment of homosexuals, including Sir Richard Burton, John Addington Symonds, Edward Carpenter, and Havelock Ellis. Unlike in Germany, however, these isolated protests never coalesced into a political movement similar to the reform movement led by the SHC. What emerged in Britain instead were scholarly societies devoted to the scientific study of sexuality.

Edward Carpenter and Havelock Ellis, in particular, were familiar with the work of Magnus Hirschfeld, and it was his example that led to the formation of the British Society for the Study of Sex Psychology (BSSP). Founded in 1914, the BSSP collaborated with Hirschfeld's SHC in advancing the scientific understanding of sexuality. Following the foundation of the ISS in Berlin in 1919, the BSSP and the ISS cooperated in the exchange of scholarly papers on sexuality, participated in international conferences, and founded the World League for Sexual Reform (WLSR). Through their collective efforts, the scientific study of sexuality was immeasurably enhanced and with it the scientific understanding of homosexuality.

The BSSP and the WLSR provided an opportunity for those interested in the reform of sex crimes codes to collaborate and exchange information. This tradition of the scientific study of sexuality reemerged after World War II and provided the basis for the establishment of the Committee on Homosexual Offenses and Prostitution, better known as the Wolfenden Committee. The committee report, in 1957, had a great impact on the development of a political consciousness among homosexuals in Great Britain as well as on the eventual reform of British law. Thus, the BSSP and the WLSR were important prewar precedents to the eventual emergence of a homosexual emancipation movement in Britain.

The German homosexual rights movement also had repercussions in the USSR. Under the czars, homosexual intercourse between men was punished under Article 995 of the Code of Laws of the Russian Empire which made anal sex between men a crime. The prescribed punishments were four to five years in prison. A 1903 revision of the legal code reduced the penalty to no less than three months' imprisonment. Originally enacted in 1845, Article 995 was abolished in 1917 along with the entire Code of Laws.

Although there had never been a homosexual emancipation movement in Russia per se, there was a burgeoning literary circle of homosexual men and women after 1905, including Mikhail Kuzmin, Nikolai Klyuev, and Sophia Parnok. The years 1905 to 1917 were a period of unprecedented freedom of expression in Russia, and many authors wrote openly of homosexuality. The abolition of 995 after the revolution was a cause for great celebration among those who had openly written in defense of homosexual love.

Even though the deletion of 995 from the Code of Laws resulted more from efforts to rid the legal code of remnants of czarist influence than those to further the cause of homosexual emancipation, the event was touted by Soviet physicians as evidence of the superiority of the new Soviet attitude toward sexuality. Magnus Hirschfeld became aware of these reforms at meetings of the WLSR and hailed the abolition of 995 as a propitious moment for the homosexual emancipation movement. Hirschfeld felt that the decriminalization of homosexuality in the USSR might enhance the chances for repeal of 175 in Germany, and he often pointed to the USSR as an example of progressive attitudes toward sexuality. Indeed, as late as 1930, official Soviet attitudes relied on Hirschfeld's claim that, because homosexuality was an involuntary biological condition, homosexual intercourse should not be prosecuted.

The German homosexual rights movement was also the inspiration for the 1924 formation of the ill-fated and short-lived Society for Human Rights (SHR), in the United States. Formed in Chicago by Henry Gerber, the idea for the SHR came from the Bund für Menschenrechte (League for Human Rights), the largest (and least political) of the three German homosexual rights groups. However, Gerber and the

SHR came under immediate attack by the Chicago police, and the SHR did not survive for more than a few months. Although Gerber continued to write and speak out intermittently on behalf of homosexuals, the movement for homosexual rights in the United States would not begin in earnest for another 25 years.

Outside of Germany, it was only in the Netherlands that the early homosexual rights movement took the form of a sustained political movement. Although the Netherlands movement was less public and less well organized than its German counterpart, the SHC inspired the creation of the Nederlandsch Wetenschappelijk Humanitair Komitee (Dutch Scientific-Humanitarian Committee [DSHC]). Founded in 1911 by Jacob Schorer, the DSHC promoted the case for homosexual love and fought for the repeal of legislation that established differential ages of consent for heterosexuals and homosexuals. There was no counterpart to Paragraph 175 in the Netherlands until 1940 when the German invasion of the Netherlands led to the criminalization of male homosexual relationships. Although the DSHC did not survive the war, its example provided the impetus for the reemergence of one of the first postwar homosexual rights groups, the Cultuur-en-Ontspannings Centrum (Culture and Recreational Center [CRC]).

The Collapse of the Early Homosexual Rights Movement

The optimism of Hirschfeld and others committed to change was short lived, as the movement for legal reform in Europe suddenly collapsed. As early as 1922 in the USSR, the first Soviet criminal code reinstituted criminal penalties for homosexual prostitution, for sex with minors, and for public lewdness. Furthermore, in the mid-1920s, the USSR reintroduced restrictive censorship laws, making it increasingly difficult to publish unconventional literary or scientific works on sexuality. Finally, in 1934, a revision of the Soviet Criminal Code reintroduced criminal penalties of up to five years' imprisonment for adult homosexual intercourse.

The consolidation of power by the Nazi Party after 1932 also spelled the end of the aspirations of the homosexual emancipation movement in Germany. Not only were German homosexual rights organizations unable to repeal Paragraph 175, the scope of offenses was broadened by the Nazis (in the form of Paragraph 175a), and homosexual rights groups were banned.

Neither the SHC, the COS, nor the GFA survived the rise of the Nazi Party in Germany in the 1930s. A similar fate befell the ISS, the WLSR, and the DSHC. The hopes of the early movement leaders were crushed by the rise of fascism and the incarceration and murder of thousands of homosexuals in Nazi concentration camps. Not even the BSSP, in Britain, survived World War II.

Although the principal objectives of the early homosexual emancipation movement were thwarted by the rise of fascism and the outbreak of war between Germany and the Allied powers, the early movement established an important precedent. Never before had homosexual rights organizations existed, and public debate about homosexuality had never been so commonplace. Although limited in scope when compared with today, the homosexual rights movement became firmly entrenched as a result of the courageous efforts of the individuals involved.

The Modern Homosexual Rights Movement (1945–1969)

The post–World War II period in Europe remained an era of overt legal oppression of gays and lesbians. The meager progress of the early homosexual rights movement had been completely undone by the rise of fascism in Central Europe and Stalinism in Eastern Europe. The legal predicament of gays and lesbians remained highly problematic. Sodomy statutes remained in the legal codes of most countries, and social tolerance of homosexuals was no greater than it was prior to World War II. Given the oppressive social and legal climate in Europe, it is remarkable that the reconstruction of the homosexual rights movement in the immediate postwar period proceeded as quickly as it did.

The homosexual emancipation movement reemerged slowly and tentatively shortly after the defeat of Germany. *Levensrecht* (Right to Live), a journal devoted to homosexual issues, reemerged in the Netherlands. Founded by Bob Angelo shortly before the German invasion of the Netherlands in 1940, its publication was suppressed by the German occupation. Its republication in 1946 found an immediate audience, which led to the formation of a close circle of like-minded persons that came to be known as the "Shakespeare Club." It was out of discussions among individuals affiliated with this reading circle that the Cultuur-en-Ontspannings Centrum (Culture and Recreational Center [CRC]) was born. Catering initially to the social needs of Dutch homosexuals, its national office opened in 1948. The Culture and Recreational Center was the first postwar organization of homosexuals in Europe.

Founded only five years after the CRC was the French Homosexual journal *Arcadie*. Like the CRC, it originated from a reading group, the Club littéraire et scientifique des pays latines (Literary and Scientific Club of the Latin Countries). Commonly referred to as Arcadie, this was the first homosexual rights organization in France, and it remained the most prominent French organization throughout the 1950s and 1960s. Arcadie played a leading role in the effort to rescind the repressive Pétain-de Gaulle law, legislation that established unequal ages of consent for heterosexuals and homosexuals.

The first homosexual rights organization in Britain was also founded during the postwar years. Established in 1958 to promote the reforms advocated by the 1957 "Report of the Committee on Homosexual Offenses and Prostitution," the Homosexual Law Reform Society (HLRS) was the mainstay of the British homosexual rights movement for roughly 15 years.

The CRC, Arcadie, and the HLRS spearheaded the effort in Europe to repeal sodomy laws, equalize age-of-consent laws, reform public opinion, and provide social venues for gays and lesbians. The most significant legal victory was the enactment of the 1967 Sexual Offenses Act in Britain. With the exception of the postwar recision of the sodomy statute imposed on the Netherlands by the Nazis during World War II, the 1967 Sexual Offenses Act marks the first success in the 70-year struggle to legalize adult homosexual intercourse in Europe. The 1967 Sexual Offenses Act accelerated the movement to repeal sodomy statutes throughout the British Commonwealth, Europe, and the United States.

The postwar social and political climate for gays and lesbians in North America was little better than in Europe. In the United States, every state in the union had a sodomy statute, often with exceptionally severe penalties. The situation in Canada was equally oppressive. Modeled on British law, the Canadian law had defined sodomy as a crime since 1859, and the crime of gross indecency, also borrowed from the British, was enacted only seven years after the 1885 Offenses on Public Decency Amendment (the Labouchère Amendment) in Britain.

Complicating the situation for gays and lesbians in North America was the absence of a North American counterpart to the early homosexual rights movement in Europe. The postwar homosexual rights movement in North America began in isolation from developments in Europe and with no indigenous history.

Founded at roughly the same time as the Shakespeare Club in the Netherlands was the Veterans Benevolent Association in the United States. Many leading scholars of the homosexual emancipation movement in the United States attribute the origins of the homosexual emancipation movement in North America to the treatment of gay servicemen during World War II.[6] Founded after the war in New York by several servicemen dishonorably discharged because of their homosexuality, the Veterans Benevolent Association is currently considered to have been "the first major gay membership organization in the United States."[7]

Several years later, and apparently in isolation from developments elsewhere in the United States and Europe, the Mattachine Society (MS) was formed. Founded in 1951 in Los Angeles by Harry Hay and others, the MS became the prototype of homosexual activism in North America until its disintegration as a national organization in 1961.

The 1950s and 1960s were years of heightened national security in the United States. This resulted not only in the political repression of left-wing political parties but also in attempts to rid the government and armed forces of "sexual deviates," such as homosexuals, who ostensibly constituted a security risk to the United States. Thousands of gay men and lesbians were dishonorably discharged from the armed services; and many more were fired from their jobs with federal, state, and local governments.

The situation for gays and lesbians in the 1950s and 1960s was rendered even more problematic by the lack of support for homosexual rights in U.S. civil society. The classification of homosexuality as a mental illness by the American Psychiatric Association was the source of personal distress for gays and lesbians as well as an impediment to social and political change. Furthermore, gays and lesbians were routinely attacked by religious groups as moral reprobates, and there were few allies in the legal profession, even among civil libertarians associated with the American Civil Liberties Union.

Founded as a clandestine organization because of the fear of exposure and arrest, the MS never exceeded several thousand members. Nevertheless, the organization had a great influence on those who directly participated in its activities. It offered the first nationwide social outlet for gay men and lesbians, aside from gay bars, and provided a forum for the discussion of relevant social, psychological, and legal issues with sympathetic professionals.

One of its principal legacies is the cadre of homosexual rights activists who honed their political acumen in activities sponsored by the MS. Long after the demise of MS as a national organization, activists associated either with individual chapters of the MS or with other gay and lesbian organizations continued the fight for the civil rights of gays and lesbians.

Another legacy of the MS was the publication of the *Mattachine Review* and *One Magazine*, the first homosexual journals in the United States. Together, the *Mattachine Review* and *One Magazine* reached thousands of gay men and lesbians with information that would have otherwise been unavailable. *One Magazine* was particularly significant because of its resistance to the 1954 censorship of its publication by the Los Angeles postmaster. In a 1958 decision by the U.S. Supreme Court, the action of the Los Angeles postmaster was set aside, and *One Magazine* was again allowed to circulate. The Supreme Court's decision resulted in a significant increase in both the number of gay and lesbian publications as well as in the total circulation of all gay and lesbian publications in the United States. The founders of *One Magazine* also initiated the Institute of Homophile Studies, the first gay and lesbian studies program in the United States.

The MS was also indirectly responsible for the formation of the Daughters of Bilitis (DOB), the first autonomous lesbian organization in North America. The DOB was founded in 1955 by Del Martin and Phyllis Lyon, among others, who concluded that lesbians could best be served by an organization devoted to the needs of homosexual women. The model for the DOB was the MS.[8] Barbara Gittings, the founder of the New York chapter of the DOB, credits the New York chapter of the MS for providing the occasion for the formation of the DOB in New York.[9] Like the MS, the DOB soon began publishing its own journal devoted to lesbian issues, the *Ladder*.

Inspired by the example of the MS and DOB in the United States, the Association for Social Knowledge (ASK) was founded in Vancouver, British Columbia, in 1964. Like the MS and DOB, ASK attempted to organize Canadian gays and lesbians to oppose Canadian statutes that criminalized sodomy and gross indecency. ASK also unsuccessfully opposed the extension of a 1948 criminal psychopath law to gay men. These laws, restricted initially to homosexual intercourse between men, had been extended to women in a 1953 revision of the Canadian Criminal Code. ASK also served as a social outlet for gays and lesbians and provided the opportunity to discuss issues pertaining to homosexuality with other like-minded individuals and psychiatric, legal, and social work professionals. Unlike they did in the United States, gays and lesbians in Canada did not form separate organizations during this period.

Viewed collectively, the MS, DOB, and ASK served important social and political functions. Given the highly repressive social and political atmosphere in North America in the postwar period, the emergence of organizations devoted to the interests of gays and lesbians was an achievement in its own right. Homosexual intercourse was illegal. The dismissal of thousands of gays and lesbians from the federal civil service and the armed services in both the United States and Canada cast a pall over attempts to organize gays and lesbians. Gays and lesbians had very few allies among lawyers, psychiatrists, or the clergy. Incapable of achieving major social, psychiatric, or legal reforms, these small groups of individuals nevertheless paved the way for the more ambitious agenda of future gay and lesbian rights activists.

Ultimately, however, the comparatively staid and reformist politics of the established gay and lesbian rights organizations were overwhelmed by the direct-action techniques of civil rights and antiwar groups. The reinvigoration of the women's rights movement also provided a platform for the public discussion of gender issues, issues that had been dormant since the adoption of the Nineteenth Amendment in 1920. Collectively, the confluence of assertive African American, antiwar, and women's rights organizations, and the reintroduction of gender issues into the public arena, created an opportunity for the emergence of more vigorous gay and lesbian rights organizations.

Two such organizations were the Society for Individual Rights (SIR) and the Washington, D.C., Chapter of the Mattachine Society (MSW). Formed in 1961, under the leadership of Frank Kameny, MSW challenged the dismissals of gays and lesbians from the federal civil service and from the armed services. In San Francisco SIR superseded the San Francisco chapters of MS and DOB as the dominant force in gay and lesbian organizing. From its founding in 1964, SIR was more overtly political than either the MS or the DOB, participating in election campaigns, endorsing candidates, taking positions on issues, and so forth. Both organizations proved to be prototypes of the more public and confrontational style of gay and lesbian organizing that became commonplace after Stonewall.

The resistance to discrimination and public humiliation displayed in New York City during the Stonewall Inn riots of 1969 have come to symbolize the attitudinal change of gays and lesbians toward their social and legal stigmatization. What began as a routine bar raid by the New York City police culminated in a full-fledged street battle between the police, bar patrons, and onlookers on the evenings of 27 and 28 June. In the immediate aftermath of the confrontation, new leaders and organizations emerged, and the era of mass resistance to discrimination had begun.

The Contemporary Gay and Lesbian Rights Movement

The contemporary gay and lesbian rights movement can be distinguished from its predecessors on a number of grounds. The first is the emergence of mass organizations. Prior to the Stonewall riots, gay and lesbian organizations were small groups of dedicated reformers who experienced little success in recruiting large numbers of individuals to the cause of gay and lesbian rights. Today, gay and lesbian groups in North America and Europe are mass-membership organizations, and they spearhead a movement of millions of individuals.

Another distinguishing characteristic of the contemporary period is the emergence of gay and lesbian rights groups outside of Western Europe and North America. The early homosexual rights movement was confined to Western Europe. During the quarter-century between the end of World War II and Stonewall, homosexual rights groups developed in North America, but it has only been since the early 1970s that gay and lesbian groups have emerged in other parts of the world. This, in turn, has led to the emergence of an international gay and lesbian rights movement, the culmination of over a century of organizational efforts.

The contemporary period has also been characterized by the broadening of the gay and lesbian rights agenda. Although elimination of existing sodomy laws remains a primary goal of the movement, the gay and lesbian rights agenda is now a much more comprehensive civil rights agenda, including such items as antidiscrimination legislation in employment, housing, and public accommodations; the acquisition of domestic partnership rights; the right to civil marriage; immigration; political asylum; and the rights of people with AIDS (PWAs).

Finally, contemporary gay and lesbian rights groups are now increasingly associated with other civil rights and civil-libertarian groups. Prior to Stonewall this was virtually unheard of. On the one hand, more well-established civil rights and civil-libertarian groups were afraid of being further stigmatized and politically isolated through support for gay rights. On the other hand, the constituency of established homosexual rights groups was so small and fragile that other civil rights and civil liberties issues would have only complicated the struggle to form gay and lesbian organizations.

Today, however, it has become increasingly common for gay and lesbian organizations to form coalitions with racial minorities and women's groups in pursuit of common objectives. This has been due, in no small part, to the broadening of the gay and lesbian rights agenda. As long as the gay and lesbian agenda remained focused on the eradication of sodomy statutes, there was little basis for coalitions with other movements for social and political equality. But the inclusion of more traditional civil rights issues in the agenda of gay and lesbian organizations has created the opportunity to form a common front, at least on a limited number of issues; and established organizations representing women, racial minorities, and civil liberties issues now increasingly recognize the need to support gays and lesbians.

The Impact of the Gay Liberation Front on the Contemporary Gay and Lesbian Liberation Movement

Founded in New York City shortly after the Stonewall Inn riots in the summer of 1969, the Gay Liberation Front (GLF) ushered in a new era by reinvigorating the effort to politicize gays and lesbians. The GLF addressed the interests of a younger, more assertive, and less-closeted spectrum of the gay and lesbian community eager to carry the fight for gay and lesbian rights into the political arena. Within two years, GLF chapters proliferated around the United States; GLF organizations began to assert themselves in England, Canada, and the Federal Republic of Germany; and GLF-type organizations, such as the Front Homosexuel d'Action Révolutionnaire (Revolutionary Homosexual Action Front [RHAF]) and the Frente Unitario Omosessuale Rivoluzionario Italiano (Italian Homosexual Revolutionary United Front) began organizing in France and Northern Italy. By challenging the comparatively staid platforms of existing homosexual rights organizations in Western Europe and North America, these organizations transformed the gay and lesbian movement into a formidable force for political change.

The aforesaid organizations shared a common ideology. They were critical of the role of psychiatry in perpetuating antiquated psychological stereotypes of gays and lesbians. They espoused a socialist agenda, often attempting to form alliances with unions and workers parties. Coalitions with women's groups and racial minorities were undertaken for the first time. They were eager to make their presence felt in the antiwar movement, and they were critical of the colonialism and neocolonialism of the Western powers.

If, as their detractors claimed, they were too radical, too idealistic, and poorly organized, it is also true that the extraordinary outpouring of energy associated with the politics of these self-styled revolutionary groups forever changed the character of the gay rights movement and were instrumental in developing it into the mass movement that it is today. Their critique of psychiatry was instrumental in forcing a reevaluation of the nature of sexual orientation and in the ultimate delisting of homosexuality as a mental illness by professional organizations such as the American Psychiatric Association. Their efforts to form coalitions with unions, socialist parties, women's groups, and racial minorities were the first such efforts and, if they resulted in little initial cooperation, they did become the prototype for contemporary coalitions between socialist parties and gay and lesbian groups, and between racial minorities, women's groups, and gays and lesbians.

The notoriety generated by GLF activities in North America and Western Europe, in addition to the reinvigoration of many established organizations, precipitated the emergence of gay and lesbian organizations in other areas of the world where the gay liberation movement had been quiescent. In Mexico, for example, the Frente de Liberación Homosexual de Mexico (Homosexual Liberation Front of Mexico), the Frente Homosexual de Acción Revolucionaria (Revolutionary Homosexual Action Front), and the Grupo Lambda de Liberación Homosexual (Lambda Homosexual Liberation Group) began organizing in the 1970s in Mexico City. Shortly thereafter, groups began to emerge elsewhere in Mexico, as well as South America, such as the Brazilian organization Somos (We Are) and, more recently, the Movimiento Homosexual de Lima (Homosexual Movement of Lima). By the 1990s, gay, lesbian, and bisexual organizations had become increasingly common throughout Latin America.

Homosexual rights organizations also became more visible in South Africa, New Zealand, and Australia during the 1970s. In South Africa, a gay liberation movement erupted on the campus of the University of Natal in 1972. Only the second homosexual rights organization in the history of South Africa, its existence was brief, but it was soon followed by much larger and more successful groups. In Australia, groups such as the Campaign against Moral Persecution (CAMP) began a movement to rescind Australia's sodomy statutes; and, in New Zealand, where the Dorian Society had been actively engaged in a similar struggle since 1964, the strength of the political coalitions committed to reform grew steadily.

The first signs of homosexual rights organizing in Eastern Europe also became evident in the 1970s with the emergence of the Homosexuelle Interessen-Gemeinschaft Berlin (Homosexual Interest Group Berlin), possibly the first homosexual rights organization in the German Democratic Republic. Homosexual groups soon multiplied in major East German cities. Sustained by the Lutheran/Evangelical Church, the environment for gays and lesbians in the GDR gradually improved and was the first example of a nationwide coalition of gay and lesbian organizations in Eastern Europe, until the collapse of the Soviet Union created opportunities for the emergence of homosexual groups in other Eastern European countries. Today there are gay and lesbian rights groups throughout most of the republics of the former Soviet Union, such as MAGNUS in Slovenia.

The first international organization of gays and lesbians, the International Gay Association, was also initiated in the 1970s. Renamed the International Lesbian and Gay Association (ILGA) in 1986, the ILGA represents the culmination of Magnus Hirschfeld's dream of an international movement devoted to the emancipation of homosexuals. The ILGA provides an invaluable source of current information concerning international issues pertaining to gays and lesbians. Its *Pink Book*, published at roughly five-year intervals, and its monthly *Euroletter* contain timely summaries of international events pertinent to gays and lesbians. The ILGA, through its subsidiary, the International Gay and Lesbian Human Rights Commission (IGLHRC), tracks the status of gay and lesbian human rights around the world. The ILGA also lobbies on behalf of gay and lesbian interests. Its activities range from lobbying individual governments to representing the interests of gays and lesbians in the current European Union negotiations.

In the 1980s the first AIDS organizations appeared to represent the interests of PWAs. At a time when the health crisis posed by HIV was being ignored by public officials in the United States and Western Europe, and at a time when gay men were being vilified for its onset, established gay and lesbian rights organizations were overwhelmed with the additional responsibilities of addressing the social and political ramifications of this new disease. The imperative need to address the public health and civil rights issues created by AIDS led to the formation of AIDS service organizations such as the Gay Men's Health Crisis in New York City. Before the end of the decade there were AIDS organizations throughout the United States and Western Europe. AIDS education and support services now also exist in Eastern Europe, Latin America, Australia, and in some regions of Africa and Asia.

Accomplishments of the Gay Liberation Movement

From the inception of the early homosexual rights movement to the present, the elimination of sodomy statutes has remained a central goal of the international gay and lesbian movement. The right of adults to have sexual relations with individuals of their choice, regardless of sex, is at the core of the gay and lesbian rights agenda. Much has been accomplished from the years just before Stonewall to the present, such as the 1967 decriminalization of adult homosexual relations in Britain, the decriminalization of adult homosexual relations in the German Democratic Republic (1968), in the Federal Republic of Germany (1969), in Canada (1969), in New Zealand (1986), and the spate of recent statutes decriminalizing homosexual relations in the republics of the former Soviet Union. In 1997, the state of Tasmania repealed two criminal sodomy statutes, thereby eliminating the last criminal laws prohibiting homosexual intercourse in Australia.[10]

The repeal of sodomy statutes, however, is no longer the exclusive focus of the gay and lesbian liberation movement. The contemporary objectives now resemble the goals of other, more established, civil rights organizations, such as the National Organization of Women. Objectives now include enacting legislation protecting gays and lesbians from discrimination in employment, housing, and public accommodations; the inclusion of gays and lesbians in "hate crime" statutes; and, most recently, the right to domestic partnership benefits and the right to marry.

There has been considerable progress in the civil rights protection afforded gays and lesbians since the passage of the first nationwide gay and lesbian civil rights act in Norway in 1981. In the United States, for example, 10 states (California, Connecticut, Hawaii, Massachusetts, Minnesota, New Hampshire, New Jersey, Rhode Island, Vermont, and

Wisconsin) provide varying degrees of civil rights protection for gays and lesbians. In addition, roughly 150 county and city governments have enacted legislation protecting the rights of gays and lesbians.[11]

Canada's civil rights record is more impressive. Beginning with the extension of civil rights protection to gays and lesbians in Quebec in 1977 and Ontario in 1986, other Canadian provinces quickly enacted their own statutes. As of 1996, only Alberta, Newfoundland, and Prince Edward Island had no provincial human rights laws protecting gays and lesbians. The Canadian Human Rights Act was also amended in 1996 to include sexual orientation: "The law forbids discrimination based on sexual orientation by federally regulated employers, landlords and services," such as "the federal government, banks, broadcasters, the telephone and telecommunications industry, railways, airlines, shipping and inter-provincial transportation." Furthermore, although sexual orientation is not specifically protected by the Canadian Charter of Rights and Freedoms, the Supreme Court has recognized that it is tantamount to the rights and protection enumerated in section 15 of the charter.[12]

The greatest progress toward achieving civil rights protection for gays and lesbians has been in Northern Europe. As early as 1981, Norway's comprehensive civil rights law became the first nationwide civil rights law to include protection for gays and lesbians. In 1985 France amended its statute prohibiting racism to include sexual orientation and, in 1987, Sweden and Denmark followed the Norwegian example by including sexual orientation in their antidiscrimination laws. In 1992 the Netherlands amended its penal code to include protection on the basis of "hetero- or homosexual orientation" and, in 1995 and 1996, Spain, Finland, Slovenia, and Iceland followed suit.[13] Although the degree of protection offered gays and lesbians by these statutes differs considerably, the most comprehensive statutes include legal prohibitions on discrimination in the public and private labor markets, public accommodations, and the inclusion of gays and lesbians in "hate crime" statutes.

In Australia, the efforts of such organizations as CAMP finally began to pay dividends in 1982 when New South Wales enacted the first statewide antidiscrimination statute. In 1991, South Australia became the second state to enact legislation protecting the rights of gays and lesbians. New Zealand, which maintained criminal penalties for consensual homosexual intercourse between adults until 1986, enacted a national human rights law in 1993, accomplishing a longstanding goal of the New Zealand Homosexual Law Reform Society.

Potentially the most significant national civil rights development, however, is unfolding in South Africa. Owing to the efforts of gay and lesbian rights groups in South Africa, in particular the individual efforts of Simon Nkoli and the Gay and Lesbian Organization of the Witwatersrand, the African National Congress succeeded in including a provision protecting the civil and political rights of gays and lesbians in the 1994 interim Constitution of South Africa. This is one of the first such constitutional provisions in the world. The adoption of the permanent Constitution of South Africa in 1996 retained the interim constitution's protections of the rights of gays and lesbians.

At the international level, the ILGA has been active in the negotiations of the European Union (EU) and its predecessor the European Community (EC), where the issue of protecting the civil and political rights of gays and lesbians has been the object of controversy for two decades. In 1981, for example, the Parliamentary Assembly of the Council of Europe adopted Recommendation 924, a provision that condemned discrimination against gays and lesbians. Similarly, the Council of Europe has required the elimination of sodomy statutes pertaining to gays and lesbians as a precondition for membership since 1993. The European Court of Human Rights has also ruled that prohibitions on homosexual intercourse is a violation of the European Convention on Human Rights. Yet another positive development was the European Parliament's adoption of the "Resolution on Equal Rights for Homosexuals and Lesbians in the EC" in 1994. In this far-reaching resolution the European Parliament called on member states to rescind sodomy laws pertaining to gays and lesbians, to prohibit civil and political discrimination against gays and lesbians, and called on the EU Commission to draft a comprehensive recommendation pertaining to the rights of gays and lesbians in the EU.[14]

The Organization for Security and Cooperation in Europe (OSCE) has also been the site of negotiations pertaining to the rights of gays and lesbians since 1992 when it was discussed at the OSCE's follow-up meeting in Helsinki. In 1995 the OSCE's Parliamentary Assembly adopted a resolution calling on member states to prohibit discrimination on the basis of "ethnicity, race, colour, language, religion, sex, sexual orientation, national or social origin or belonging to a minority."[15]

The United Nations (UN) has also begun to take action on the issue of the civil and political rights of gays and lesbians. On 31 March 1994, in *Toonen vs. Australia,* the UN Human Rights Committee ruled that statutory prohibitions on consensual adult homosexual intercourse violated Article 17 of the International Covenant on Civil and Political Rights (ICCPR). Its opinion also asserted that sections 2(1) and 26 of the ICCPR were also applicable to sexual orientation.

Another striking development in recent years has been the movement to extend the right of civil marriages to gays and lesbians. Initiated by the Danish Registered Partnership Act in 1989, gays and lesbians now also enjoy the right to registered partnerships in Norway, Sweden, Iceland, and Greenland. In 1996, Hungary became the first Eastern European country to recognize same-sex partnerships when the Hungarian Parliament voted to extend the privilege of common-law marriages to gays and lesbians. Although the right to a registered partnership is not the legal equivalent of a heterosexual marriage (registered partnerships do not entitle one to a church marriage, for example), registered partnerships do entitle gays and lesbians to most of the privileges of a traditional marriage. Similar legislation was recently enacted in the Netherlands and is pending consideration in Finland and in the state of Hawaii.

Finally, AIDS organizations such as the AIDS Coalition to Unleash Power (ACT-UP) in the United States, Europe, and Australia, and AIDS Action Now! in Canada led the fight to increase public awareness about the disease and public and privately funded research into the causes and cure of AIDS. In North America and Europe there are now innumerable public as well as private AIDS organizations, often serving specific ethnic and racial groups. AIDS organizations in Latin America, Africa, and Asia have not only increased public awareness about AIDS but have also been invaluable sources of information about gays and lesbians in cultures where, heretofore, there had been relatively little public discussion about homosexuality. Although the AIDS movement has outgrown its roots in the contemporary gay and lesbian movement, the initial impetus for AIDS organizing can be attributed to the work of gay men and lesbians.

Goals of the Contemporary Gay Liberation Movement

Despite the remarkable progress since Stonewall, much remains to be done to improve the legal situation of gays and lesbians. Although many nations have decriminalized homosexual intercourse in the last 30 years, for example, there are still 86 countries that continue to ban gay sex (44 of which ban lesbian sex). The United States is one of the 86.[16]

In the United States, in 1955, at a time when all but two U.S. states had criminal penalties for sodomy,[17] the American Law Institute's (ALI) model penal code proposed the abolition of sodomy laws, beginning the slow process of decriminalization. In the four decades between the ALI's draft penal code and the 1986 U.S. Supreme Court's precedent-setting *Bowers v. Hardwick* decision, roughly one-half of the states had excised sodomy from their codes of criminal justice. Advocates of gay and lesbian rights pinned their hopes for the elimination of the remaining sodomy laws in the United States on the *Bowers v. Hardwick* case, a challenge to the constitutionality of sodomy statutes. In

1986, however, the high court upheld the constitutional right of states to criminalize sexual practices between homosexuals and thus set back the movement to decriminalize homosexual intercourse in the United States. A decade after this historic Supreme Court decision, the law codes of 18 states and the District of Columbia still contained criminal penalties for sodomy.

Thus, despite the progress in decriminalizing homosexual intercourse in recent years, gays and lesbians still lack the basic freedom to engage in sexual relations with individuals of their choice in many U.S. states as well as in 85 other countries. Penalties for engaging in homosexual relations are typically severe, ranging from monetary fines and incarceration to the death penalty. Amnesty International reports that a number of countries, such as Iran, Mauretania, and Yemen still retain the death penalty for private, consensual homosexual relations. Furthermore, even where homosexuality is not specifically mentioned in the code of laws, some countries, such as Oman, Pakistan, Saudi Arabia, and the Sudan, have interpreted homosexual intercourse to be a capital offense.[18]

Similarly, despite the recent advances in human rights laws pertaining to gays and lesbians, few nations provide protection for the civil and political rights of homosexuals. There are currently only 11 countries that have nationwide civil rights laws pertaining to gays and lesbians. Other countries, such as the United States, only provide partial protection through state and municipal statutes. Most countries, however, provide no legal recourse whatsoever against discrimination based on sexual orientation. In extreme cases, gays and lesbians are targeted by political authorities for their advocacy of gay and lesbian rights. In 1992, Nicaragua amended its penal code to provide that "anyone who induces, promotes, propagandizes or practices in scandalous form sexual intercourse between persons of the same sex commits the crime of sodomy and shall incur one to three years imprisonment"[19] In Turkey, the First Congress of Homosexual Solidarity planned for July 1993 was banned, its organizers arrested, and the international delegates detained before being expelled from the country. And, in 1995, Gary Wu was imprisoned for organizing a social event for lesbians attending the Fourth Annual Conference on Women in Beijing and denied an exit visa from the People's Republic of China.

Furthermore, aside from the half-dozen countries that recognize the legality of gay and lesbian domestic partnerships, there are no other countries in the world where gays and lesbians have the legal rights of married heterosexuals. Even in countries where registered partnerships exist, gay and lesbian partnerships are not the full legal equivalent of their heterosexual counterparts (gays and lesbians, for example, are generally not entitled to church weddings and are prohibited from adopting children). There are also signs of increasing resistance to such unions, as in the United States where Congress and the president recently enacted the Defense of Marriage Act. It is impossible to foresee whether the current impetus to afford gays and lesbians rights traditionally reserved to heterosexual couples will expand significantly beyond the handful of countries that already afford such rights.

Also, without diminishing the significance of recent efforts to include gay and lesbian rights in international human rights law through the lobbying efforts of such groups as the ILGA, the lack of enforcement mechanisms diminishes the practical relevance of international institutions to the everyday lives of gays and lesbians. Despite the growing impetus to include gay and lesbian rights in international covenants, the future enforcement of such covenants still depends on the goodwill of the individual signatories. Thus, although recent proclamations of the EU, the OSCE, and the UN are promising, they are not binding, and therefore the utility of such declarations might not become apparent for decades, if ever.

Amnesty International also reports that gays and lesbians have been the victims of extrajudicial "disappearances" and executions. An example of such behavior was the murder of José dos Santos in Coqueiro Sêco, Brazil. A member of the city council, dos Santos was repeatedly threatened with death by the mayor and other officials, including police officers, because of his acknowledged bisexuality. On 14 March 1993, dos Santos was abducted from his house and beheaded. His family and friends suspect plainclothes officers in his death. Other recent reports of extrajudicial executions and disappearances include the recent policy of "social cleansing" in Colombia, where homosexuals, petty criminals, and vagrants have been the chief targets.[20]

Aside from the obvious inadequacies of national and international laws, gays and lesbians face the herculean task of transforming social attitudes toward sexuality and gender, a goal that has often been eclipsed by the drive to achieve equal rights. Rights-based movements are only relevant in the context of a limited number of political systems and, even within these political cultures, the acquisition of legal rights does not ensure the happiness or well-being of most gays and lesbians. Thus, much remains to be done to educate the public regarding the desirability of alternatives to the dominant heterosexual sex/gender model.[21]

Finally, the eradication of AIDS, and the care of PWAs, also remains a primary goal of the contemporary gay and lesbian movement. Despite the remarkable medical progress in recent years, most PWAs in the developing world, as well as many in the developed world, have no access to state-of-the-art medical treatments; and public and private resources devoted to the prevention of AIDS, and the care of PWAs, remain woefully insufficient.

The Future of the Gay and Lesbian Liberation Movement: Organizational Dilemmas

The maturation of the gay and lesbian liberation movement has resulted in a host of organizational dilemmas. For most of its history the focus of the movement has been on the elimination of discriminatory laws and practices affecting gay men and lesbians. This single-issue focus has been the source of recurrent controversy throughout its history and has been particularly acute during the contemporary period. Although few have disputed the necessity of addressing overt forms of discrimination perpetrated against gays and lesbians, many have argued that this has neglected the concerns of lesbians and racial minorities, as well as bisexuals and transgendered people.

The early homosexual rights movement, for example, was riven with controversy over the women's rights movement. Magnus Hirschfeld and the SHC argued that there was a natural affinity between the movement for women's rights and the homosexual rights movement and attempted to forge coalitions between the two movements. Because Paragraph 175 pertained only to sexual relations between men, however, many lesbians devoted their energy to the women's movement and resented the preoccupation of the homosexual rights movement with the repeal of Germany's sodomy statute. Further problematizing relations between gay men and lesbians were individuals such as Adolph Brand and Benedict Friedländer who espoused a misogynist philosophy and were not only uninterested in women's rights but unsympathetic to the plight of lesbians. This, among other things, caused a rupture between the SHC and the COS as well as the alienation of many lesbians from the initial movement for homosexual rights.

The apparent insensitivity of contemporary mainstream gay rights groups to the women's movement has also been a source of controversy in the United States since the inception of the modern homosexual rights movement in the 1950s. Homosexual rights leaders, most of whom were men, failed to appreciate the significance of women's rights to lesbians. This resulted in the creation of the Daughters of Bilitis, the first lesbian rights organization in North America. Male leaders also failed to appreciate the political potential of building coalitions with women's rights groups. Although women's rights groups were equally ambivalent about endorsing gay and lesbian rights and were uneasy about the presence of lesbians in their ranks, many lesbians felt that their interests were better served by the women's rights movement, or by lesbian separatist groups, than by mainstream gay and lesbian organizations.

Another source of controversy during the modern period was racism within the gay and lesbian community. Racial minorities have often been subjected to the same forms of overt discrimination by gay and lesbian establishments, and by gay and lesbian groups, as they have faced in the wider world. Racial minorities have also complained about the apathy displayed by the gay and lesbian movement toward the movement for racial justice. The situation was complicated by the historic unwillingness of most black, Hispanic, and Asian civil rights groups to endorse the gay and lesbian rights agenda, creating a dilemma of divided loyalties for nonwhite gays and lesbians.

There have been noteworthy efforts to bridge the gaps between the interests of gays, lesbians, and racial minorities. In the years following Stonewall, for example, the GLF challenged established homosexual rights groups to broaden the gay and lesbian civil rights agenda. Among other things, the GLF was committed to building a broad revolutionary coalition with antiwar activists, African American civil rights groups, and women's rights organizations. However, the GLF's efforts to develop a broad movement for social justice foundered, and the GLF rapidly fell into disarray. Special-interest groups in Western Europe and the United States, such as the Gay Activist Alliance, reemerged and set the tone for the gay and lesbian rights movement for the 1970s and 1980s.

At the same time, lesbian feminist critiques of the gay male subculture in North America and Western Europe further alienated many gay men from lesbians, and mainstream gay and lesbian organizations proved to be no more receptive to racial issues than they had been prior to Stonewall. This has resulted in the proliferation of lesbian feminist organizations as well as groups of Asian, black, and Hispanic gay and lesbian organizations during the contemporary period.

More recently, however, renewed efforts to build coalitions between the women's rights movement, the movement for racial justice, and the gay and lesbian rights movement have emerged. In the United States, in 1982, the Human Rights Campaign Fund (now the Human Rights Campaign), for example, became a member of the Leadership Council on Human Rights (LCHR). The LCHR was founded in 1950 to battle racial discrimination but has subsequently broadened its agenda to include women's rights and gay and lesbian rights issues. Thus, since 1982, as a member of the LCHR, the HRC has lobbied for abortion rights and African American rights legislation, such as the 1988 Fair Housing Act, and African American and women's rights members of LCHR have actively lobbied on behalf of the Employment Non-discrimination Act.

The most significant example of cooperation between the movement for racial justice and the gay and lesbian rights movement, however, occurred fairly recently in South Africa. The modern homosexual rights movement in South Africa, which dates from the founding of the Homosexual Law Reform Fund in 1968, historically excluded blacks. Through the efforts of many individuals, such as Simon Nkoli, however, interracial gay and lesbian organizations slowly came into being and the gay and lesbian rights movement ultimately joined the anti-apartheid movement. Because of the efforts of individuals like Nkoli, who was also a member of the African National Congress (ANC), the ANC endorsed the principle of gay and lesbian rights when it included antidiscrimination language to protect the rights of gays and lesbians in the 1996 permanent Constitution of South Africa.

Nevertheless, examples of cooperation between gay and lesbian rights groups, women's rights groups, and the movement for racial justice remain the exception to the rule. A single-issue focus continues to be the current emphasis of most contemporary gay and lesbian rights groups. As Colombian human rights activist Juan Pablo Ordenz complained:

> While our primary concern may be lesbian and gay people branded as "desechables"—"disposables," sexual orientation is only one of many reasons why people are so stigmatized. Those who oppress and kill "disposables" do not trouble themselves to treat them in discrete categories . . . it is absolutely crucial for gay and lesbian rights groups to make coalitions with diverse, broad-based human rights organizations to accomplish the hoped-for goal.[22]

This sentiment was echoed by U.S. activist Urvashi Vaid, former executive director of the National Gay and Lesbian Task Force (NGLTF), who wrote that many white male supporters of the NGLTF complained every time the NGLTF supported black civil rights or women's rights issues because these issues were not "our" issues, "women and people of color are asked by the movement to suppress those identities in order to participate in the movement."[23] From Vaid's point of view, the exclusive focus on issues pertaining to sexual orientation by the contemporary gay and lesbian rights movement tacitly reinforces existing gender and racial hierarchies and is therefore inimical to the interests of many gays and lesbians.

Thus, the future success of the gay and lesbian rights movement will depend, in part, on the ability of gay and lesbian organizations to represent the diverse needs of its constituents. Other fundamentally divisive issues confronting the contemporary gay and lesbian rights movement are bisexuality and transgenderism. The modern Western concepts of "homosexuality" and "sexual orientation," or the terms *gay* and *lesbian*, conceptualize identity on the basis of sexual object choice. This construction of identity implies an exclusivity of sexual desire as well as a traditional conception of gender roles (with the exception of sexual object choice). Bisexuals and transgendered people have challenged the contemporary gay and lesbian movement to become more inclusive on both accounts.

It is important to recall that the history of the gay and lesbian movement has been more multifaceted than the terms *homosexual*, *gay*, or *lesbian* imply. Many of the most prominent advocates of homosexual rights, for example, such as John Addington Symonds and Harry Hay were married to women. Although this does not mean that they were bisexual, neither can it be said that they were monosexual. At the same time, many advocates of gay and lesbian rights, such as Benedict Friedländer and Adolph Brand, have lived openly bisexual lives, and advocated bisexuality.

It should also be recalled that the early homosexual rights movement embraced a sex/gender model (the "third sex") that implied a transgendered psychosexual state of being. Thus, at the very inception of the homosexual rights movement, it was assumed that same-sex desire implied more than an inversion of sexual object choice; it also implied an inversion of gender roles. It is only relatively recently that *homosexuality* has been defined exclusively in terms of sexual object choice. This issue has reemerged in recent years with the demand by transgendered people for inclusion in gay and lesbian rights organizations, raising further questions about the validity of the heterosexual/homosexual binary as an organizational principle.

Outside the Western experience, the multifaceted nature of sexual identities becomes even more apparent. Whether thinking of the history of the Japanese samurai and the Chinese catamite, the North American "berdache," the "boy-inseminating" practices in Melanesia, the Zuni "man-woman," or the Latin American "cochón" and "hombre-hombre," the cultural relativity of "homo-sexual" expression becomes undeniable.[24]

If gays and lesbians are to succeed in mobilizing an international movement, their leaders will have to recognize not only the relevance of women's rights and the rights of racial minorities to the gay and lesbian movement but also the interests of bisexuals and transgendered people. Most important, perhaps, is a recognition of the cultural relativity of the modern Western sex/gender model.

The limitations of the Western sex/gender model was recognized by the ILGA in its 1993 *Pink Book*, in which the authors acknowledged that there "is no such thing as *the* lesbian or *the* gay man" and that "same-sex lifestyles differ from place to place and from time to time." [25] This nominal recognition of the need to embrace a more inclusive model of sexual minorities as the basis for the future of the movement was a necessary first step in what will undoubtedly be a long and difficult road in forging a unified movement of sexual minorities that is international in more than name only.

Notes

1. The demarcation of the early period was first suggested by John Lauritsen and David Thorstad, *The Early Homosexual Rights Movement (1864–1935)* (New York: Times Change Press, 1974).

2. See, for example, John Boswell, *Christianity, Social Tolerance, and Homosexuality* (Chicago: University of Chicago Press, 1980); James A. Brundage, *Law, Sex, and Christian Society in Medieval Europe* (Chicago: University of Chicago Press, 1987); Vern Bullough and James Brundage, eds., *Sexual Practices and the Medieval Church* (Buffalo: Prometheus Books, 1982).

3. Karl Heinrich Ulrichs, *The Riddle of "Man-Manly" Love: The Pioneering Work on Male Homosexuality*, 2 vols., trans. by Michael A. Lombardi-Nash (Buffalo, N.Y.: Prometheus Books, 1994).

4. Harry Oosterhuis, "Homosexual Emancipation in Germany before 1933: Two Traditions," in *Homosexuality and Male Bonding in Pre-Nazi Germany*, ed. Harry Oosterhuis (New York/London: Haworth Press, 1991), 12.

5. James Steakley. *The Homosexual Emancipation Movement in Germany* (New York: Arno, 1975), 100 n 25.

6. See, for example, John D'Emilio, *Sexual Politics, Sexual Communities: The Making of a Homosexual Minority in the United States, 1940–1970* (Chicago: University of Chicago Press, 1983), Chap. 2.

7. Allan Bérubé, *Coming Out under Fire: The History of Gay Men and Women in World War Two* (New York: Plume, 1990), 249.

8. D'Emilio, *Sexual Politics, Sexual Communities*, 103.

9. Jonathan Katz, *Gay American History: Lesbians and Gay Men in the U.S.A.* (New York: Thomas Crowell, 1976), 424.

10. *The Advocate*, Issue 735 (June 1997): 22.

11. Urvashi Vaid. *Virtual Equality: The Mainstreaming of Gay and Lesbian Liberation* (New York: Anchor Books, 1995), 8.

12. ILGA, *Euroletter*, no. 45 (November, 1996): 18.

13. ILGA, *Euroletter*, no. 45, 19.

14. ILGA, *Euroletter*, no. 45, 15–16.

15. ILGA, *Euroletter*, no. 45, 17.

16. Rex Wockner, *ILGA Euroletter*, no. 46 (December 1996): 10.

17. D'Emilio, *Sexual Politics, Sexual Communities*, 14.

18. Amnesty International, *Breaking the Silence: Human Rights Violations Based on Sexual Orientation* (New York: Amnesty International Publications, 1994), 34.

19. Amnesty International, *Breaking the Silence*, 25.

20. Amnesty International, *Breaking the Silence*, 12–13.

21. For a critique of the limitations of rights-based political organizing, see Didi Herman, *Rights of Passage: Struggles for Lesbian and Gay Legal Equality* (Toronto: University of Toronto Press, 1994).

22. Herman, *Rights of Passage*, 8.

23. Vaid, *Virtural Equality*, 283.

24. See, for example, Fang-fu Ruan, *Sex in China: Studies in Sexology in Chinese Culture* (New York: Plenum Press, 1991); Gilbert Herdt, ed., *Ritualized Homosexuality in Melanesia* (Berkeley: University of California Press, 1984); Stephen O. Murray, *Latin American Male Homosexualities* (Albuquerque: University of New Mexico Press, 1995); Will Roscoe, ed., *Living the Spirit: A Gay American Indian Anthology* (New York: St. Martin's Press, 1988); and, Jun'ichi Iwata, *Love of the Samurai: A Thousand Years of Japanese Homosexuality* (London: Gay Men's Press, 1989).

25. Aart Hendriks, Rob Tielman, and Evert van der Veen, eds., *The Pink Book: A Global View of Lesbian and Gay Liberation and Oppression* (Buffalo: Prometheus Books, 1993), 18.

The Dictionary

A

ACT OF 25 HENRY VIII, C.6 (1533). Great Britain's notorious "buggery" statute enacted during the reign of Henry VIII that criminalized acts of sodomy. It was applicable to acts of anal intercourse between men and women, between men, and to acts of bestiality. The act, which superseded ecclesiastical law, prescribed the penalty of death together with the confiscation of all property. It was applicable to civilians as well as military personnel and those in the merchant marine. In 1861 the Offenses against the Person Act reduced the penalty to 10 years to life imprisonment in England and Wales; the reduced penalties were not adopted in Scotland until 1889.

This statute was the principal means used to incarcerate male homosexuals until the enactment of the Labouchère Amendment (q.v.) to the Criminal Law Amendment Act in 1885. Although not all men convicted under the statute before the recision of the death penalty incurred hanging, many did. Accurate statistics do not exist, but there are recorded incidents of executions for breach of this statute. Many men also incurred life sentences after the recision of the death penalty.

It was not until the appointment of the Committee on Homosexual Offenses and Prostitution (q.v.), better known as the Wolfenden Committee, in 1954, that a serious attempt to reform British law was undertaken. Fourteen years later, in 1967, the Sexual Offenses Act (q.v.) decriminalized adult male homosexuality and effectively rescinded both the statute of 1533 and the Labouchère Amendment. *See also* Sodomy Statutes.

AFRICA. With the notable exception of the country of South Africa, the gay and lesbian rights movement is in its infancy in Africa. Overwhelming poverty and strong social taboos against homosexuality leave little social space for gays or lesbians to congregate. The rise of Islamic fundamentalism in North Africa has problematized sexual relations between men in a region that was once tolerant of male homosexual behavior, and strong social sanctions are common

31

in East as well as West Africa. Furthermore, many countries, such as Algeria, Ethiopia, Ghana, Kenya, Nigeria, Morocco, Sudan, Mozambique, Tanzania, Uganda, Zambia, and Zimbabwe have highly punitive sodomy statutes (q.v.) or other legal proscriptions against homosexuality. Consequently, the emergence of gay and lesbian groups is exceedingly rare, and incipient organizations, such as the Gay Liberation Group (Ghana), the Rainbow Project (Namibia), and Gays and Lesbians in Zimbabwe (GALZ), operate under extremely repressive regimes. In 1995, for example, GALZ was prohibited from participating in the 1995 Zimbabwe International Book Fair. Most recently, President Robert Mugabe denounced the intention of the World Council of Churches to include GALZ in its 1998 meeting in Harare and demanded the exclusion of the group.

In South Africa, on the other hand, the gay liberation movement has a relatively long history, next only to Europe and North America (qq.v.). Beginning with the establishment of the Homosexual Law Reform Fund (q.v.), in 1968, an organization devoted to resisting the enactment of a South African sodomy statute, a number of other gay and lesbian organizations came into being in the 1970s and 1980s, including Gay Aid Identification Development and Enrichment (GAIDE), the Gay Association of South Africa (GASA), and the Gay and Lesbian Organization of the Witwatersrand (GLOW) (qq.v.). Today, lesbian and gay organizations are increasingly common throughout South Africa.

Through the efforts of GLOW and individuals such as Simon Nkoli (q.v.), the gay and lesbian movement became allied with the antiapartheid movement and the African National Congress (ANC). Not only did this represent a great breakthrough in the effort to desegregate gay and lesbian organizations, but it became an opportunity for gay and lesbian organizations to influence public policy after the accession of the ANC. In the end, the ANC embraced the principle of gay and lesbian rights and fought successfully for antidiscrimination language in the interim South African Constitution. Consequently, South Africa is one of only a few countries in the world, such as Canada and the Netherlands, to offer constitutional rights to lesbians and gays.

AGE OF CONSENT LAWS. Age of consent laws establish the age at which an individual may legally consent to sexual relations with another person. Although most age of consent laws only penalize sexual relations between an adult and a minor, some penalize sexual relations between minors as well.

A long-term objective of the gay and lesbian rights movement has been the international campaign to equalize age of consent laws for homosexuals and heterosexuals. Most typically, age of consent laws discriminate against gay men by stipulating higher ages of consent for sexual relations between men than for sexual relations between women or between men and women. Often, however, there are higher ages of consent stipulated for both gay and lesbian sexual relations than for heterosexual relations. In many places unequal age of consent laws are one of the last vestiges of de jure discrimination against gay men and lesbians.

Even in jurisdictions where there are no sodomy statutes (q.v.), or where gays and lesbians enjoy the protection of civil rights (q.v.) laws, including the right of military service (q.v.), or marriage (q.v.), there are often higher statutory age of consent requirements for homosexuals than for heterosexuals.

In France, for example, where sodomy was expunged from the criminal code in 1791, and where gays and lesbians had often sought refuge from persecution, unequal age of consent laws were introduced in 1942 to discriminate against homosexual intercourse. Applicable to both lesbians and gay men, the age of consent for homosexuals was five years higher than for heterosexuals. Penalties were severe and acted as an impediment against younger gays and lesbians coming out. *See also Arcadie.*

Although France enacted legislation in 1982 equalizing the age of consent for homosexual and heterosexual relations, other countries, such as England, still retain unequal age of consent laws in spite of the fact that homosexual intercourse has been legal for over 30 years. Other legal anomalies include countries where unequal ages of consent persist alongside statutory protections of gay and lesbian civil rights, such as Finland, or where gays and lesbians can marry, such as Hungary, or where gays and lesbians can enlist for military service, such as Israel. One setback recently occurred in Portugal. In 1995, 50 years after abolishing unequal age of consent provisions in Portuguese law, Portugal reintroduced an unequal age of consent law that discriminates against homosexual intercourse; and this at a time when Parliament was actively considering the enactment of a registered partnership act!

AKTIONSAUSSCHUSS/ACTION COMMITTEE (AC). Founded in 1920, the AC was a nationwide coalition of the three most prominent homosexual rights organizations in Weimar Germany: the Wissenschaftlich-humanitäres Komitee (Scientific Humanitarian Committee [SHC]), the Gemeinschaft der Eigenen (Community of the Special [COS]), and the Deutscher Freundschaftsverband (German Friendship Association [GFA]) (qq.v.). The SHC was founded in 1897, the COS, in 1902, and the GFA, in 1919. The purpose of the AC was to bridge philosophical differences among the three organizations and to develop a broad-based homosexual rights constituency. The coalition's primary objective was to repeal Paragraph 175 (q.v.) of the German law code. Kurt Hiller, a member of the board of directors of the SHC, was named to head the new organization. The coalition fell apart in 1923 when tensions within the GFA led to a discontinuation of its efforts to secure legal reform and thus its participation in the coalition.

ALBANY TRUST (AT). In May 1958 the AT was established as an arm of the Homosexual Law Reform Society (HLRS) (q.v.), a British homosexual rights organization. The primary purpose of the HLRS was to implement the proposals of the 1957 Report of the Committee on Homosexual Offenses and Prostitution (q.v.), better known as the Wolfenden Report. The AT supplemented the legal projects of the HLRS through psychological counseling, education, and other social work activities. In 1965 it became a recognized charity and qualified for tax rebates. The first secretary of the organization was the Reverend Andrew Hallidie Smith.

The AT fostered a wide variety of activities in support of the homosexual liberation movement. It attempted, for example, to facilitate contacts with international homophile organizations. The Club littéraire et scientifique des pays latines (Literary and Scientific Club of the Latin Countries), a French homophile organization better known as Arcadie, and the Cultuur-en-Ontspannings Centrum (Cultural and Recreational Center [CRC]), a Dutch group, (qq.v.) were two organizations with which the AT remained in regular contact. In 1966, at the request of Ted McIlvenna, the president of the Council on Religion and the Homosexual (q.v.), an American group, the AT convened a conference entitled "Anglo-American Consultation on the Church, Society, and the Homosexual," which featured presentations by John Gagnon and William Simon of the Institute for Sex Research at the University of Indiana and Antony Grey (q.v.) as well as other British and American social workers and clergy. The conference stimulated further contacts between the AT and sympathetic individuals and groups in the United States. In 1967, Grey spent four weeks in the United States on a lecture tour sponsored by the Erikson Educational Foundation and One Inc. (q.v.). The primary topic of interest was the 1967 Sexual Offenses Act (q.v.), which the HLRS and the AT had worked hard to enact.

Another major initiative of the AT was its cosponsorship of the York Social Needs Conference in 1970. The purpose of the conference was to assess the continuing needs of gays and lesbians after the passage of the 1967 Sexual Offenses Act. One product of the conference was the creation, in 1971, of the National Federation of Homophile Organizations (NFHO) (q.v.). Like the North American Congress of Homophile Organizations (NACHO) (q.v.) in the United States, the NFHO attempted to forge a national agenda and a more centralized approach to gay and lesbian issues. Also like NACHO, it was shortlived. Two of its major constituents, the Scottish Minorities Group and the Campaign for Homosexual Equality (qq.v.), walked out in 1973. The experiment with a nationwide homophile organization foundered over philosophical and organizational disputes, and the NFHO disappeared.

The AT dissolved in 1980. In 1975 the AT participated in a number of meetings with representatives of the Paedophile Action for Liberation (PAL) and the Paedophile Information Exchange (PIE). Although the AT never endorsed the objectives of either the PAL or PIE, its interest in counseling motivated the AT to explore pedophilia believing that it might contribute to a better understanding of the issue. Nevertheless, the association of the AT with pedophile groups was enough to generate a whirlwind of criticism from moral majority groups and from politicians hostile to homosexual rights. As the AT had never enjoyed financial stability, when the Thatcher government terminated all support for the activities of the AT in 1979 it had no alternative but to end its 22-year campaign for gay and lesbian rights. Only its counseling group survived its demise.

ANGELO, BOB (NIEK ENGELSCHMAN) (1913–1988). An actor by profession, Bob Angelo founded one of the first journals dealing with the subject of homosexuality. Founded in the Netherlands in 1940, *Levensrecht* (Right to Live) was suppressed by the Germans shortly after the invasion of Holland, but it reemerged immediately after the war in 1946. The republication of *Levensrecht* spawned a discussion group, the "Shakespeare Club," which in turn soon led to the creation of the Cultuur-en-Ontspannings Centrum (Culture and Recreational Center [CRC]) (q.v.).

The CRC's national office opened in Amsterdam in 1948. Bob Angelo was its first director. Branches in other Dutch cities such as The Hague and Rotterdam soon opened. These centers typically included dance floors, meeting rooms, and bars. They facilitated discussion groups as well as a variety of other cultural activities. The recreational and self-help activities of the CRC became a model for other homosexual rights groups, such as the Albany Trust (q.v.).

In recognition of his many contributions to the Dutch gay and lesbian community, Bob Angelo was awarded the Grand Cross of the Order of Orange-Nassau, similar in significance to knighthood in Great Britain.

ARCADIE. Founded in 1953 by André Baudry, *Arcadie* is widely regarded to have been the first gay and lesbian rights journal in France. Although it was preceded by the journal *Futur*, in 1952, *Futur*'s existence was a virtual secret and its circulation very small. Affiliated with *Arcadie* was the Club littéraire et scientifique des pays latines (Literary and Scientific Club of the Latin Countries). Commonly known as Arcadie, it was a social club similar to the Cultuur-en-Ontspannings Centrum (Culture and Recreational Center [CRC]) (q.v.) in the Netherlands.

The toleration of homosexuality in France after World War II was at a low ebb, and publications such as *Futur* and *Arcadie* were not designed for mass circulation for fear of repression by the authorities. But whereas *Arcadie* survived for over 30 years, *Futur* ceased publication in 1955.

Although private homosexual acts between consenting adults have been legal in France since the promulgation of the 1791 penal code by the Constituent Assembly, the political milieu during World War II and the immediate postwar years was not congenial to gays and lesbians. The Vichy government, the collaborationist regime that ruled France during the Nazi occupation, introduced changes in the age of consent laws designed to discriminate against gays and lesbians. Theretofore, the age of consent had been 16 for heterosexuals and homosexuals alike. Marshal Pétain's decree (Article 334), however, raised the age of consent for homosexual intercourse to 21. This article was applicable to lesbians as well as gay men, even if both parties were below the age of 21 and the intercourse was consensual. Prison sentences of up to three years were prescribed by the statute. Charles de Gaulle incorporated these changes into Article 331 of the postliberation French penal code in 1945 (the Pétain-de Gaulle law). Furthermore, in 1960, de Gaulle was also responsible for introducing changes into the statute on public indecency, penalizing gays and lesbians more severely than heterosexuals for comparable offenses.

The postwar years also witnessed a resurgence in Thomistic thought, with its characteristic condemnations of the immorality of homosexuality and the polemics of the psychiatric profession's insistence that homosexuality constituted a mental illness. The French psychiatrist Dr. Eck no less than his American counterparts Dr. Irving Bieber and Dr. Charles Socarides, saw homosexuality as a threat to family, nation, race, and even civilization itself. Police crackdowns on homosexuals reached new heights, and pronouncements by public officials condemning homosexuality became increasingly common.

It was in this atmosphere of increasing intolerance that *Arcadie* was born in 1953. As the voice of its parent homophile organization Arcadie, the journal *Arcadie* championed the repeal of the Pétain-de Gaulle law as well as an end to the differential punishments for infractions of the public indecency statute. *Arcadie* criticized the attitudes of the Marxist Left, the mass media, the church, and psychiatry for perpetuating outmoded stereotypes of gays and lesbians.

Like the Mattachine Society (MS) (q.v.) and the Daughters of Bilitis (DOB) in the United States, the Committee for Homosexual Equality (CHE) (q.v.) in Britain, and the CRC in the Netherlands, Arcadie was a reformist organization devoted to legal equality and the assimilation of gays and lesbians into French society. As the Gay Liberation Front (GLF) (q.v.) posed philosophical and organizational challenges to the MS, DOB, and CHE in the United States and in Britain, Arcadie was challenged by the emergence of the Front Homosexuel d'Action Révolutionnaire (Revolutionary Homosexual Action Front [RHAF]) (q.v.) in 1971. The RHAF saw Arcadie's program of political action as too reformist and proposed instead a coalition of minority groups and a socialist platform. But, at the time of *Arcadie*'s 20th birthday in 1973, the RHAF had already disappeared from the scene.

The RHAF was superseded by the Groupe de Libération Homosexuelle (Homosexual Liberation Group) and, in the late 1970s, the Comité d'Urgence Anti-Répression Homosexuelle (Emergency Committee against the Repression of Homosexuals [ECARH]) (qq.v.), a coalition of 16 French gay and lesbian organizations. Arcadie was not among them. Arcadie's long tradition of emphasizing social functions and its apolitical posture isolated it from participation in such an overt political coalition.

Beginning in 1978, demands to rescind the Pétain-de Gaulle law were initiated in the Senate and, in 1979, were first considered by the National Assembly. The ECARH supported the candidacy of François Mitterrand in 1981 because of Mitterrand's promise to end discrimination against gays and lesbians. In 1982, the Pétain-de Gaulle law was repealed and the age of consent for both heterosexuals and homosexuals was established at 15.

At its height, Arcadie could claim to be one of the oldest gay and lesbian rights organizations in the world and boasted a membership in excess of 50,000. After Mitterrand's election, however, Arcadie, along with its journal *Arcadie*, ceased operations. Its closure, in 1982, after almost 30 years was a reflection of changing times. New gay and lesbian political and social organizations had emerged and eclipsed Arcadie's historic role.

ARTICLE 121.1. Enacted in 1960, Article 121 of the Soviet penal code penalized various aspects of anal intercourse between men. Article 121.1 penalized voluntary male homosexual intercourse, with prison sentences not to exceed five years' duration. Homosexual intercourse between women had never been an object of the Soviet criminal code or of the Czarist codes that preceded it. Article 121 replaced Article 154a, a Stalinist-era sodomy statute (q.v.) that was enacted in 1934. The enactment of 154a ended a 17-year period of relative sexual freedom in the USSR in which homosexual intercourse, among other things, remained beyond the purview of the law.

Prior to 1917, sodomy between men was punishable under the code of laws of the Russian Empire. Article 995, enacted in 1845, punished anal intercourse between men with maximum prison sentences of four to five years. A revision of the penal code in 1903 imposed minimum sentences of no less than three months. The entire Czarist code of laws was abolished in 1917, including Article 995.

The relaxation in the moral code under the Bolsheviks was short-lived, however. Article 154a reenacted the provisions of Article 995 with similarly harsh sentences (three to five years for voluntary anal intercourse). Article 121.1, by comparison, contained no stipulated minimum sentence, reflecting the liberalization of the Soviet penal code after Stalin's death.

Opposition to Article 121.1 among Soviet psychiatric and legal professionals was widespread. Opposition from gay and lesbian rights groups did not occur until the founding of the Sexual Minorities Association (q.v.) in 1989, owing to the repression of gay and lesbian organizations by the Communist Party. Only four years later, in 1993, however, Boris Yeltsin rescinded Article 121.1. Only those aspects of Article 121 that penalize involuntary anal intercourse or intercourse with minors remain on the books in Russia.

ASIA. Although male homosexuality has a long history in Asia (male homosexuality was a venerated tradition among certain groups such as the Japanese samurai), and although there is a correspondingly rich literary record of male homosexual practices, the development of an Asian gay and lesbian identity, culture, and political movement has been relatively recent in comparison with Europe or North America (qq.v.).

The situation of gays and lesbians varies considerably from one country to the next. On the one hand, there are countries such as the Philippines or Thailand where there is comparatively little official oppression of male homosexuality and where the practice is tolerated if not universally accepted. On the other hand, official proscription of homosexual relations in the form of sodomy statutes (q.v.) still exists in such countries as India, Malaysia, and Singapore,

where they are legacies of British colonialism. Even where sodomy laws do not exist, such as in the People's Republic of China, official repression of homosexuality is manifested in the prosecution of homosexuals as "hooligans."

Just as important, perhaps, are the overwhelming familial and economic pressures that exist throughout Asia, the close family ties, the need to marry and bear children to satisfy social expectations, the lack of resources to rent a living space of one's own, and so on. Even where homosexual intercourse is not criminalized and where the practice of male homosexuality is tolerated, gays and lesbians rarely have the luxury of living independently, or of interacting within a Western-style gay and lesbian subculture.

A gay and lesbian identity and culture is slowly beginning to develop throughout Asia, however, and with it the beginnings of gay and lesbian political organizing. Organizations such as the Ten Percent Club in Hong Kong and the International Lesbian and Gay Association-Japan (ILGA-J) (qq.v.) have established roots. They provide social venues for their members and have begun to engage in educational and social service functions such as AIDS education. They have also begun to engage in political activities, such as the opposition of the Ten Percent Club to Hong Kong's criminal statutes prohibiting homosexual intercourse. Similar groups have formed in other Asian countries such as Malaysia (Pink Triangle), Indonesia (KKLGN), India (Bombay Dost), and the Philippines (the Library Foundation). A measure of international cooperation among Asian organizations has also begun to emerge with the establishment of the annual conferences of Asian Lesbians and Gays. Even in the People's Republic of China, where there is no official toleration of homosexuality, there is evidence of underground groups and pioneers of gay and lesbian rights such as Gary Wu (q.v.).

Whether gay and lesbian culture and politics in Asia will evolve by adopting Western-style values, or whether it will develop its own distinctive values and objectives remains to be seen. On the one hand, Western media and tourism have apparently had an impact on the development of commercial establishments serving gay males and the development of a Westernized gay identity, at least in many urban areas. On the other hand, some Asian activists feel that the Westernization of Asian gay and lesbian culture is unwelcome. A manifesto drafted at a December 1997 conference of some 200 gays and lesbians in Hong Kong "rejected the need to protest, lobby, or come out," stressing instead " 'social harmony' . . . as most conducive to 'achieving tongzhi liberation in the family-centered, community-oriented Chinese society.' " (*The Advocate*, 24 June 1997, 72.).

ASSOCIATION FOR SOCIAL KNOWLEDGE (ASK). Founded in 1964 in Vancouver, British Columbia, by John MacKinnon, Bruce Somers, Gerrald Turnball, and others, ASK was the most prominent gay and lesbian rights organization in Canada prior to Stonewall (q.v.).

The impetus for the formation of ASK were the Mattachine Society (MS) (q.v.) and the Daughters of Bilitis (DOB), organizations that emerged in the United States during the early 1950s. Unlike the MS and the DOB, however, ASK included both lesbians and gay men.

ASK maintained a community center, published a newsletter, and maintained informal ties with citywide chapters of the MS and DOB (the national organizations of both the MS and the DOB ceased to exist prior to the founding of ASK), the Society for Individual Rights, and the Council on Religion and the Homosexual (qq.v.). ASK was also a member of the short-lived North American Conference of Homophile Organizations (q.v.).

ASK's approach to organizing gays and lesbians was borrowed from the MS. The focus of the organization was to recruit respectable individuals who were interested in informing themselves and others about the problems confronting homosexuals in Canada. Like the MS, it relied heavily on experts in psychology and medicine to educate the membership on the nature of homosexuality and to argue that existing criminal penalties punishing homosexual behavior were irrational.

Although ASK was not instrumental in the parliamentary debates that ultimately led to the passage of the Canadian Criminal Code reform (q.v.) of 1969, it was influential in mobilizing gays and lesbians in support of decriminalizing private consensual sex between adult homosexuals. ASK sponsored speeches and used its newsletter to attack the criminal penalties attached to homosexual relationships. It thus helped forge an incipient political consciousness among gays and lesbians in Canada at a time when few dared risk the consequences of public pronouncements in defense of homosexual rights.

ASK disappeared on the eve of the passage of the Canadian Criminal Code reform of 1969. In its place emerged the University of Toronto Homophile Association, the first post-Stonewall group in Canada, and then, in the 1970s, numerous groups such as the Vancouver Gay Liberation Front, Toronto Gay Action, and Front de Libération Homosexuelle (Homosexual Liberation Front) in Montreal. Like other Gay Liberation Front (q.v.) groups in the United States and Europe, these organizations disappeared within a few years and were replaced by more reformist single-issue organizations, such as the

Coalition for Gay Rights in Ontario (q.v.), an organization whose objectives were more similar to those of ASK.

ASYLUM. In recent years, as the international movement to extend civil rights (q.v.) protections to gays and lesbians has gained in strength, so too has the movement to protect gays and lesbians from antigay persecution. Ten countries now grant asylum from persecution on the basis of sexual orientation: Australia, Belgium, Canada, Finland, Germany, Ireland, the Netherlands, New Zealand, the United Kingdom, and the United States. Most refugees have come from areas of the world where homosexuality is least tolerated, such as Africa, Asia, (Eastern) Europe, Latin America, and the Middle East (qq.v.).

AUSTRALIA/NEW ZEALAND. Next only to Europe and North America (qq.v.), Australia and New Zealand have the longest history of gay and lesbian political organizing in the world. Beginning with New Zealand's Dorian Society (DS), in 1964, and Australia's Campaign against Moral Persecution (CAMP) (qq.v.), in 1970, gay and lesbian rights activists challenged sodomy statutes (q.v.), the legacy of British colonialism.

Although 22 years passed between the foundation of the DS and the decriminalization of sodomy in New Zealand, in 1986, the results of gay and lesbian organizing have been dramatic. Shortly after the foundation of CAMP, sodomy was decriminalized in the federal territories of Australia, in 1973. This set in motion the decriminalization of sodomy in Australian states, which culminated in 1997 with the decriminalization of sodomy in Tasmania, a long-term goal of the Tasmanian Gay and Lesbian Rights Group.

Progress on the civil rights (q.v.) front has also been encouraging. In 1977, New South Wales became the first Australian state to enact civil rights protections for gays and lesbians. The state of South Australia followed suit in 1984. In 1993, New Zealand enacted a nationwide gay and lesbian civil rights statute, making it one of the few counties in the world to have established this precedent.

There has also been progress in other respects. In 1992, Australia dropped its prohibition on homosexuals in the military service (q.v.), something that has yet to be achieved in the United States. Although marriage (q.v.) between individuals of the same sex is not yet recognized, Australia took a step in this direction in 1991, when homosexual relationships were recognized as legitimate relationships for purposes of immigration, and, in both Australia and New Zealand, there are efforts to establish the legitimacy of gay and lesbian domestic partnerships.

AXGIL, AXEL (1915–   ). Founder, in 1948, in Ålborg, Denmark, of the Landsforeningen for Bøsser og Lesbiske (National Organization of Gays and Lesbians) (NOGL) (q.v.), which is the current national Danish gay and lesbian organization. Due to the notoriety associated with the foundation of this group, Axgil lost both his job and his apartment in Ålborg. He soon fled to Copenhagen, where he served as chair of the rapidly growing group until 1952.

In 1957 Axel and roughly 80 other men affiliated with the NOGL were arrested in a pornography scandal. Among the others arrested was his lover, Eigil. After their release from prison in 1958 they adopted a common surname, Axgil. They have remained together ever since and have devoted much of their time to advancing the interests of gays and lesbians.

One of their chief concerns was the campaign for a partnership law, one that would give gays and lesbians the same rights as married heterosexual couples. Their efforts were rewarded when the Danish Registered Partnership Act (q.v.) was passed by the Folketing, the Danish Parliament, in May 1989. In October of the same year Axel and Eigil were honored as the first to be married under the provisions of the statute.

B

***BAEHR V. LEWIN* (1993).** A Hawaii Supreme Court decision ordering the attorney general of the state of Hawaii to justify the state's refusal to issue marriage licenses to gay and lesbian couples.

Pursuant to the court's order, the attorney general of the state of Hawaii appeared before a state trial court judge in 1996 to defend the state's contention that there existed a compelling state interest in denying Ninia Baehr and Genora Dancel, Joseph Melillo and Patrick Lagon, and one other lesbian couple the right to marry.

The state trial court ruled that Hawaii had failed to demonstrate a compelling state interest and, therefore, that gays and lesbians were guaranteed the right to marry by the Hawaiian constitution. The decision (*Baehr v. Miike*) is on appeal to the Hawaii Supreme Court.

The gay and lesbian marriage issue became more complicated in April 1997 when the Hawaiian legislature passed a constitutional amendment that would give the legislature the power to define marriage (q.v.) eligibility. Ratification by voters is scheduled for the November 1998 elections.

Thus, the outcome of the effort to legalize homosexual marriages in Hawaii is very much in doubt. If Hawaii legalizes same-sex marriages, it will be the first political jurisdiction in the Americas to do so. Although a number of U.S. cities allow gay and lesbian couples to register their partnerships (which might even qualify the couples for a limited range of benefits), these partnerships are in no sense legal marriages.

In response to the eventuality of civil marriages for gay and lesbian couples in Hawaii, many state legislatures have enacted legislation prohibiting the legal recognition of such unions in their states. The U.S. Congress has also adopted the Defense of Marriage Act (q.v.). Among other things, this statute prohibits the federal government from recognizing the validity of gay and lesbian unions performed in U.S. states or in other nations and would preclude gay and lesbian couples from receiving federal benefits accorded to married heterosexual couples.

BAEHR V. MIIKE. *See* BAEHR V. LEWIN.

BENKERT, KARL MARIA. *See* KERTBENY, KARL MARIA.

BOWERS V. HARDWICK (1986). In this precedent-setting case the U.S. Supreme Court ruled in a 5–4 decision that the U.S. Constitution does not prohibit states from enacting and enforcing sodomy statutes (q.v.).

The federal structure of the U.S. Constitution reserves to the states the right to enact legislation except where such right has been explicitly delegated to the federal government or where such legislation violates rights guaranteed in the Constitution. Legislation prohibiting acts of sodomy has traditionally been the province of the states.

A challenge to the state of Georgia's sodomy statute by Michael Hardwick formed the basis for the Supreme Court's historic *Bowers v. Hardwick* decision. At the time of Mr. Hardwick's arrest in Atlanta, the maximum penalty for violation of Georgia's statute was 20 years. In ruling that states had the legal authority to prohibit sexual acts between consenting adult homosexuals, the Supreme Court denied that a constitutional right to privacy forbade such laws. Today, roughly 30 years after the British Parliament abolished criminal penalties for private sexual behavior between adult homosexuals, almost 40 percent of the U.S. states still retain such criminal penalties, though few are as severe as was Georgia's statute in 1986.

BRAND, ADOLF (1874–1945). Anarchist, German homosexual activist, cofounder of the Gemeinschaft der Eigenen (Community of the Special [COS]) (q.v.), and publisher of *Der Eigene* (The Special) (q.v.).

Adolf Brand's interest in the homosexual emancipation movement was awakened by his reading of Magnus Hirschfeld's (q.v.) *Sappho und Sokrates*. They met in 1896 and laid plans for a movement to repeal Paragraph 175 (q.v.), the section of the German criminal code that penalized adult male homosexual relations.

Brand was also an early supporter of the Wissenschaftlich-humanitäres Komitee (Scientific-Humanitarian Committee [SHC]) (q.v.), the homosexual rights organization founded by Hirschfeld to spearhead the campaign for homosexual emancipation. Although Brand and Hirschfeld continued to cooperate intermittently throughout their careers, their association became increasingly inimical owing to theoretical differences.

Hirschfeld, a physician, focused on biological etiologies of homosexuality, whereas Brand emphasized the cultural roots and ethical qualities of male friendship. Brand used the term *homosexuality* reluctantly because of its roots in the medical model (q.v.) of homoeroticism. These theoretical differences resulted in the growing animosity between followers of the COS and those of the SHC.

The COS was founded by Brand, Benedict Friedländer (q.v.), and others in 1902. More of a literary circle, or a circle of friends, it was not open to women and was not as influential as the SHC. Relations between the COS and the SHC reached a low point when Friedländer resigned from the SHC in 1906, attempting to lead others with him to the COS. This action failed, and the COS never again rivaled the SHC's importance in the homosexual emancipation movement.

The philosophy of the COS was spelled out in the pages of *Der Eigene*. Founded by Brand in 1896, the journal published literary, artistic, historical, and polemical articles on the subject of love among men, including man-boy love, or pedagogical eros. Attacks on the medical model of homosexuality, Magnus Hirschfeld and the SHC in particular, also featured prominently in the pages of the journal. It ceased publication in 1931, on the eve of the rise of the Nazi Party.

Brand was imprisoned on two occasions. In 1903, he was sentenced to prison for two months as a result of his conviction for publishing photographs of nude youths in *Der Eigene*. He was also sued for libel by the prime minister Bernhard von Bülow as a result of a 1907 article in which he accused the prime minister of being a homosexual. Brand's motivation was to discredit the prime minister, whom Brand believed to be the source of a journalist's exposé of a circle of homosexuals close to Kaiser Wilhelm II. (The matter was known as the Harden-Eulenburg scandal). Bülow's libel suit resulted in Brand's conviction and a prison sentence of 18 months.

Brand's activism came to an end in the early 1930s when the Nazi Party banned the activities of the COS and the publication of *Der Eigene*. Adolf Brand and his wife died in an air raid in 1945.

BRITISH SEXOLOGICAL SOCIETY. *See* BRITISH SOCIETY FOR THE STUDY OF SEX PSYCHOLOGY.

BRITISH SOCIETY FOR THE STUDY OF SEX PSYCHOLOGY (BSSP). The BSSP was founded in 1914 on the eve of World War I. The impetus for the formation of the BSSP was most likely the Fourteenth International Medical Congress in 1913. Magnus Hirschfeld (q.v.) traveled to London for this meeting and delivered a speech on *intermediate types*, a term frequently used in medical circles to refer to homosexuals. In attendance were Havelock Ellis and Edward Carpenter (qq.v.), two of the most prominent British authorities on human sexuality. Inspired by the work of Hirschfeld and the Wissenschaftlich-humanitäres Komitee (Scientific Humanitarian Committee) (q.v.) in Berlin, Ellis and Carpenter sought to replicate its research and educational activities in London. Political and legal reform, the founders hoped, would follow in the wake of public education. Carpenter was named the first president of the BSSP in 1914.

Although World War I interfered with the initial activities of the BSSP, the society continued to organize. One of its first campaigns was the establishment of a library committee. In the process of building up a library for its own use, the society fought for access to the Private Case Books Catalogue of the British Museum, a catalogue not open to the general public. Many books on sexuality, including Edward Carpenter's *Intermediate Sex*, were housed there and the society rightly felt that it should be allowed access to the collection. The privilege of using the collection was never extended to the BSSP despite the scholarly credentials of its members.

The BSSP championed the cause of women's rights as well as the rights of homosexuals, taking the position that the two issues were intertwined and had to be addressed simultaneously. Consequently, birth control and women's suffrage were principle concerns of the BSSP from the beginning. Stella Browne was instrumental in developing the BSSP's role on both issues. Pamphlets published by the BSSP relevant to women's rights issues include her *Sexual Variety and Variability among Women* and Havelock Ellis's *Erotic Rights of Women*.

The BSSP maintained a special subcommittee on homosexuality. The membership of this committee was drawn to a considerable degree from the Order of Chaeronea (q.v.). Among the pamphlets on homosexuality published by the BSSP were F. A. E. Crew's *Sexual-*

ity and Intersexuality, Laurence Housman's (q.v.) *The Relation of Fellow-Feeling to Sex*, and H. D. Jennings White's *Psychological Causes of Homoeroticism and Inversion*.

The BSSP enjoyed wide support among progressives in England as well as abroad. E. M. Forster, Radclyffe Hall and her companion, Una Troubridge, Oscar Wilde's son Vyvyan Holland, Bertrand Russell and his wife, Dora Russell, and George Bernard Shaw were all members. The society developed professional affiliations with the SHC and the Institut für Sexualwissenschaft (Institute for Sexual Science) (q.v.) in Berlin, Margaret Sanger (the American birth control advocate), and even the short-lived Society for Human Rights (q.v.) in Chicago.

Members of the BSSP (renamed the British Sexological Association in the 1920s) were also instrumental in the formation of the World League for Sexual Reform (q.v.) in 1921. An association of medical professionals, lawyers, and others committed to sex education, the legal equality of men and women, abortion rights, and the rights of homosexuals, the league attracted an international membership. Havelock Ellis was named as one of its first honorary presidents. Neither the league nor the BSSP survived the rise of fascism in Germany and World War II.

BUND FÜR MENSCHENRECHTE. *See* DEUTSCHER FREUND-SCHAFTSVERBAND.

BURTON, SIR RICHARD (1821–1890). In 1885 Sir Richard Burton's translation of *Arabian Nights* was published. Appended to the translation was his "Terminal Essay," an essay on pederasty. He claimed that his own interest in the subject was awakened in 1845 when, in India, he observed eunuchs and boy prostitutes for hire in Karachi. The "Terminal Essay" immediately became the object of censorship and was deleted from the popular edition. Reissued in 1887 as the *Sotadic Zone*, Burton's geographical survey of the practice of pederasty created controversy among the reading public, because of his forthright discussion of homosexual practices throughout the world.

Drawing on his own observations as well as on works of anthropology, history, literature, and philosophy, Burton concluded that the practice of pederasty was a geographical and climatic phenomenon. He claimed that there was a "sotadic zone" within which the practice was common. Outside the zone, it was practiced with infrequency and was often the subject of moral and legal sanction. The borders were mapped latitudinally. The latitudinal breadth varied considerably depending on longitude. For example, in Europe and

Africa, the zone included those regions bordering or encompassed by the Mediterranean; in Asia it included the entirety of China, Japan, and Turkistan; and it encompassed, as well, the New World.

Burton maintained that the cause of pederasty was a mixing of masculine and feminine temperaments, a phenomenon more common in the sotadic zone than to the north or south of it. Both males and females were known to exhibit such temperaments. Although such individuals were not unknown outside the zone, Burton claimed that they were comparatively rare.

The balance of the essay is devoted to tracing the recorded history of pederasty in Europe, North Africa, Persia, Asia, and the Americas. Burton used Greek and Roman history, Christian and Islamic texts, observations from Turkey and China to the Aleutian Islands and the Mayan and Incan civilizations of the Americas to emphasize the extent of the practice.

The significance of the *Sotadic Zone* lies in its scientific discussion of a long-neglected subject by a recognized scholar. Although Burton does not attempt an explanation of the fusion of temperaments characteristic of the pederast, his idea is similar to that of Karl Heinrich Ulrichs's (q.v.) *urning*, a concept with which Burton was unfamiliar. Regardless of the differences in analysis, Burton's essay, like the work of Ulrichs and other leading medical authorities of the day, underscored the naturalness of homosexuality and helped in no small measure to liberate the discussion of the subject from its religious trappings.

C

CAMPAIGN AGAINST MORAL PERSECUTION (CAMP). Established in Sydney, New South Wales (NSW), by John Ware and Christobel Poll in 1970, CAMP Inc. (as it was originally known) was the first gay and lesbian organization in Australia devoted to the rights of gays and lesbians. It published a journal, *CAMP Inc.*, as well as a newsletter, *CAMP NSW Newsletter*. In the mid-1970s the organization became known as CAMP NSW. One of CAMP's accomplishments was the establishment of a network of CAMP affiliates, using its publications as a basis for communications among its various chapters.

The foundation of CAMP is illustrative of the international impact of the Stonewall (q.v.) riots on the gay and lesbian movement. Prior to 1970, small support groups of gays and lesbians existed in Australia, but, as was true in most other countries, they were semisecret organizations with no political agenda. The Stonewall riots, and the subsequent foundation of the Gay Liberation Front (GLF) (q.v.), transformed the role of gay and lesbian organizations. Although CAMP eschewed the more confrontational tactics of GLF groups, it emphasized the necessity of "coming out" as a first step in the eventual liberation of gays and lesbians, an emphasis inspired by the GLF. CAMP's programs, however, were more reformist than the activities of the GLF, bearing a closer resemblance to Arcadie or the Mattachine Society (qq.v.) than to the GLF. CAMP focused on public education, the provision of social and psychological support services for its members, and periodic public rallies. Perhaps its most influential outreach activity was a telephone counseling service, Phone-A-Friend (PAF). PAF steadily grew in popularity throughout the 1970s and increasingly became a source of controversy within the organization. Those who were interested in overt forms of political activity saw PAF as a capitulation to the mental health establishment and a reinforcement of the medical model of homosexuality (q.v.), whereas those who were active in PAF argued that many homosexuals were in need of counseling because of straight society's ostracism of gays and lesbians.

Another source of controversy within CAMP was the perception by lesbians that the group catered primarily to the interests of gay males as opposed to the interests of lesbians. In part, this was a by-product of CAMP's preoccupation with the elimination of sodomy laws, which, in Australia, were applicable only to men. In part, also, CAMP was much more attentive to the social requirements of gay men than it was to the needs of lesbians. Attempts on the part of lesbians to create separate social spaces were (in part) successful, but these separatist initiatives eventually created conflict within CAMP over the exclusionary nature of lesbian subgroups such as the Radical Lesbians Group.

CAMP's demise as a political organization came in 1978, shortly after it joined with other groups such as the Gay Task Force and the Lesbian Feminist Action Front, in an NSW-wide coalition known as Gayfed. The affiliation was shortlived. CAMP withdrew because of misgivings about Gayfed's leadership, which CAMP felt was too politically radical. CAMP's leadership, on the other hand, was more interested in becoming a service organization. Shortly after CAMP's initial affiliation with Gayfed, CAMP became a state-chartered charity, and its focus shifted to addressing the social and psychological needs of the gay male community. In 1981, the organization's name was changed to The Gay Counseling Service of NSW.

It was through the efforts of CAMP, as well as other Australian gay and lesbian organizations, that homosexual intercourse between men was eventually decriminalized. In 1973 the federal government decriminalized sodomy in those areas under its jurisdiction. Australian states soon followed suit; in 1997, the state of Tasmania repealed the last homosexual sodomy statute in Australia. Likewise, CAMP initiated the movement to enact antidiscrimination laws protecting the rights of gays and lesbians. In 1982, New South Wales was the first state to enact legislation protecting gays and lesbians, and South Australia was the second, in 1991.

CAMPAIGN FOR HOMOSEXUAL EQUALITY. *See* COMMITTEE FOR HOMOSEXUAL EQUALITY.

CANADIAN CHARTER OF RIGHTS AND FREEDOMS (1982). The Canadian Charter of Rights and Freedoms, a constitutional revision guaranteeing fundamental rights, such as the freedom of expression and association, due process of law, and equality, was adopted in 1982. Section 15 of the charter (adopted in 1985) prohibits specific forms of discrimination and provides for the legal equality of all individuals. Although discrimination on the basis of sexual orientation was not one of the specifically enumerated forms of discrimination prohibited by Section 15, subsequent federal appellate court decisions, as well as Supreme Court decisions, have interpreted Section 15 to prohibit discrimination against gays and lesbians. In addition, in 1992, the Ontario Court of Appeal declared that Canada's federal human rights act violated Section 15 of the charter because it failed to protect the rights of gays and lesbians. The federal government, in an unexpected turnaround, accepted the court's judgment and ordered the Canadian Human Rights Commission to interpret Section 15 to include sexual orientation in its future deliberations.

The Canadian Human Rights Act was subsequently amended (in 1996) to include sexual orientation. The constitutional protection of the rights of gays and lesbians was a long-standing goal of such provincial gay rights groups as the Coalition for Gay Rights in Ontario (q.v.) as well as of the national gay rights lobby Equality for Gays and Lesbians Everywhere and the openly gay Member of Parliament Svend Robinson (q.v.). Canada is thus one of the few countries in the world that affords constitutional protection on the basis of sexual orientation.

CANADIAN CRIMINAL CODE REFORM (1969). Canadian laws on homosexuality were influenced by British law. Based on the 16th-century Act of 25 Henry VIII, Ch. 6 (q.v.), Canada enacted its own "buggery" statute in 1859. Like its British counterpart, it carried the death penalty. Similarly, in 1892, Canada enacted a gross indecency statute modeled on the 1885 British Labouchère Amendment (q.v.).

The crime of gross indecency broadened the scope of criminal penalties pertaining to sexual behavior between males beyond anal intercourse to include all sexual relations between males. But whereas infractions of the Labouchère Amendment carried the punishment of two years, the Canadian statute carried a maximum of five years, with provisions for flogging. Also, unlike its British counterpart, the Canadian law ultimately became applicable not only to gay men but also to lesbians, in the criminal code revisions of 1953–1954.

Canadian gays and lesbians were also liable to prosecution as criminal sexual psychopaths. In 1948 Canada enacted a criminal sexual psychopath law. Under this statute, anyone convicted of offenses enumerated in the law could be tried as a criminal sexual psychopath, and conviction carried an indeterminate sentence. Although gross indecency and buggery were not part of the original legislation, they were subsequently added to the list of trigger offenses. Thus, gays and lesbians convicted of consensual homosexual relations in private were liable to prosecution as criminal psychopaths. A 1961 reform changed the offense to "dangerous sexual offender."

Everett Klippert's 1965 conviction for gross indecency and his subsequent classification and indefinite detention as a dangerous sexual offender became a *cause célèbre* in the movement to reform Canada's criminal codes pertaining to sexual offenses. Klippert's classification was upheld by Canada's Supreme Court in 1967. This decision was the subject of much public controversy. It was criticized by the mainstream press as well as the gay and lesbian press and is widely regarded as the single-most important impetus to the reform of Canadian law.

The debate over law reform in Canada was influenced by the reform movement in Britain. In 1957, the report of the Committee on Homosexual Offences and Prostitution (q.v.), commonly known as the Wolfenden Report, recommended the decriminalization of consensual male homosexual relations in private. The recommendations contained in the Wolfenden Report, and the eventual enactment of the 1967 Sexual Offenses Act (q.v.), which repealed criminal penalties for private consensual sexual relations between men in England and Wales, had a profound effect on the debate over law reform in Canada. The Association for Social Knowledge (q.v.), and the most prominent pre-Stonewall homosexual publications, *Gay* and *Two*, used the Wolfenden Report and the provisions of the 1967 Sexual Offenses Act in their appeals for the reform of Canadian law. The Wolfenden Report and the 1967 Sexual Offenses Act also provided much of the official rationale for the revision of Canadian law. In 1969, under the leadership of Pierre Trudeau and the Liberal Party, Canada enacted a sexual offenses reform bill. Like the Sexual Offenses Act in Britain, the Canadian reform only decriminalized consensual homosexual acts between persons 21 years of age or older in private (i.e., in a nonpublic venue and between no more than two persons). Nevertheless, the 1969 reform contributed to the legitimation of gay and lesbian sexual relationships and provided an impetus to further political organizing by gays and lesbians.

CARPENTER, EDWARD (1844–1929). British Socialist, feminist, and homosexual rights advocate, Edward Carpenter was a prolific writer. Like J. A. Symonds and Havelock Ellis (qq.v.), he was influenced by the American poet Walt Whitman (q.v.). His publications on homosexuality include *Homogenic Love, and Its Place in a Free Society* (1895), a text initially suppressed in the wake of the trials of Oscar Wilde (q.v.) but subsequently reissued by the Labor Press. *Love's Coming of Age* (1902), *Iolaus: An Anthology of Friendship* (1902), the *Intermediate Sex* (1908), and *Intermediate Types among Primitive Folk* (1914) were all published in Great Britain despite the oppressive social and legal atmosphere pertaining to discussions of sexuality. Carpenter's autobiography, *My Days and Dreams*, contains references to his longtime companion, George Merrill, as well as to aspects of his sexual awakening and his political philosophy.

Carpenter was deeply influenced by the socialist movement in England. He read H. M. Hyndman's *England for All*, a popular distillation of socialist principles, was active in several socialist organizations, and spoke on socialist topics throughout England.

He was also moved by his reading of the *Bhagavad Gita*, his introduction to Hinduism and by his travels to India and Ceylon. Eastern religions were important to Carpenter because of the alternatives they posed to Western rationalism and Christianity, which fostered ways of living that he felt were destructive to human spirituality.

Carpenter attributed his emotional maturation as a homosexual to Walt Whitman, whose *Leaves of Grass* he read while a student at Cambridge in 1869. Whitman appealed to Carpenter's egalitarian nature, to his disdain of crass materialism, and to his appreciation of close male camaraderie. The "Calamus" section extolled "manly love" and, according to Carpenter, was the first work of poetry that put into writing his own feelings. This encounter with Whitman's writings precipitated an extensive correspondence with the American poet, which culminated in a meeting between the two in the United States in 1877. In 1883 Carpenter published his own Whitmanesque poem, "Towards Democracy," in which he expressed his views on industrial democracy, egalitarianism, and the sexual revolution of the late 19th century. His published essays on Walt Whitman include

Days with Walt Whitman (1906) and *Some Friends of Walt Whitman: A Study in Sex Psychology* (1924).

Carpenter (unlike many other male homosexual rights advocates of the day) saw the significance of the women's movement and its relation to the movement for homosexual emancipation. He was outspoken in his criticism of the emphasis on procreation in the Hebraic and Christian teachings on sexuality. Carpenter was enamored with the spiritual potentialities of sexuality, and he felt that the overemphasis on procreation denigrated the role of women in society. He also felt that this assumption was a fundamental aspect of the prejudice against homosexuals. He advocated birth control and the emancipation of women from archaic forms of economic and social dependence on men and argued that the women's movement was integral to the homosexual emancipation movement.

Like Karl Heinrich Ulrichs (q.v.), Carpenter felt that the urning, or homosexual, was a blend of masculine sex characteristics and feminine temperament. Carpenter differed from Ulrichs in his lack of enthusiasm for biological models of homosexuality and espoused his own unique view that urnings were androgynous individuals and that bisexuality was a potentiality in all persons. Because urnings embodied androgyny, he considered them more highly evolved in a moral sense than heterosexuals.

Carpenter succeeded in establishing an international reputation through his books and essays, which were translated into many European languages as well as Japanese. His influence also extended to the United States, where his ideas were discussed in New York and on the West Coast. Carpenter had a deep influence on novelists E. M. Forster and D. H. Lawrence. Forster's novel *Maurice* was inspired by a visit to Carpenter's home at Millthorpe, which he shared with George Merrill. And if D. H. Lawrence ultimately rejected feminism and never completely embraced love between men, his early ideas on these subjects were influenced by Carpenter.

Edward Carpenter and Havelock Ellis were the principal figures behind the formation of the British Society for the Study of Sex Psychology (BSSP) (q.v.). Devoted to the scientific study of sexuality, the society was instrumental in advancing the understanding of homosexuality in scientific circles. Because of his reputation as a pioneer in the study of sexuality, Carpenter was named its first president in 1914. Together with the Wissenschaftlich-humanitäres Komitee (Scientific Humanitarian Committee) and the Institut für Sexualwissenschaft (Institute for Sexual Science) (qq.v.) in Berlin, the BSSP was instrumental in the formation of the World League for Sexual Reform (q.v.) in 1921.

Throughout his life Edward Carpenter extolled the virtues of socialism, a simple rural existence, the cause of women's rights, and love between men. They were all interconnected in his mind and harbingers of a more humane society.

CIVIL RIGHTS. A principal objective of the contemporary gay and lesbian liberation movement has been the enactment of statutes protecting gays, lesbians, and bisexuals from discrimination in employment, housing, and public accommodations. Prior to Stonewall (q.v.) the efforts of gay and lesbian groups focused primarily on creating safe social spaces for gays and lesbians to congregate and secondarily on opposition to sodomy statutes (q.v.). Over the last 30 years, the focus has broadened to include civil rights issues, the right of gays, lesbians, and bisexuals to engage in military service (q.v.), marriage (q.v.) rights, as well as the right to asylum (q.v.).

Among the first jurisdictions to enact civil rights legislation protecting the rights of gays and lesbians were Dade County, Florida, and the Canadian province of Quebec in 1977. As is true of the contemporary movements to legalize gay marriages and to integrate gays and lesbians into the armed services, however, Scandinavian countries have led the international trend to enact comprehensive nationwide statutes protecting gay and lesbian civil rights. The first nation to enact civil rights legislation for gays and lesbians was Norway in 1981. In 1987, both Denmark and Sweden followed. Other European countries offering civil rights protection include France (1985) and the Netherlands (1992).

The most recent national gay and lesbian civil rights statutes to be enacted were in the Netherlands and in New Zealand in 1993. In the Netherlands the General Equal Treatment Act forbids discrimination in the private sector on the basis of sexual orientation, a longtime goal of the Nederlandse Vereniging tot Integratie van Homoseksualiteit COC (Netherlands Organization for the Integration of Homosexuality COC) (q.v.). The New Zealand statute, coming only seven years after the decriminalization of sodomy, represents remarkable progress in just three decades since the founding of the Dorian Society (q.v.).

Countries that have constitutional protections of gay and lesbian civil rights include, Canada, the Netherlands, and South Africa. The Netherlands was the first country in the world to incorporate protections for gays and lesbians in their constitution. South Africa became the second country to do so in 1994 when it incorporated the principle of gay and lesbian rights in the 1994 interim Constitution of South Africa. This achievement was largely due to the efforts of Simon Nkoli and the Gay and Lesbian Organization of the Witwatersrand (qq.v.). By contrast, constitutional protection for gays and lesbians in Canada was accomplished through federal court interpretations of the Canadian Charter of Rights and Freedoms (q.v.). Numerous individuals and organizations were responsible for this accomplishment, including the Coalition for Gay Rights in Ontario (q.v.), Equality for Gays and Lesbians Everywhere, and Svend Robinson (q.v.), an openly gay Member of Parliament.

In other countries where nationwide civil rights protections have yet to be achieved, such as Australia and the United States, significant civil rights statutes have been enacted by local and regional jurisdictions. In Australia, in 1982, the state of New South Wales became the first Australian state to pass a gay and lesbian rights ordinance; South Australia became the second, in 1991. The groundbreaking work of organizations such as the Campaign against Moral Persecution (q.v.) laid the foundation for these breakthroughs. At the federal level, the 1986 Human Rights and Equal Opportunity Commission Act provides for investigations of complaints of discrimination on the basis of sexual preference. In the United States, the goal of extending civil rights to gays and lesbians has been the longtime objective of movement leaders such as Harry Hay and Frank Kameny (qq.v.), modern homosexual rights organizations such as the Daughters of Bilitis and the Mattachine Society (q.v.), as well as contemporary organizations such as the Human Rights Campaign and the National Gay and Lesbian Task Force (qq.v.). Although nationwide statutes such as the proposed Employment Non-Discrimination Act (q.v.) have yet to be enacted, 10 states and roughly 150 cities and counties offer varying degrees of civil rights protections for gays and lesbians.

Constitutional and/or statutory protections for the rights of gays and lesbians do not exist in Asia, Africa (except for South Africa), or Eastern Europe (qq.v.). The movement for civil rights protection in Latin America (q.v.) is in its infancy.

CLAUSE 28 (1988). British statute prohibiting the promotion of homosexuality or teaching its acceptability as a "pretended family relationship" through local government expenditures. Section 28 of the Local Government Act was enacted during the regime of Prime Minister Margaret Thatcher to thwart the growing influence of Britain's gay and lesbian movement.

Stonewall and the rise of the Gay Liberation Front (GLF) (qq.v.) had a profound impact on the British gay and lesbian movement. Theretofore, British organizations such as the Homosexual Law Reform Society and the Albany Trust (qq.v.) focused on legal reform such as the enactment of the Sexual Offenses Act (q.v.).

The impact of the GLF changed the direction of the lesbian and gay liberation movement. Although law reform remained a goal, social visibility became an objective for the first time. Lesbians and gays demanded cultural recognition, such as objective coverage in the mass media and commercial establishments catering to their needs. The 1970s and 1980s saw a growing willingness of the mass media to cover lesbian and gay issues and a profusion of commercial establishments catering to gays and lesbians. Among other demands of post-Stonewall gay and lesbian rights organizations was the demand that educational institutions include discussions of gay and lesbian history and culture in public schools.

Clause 28 was an attempt to stem the growing tide of public visibility and acceptance through prohibiting discussions of homosexuality in public schools that equated homosexual relationships with traditional familial relationships. Clause 28 also prohibited the expenditure of any local public revenues on activities that promoted the acceptability of gay or lesbian lifestyles. Thus, for example, gay or lesbian organizations such as the London Gay Teenage Group could no longer apply for funds from local governments to underwrite their activities.

The enactment of Clause 28 precipitated the largest gay and lesbian rights rally in London in the spring of 1988. Established gay and lesbian rights organizations such as the Campaign for Homosexual Equality and the Scottish Homosexual Rights Group (qq.v.) were joined by newer organizations such as Stonewall and the gay and lesbian press in voicing opposition to the bill. Despite the determined opposition of gay and lesbian organizations, however, Clause 28 remains on the statute books a decade after its original enactment. A newly formed group, the Equality Alliance, coordinated nationwide demonstrations protesting the statute in 1998, the 10th anniversary of the enactment of Clause 28, and YouthSpeak delivered a petition to the Prime Minister calling for its repeal.

COALITION FOR GAY RIGHTS IN ONTARIO (CGRO). Founded in 1975 by a number of gay and lesbian groups in the province of Ontario, Canada, it was subsequently renamed the Coalition for Lesbian and Gay Rights in Ontario. The CGRO (as it is commonly referred to) was instrumental in advancing the cause of gay and lesbian rights in Ontario as well as throughout Canada during the 1970s and 1980s. Its principal objective was the amendment of the Ontario Human Rights Code.

In 1976, the CGRO, together with other interested parties, began a campaign to amend the Ontario Human Rights Code to protect the rights of gays and lesbians. Shortly thereafter, Quebec became the first province to protect the rights of gays and lesbians when the

Quebec Human Rights Charter was amended in 1977 to include sexual orientation as a protected category. During the ensuing 10-year struggle in Ontario, the Quebec precedent provided inspiration to those involved in building political support for a similar amendment in Ontario.

After numerous attempts to amend the Ontario Human Rights Code, the efforts of the CGRO and other groups, such as the Right to Privacy Committee, eventually prevailed in 1986. Bill 7, a proposed revision to the human rights code, was amended in committee deliberations to include sexual orientation. The floor debate was preceded by a classic political confrontation between New Right organizations, such as the Coalition for Family Values, and the CGRO and its allies. Bill 7, including its sexual orientation provision, was adopted in December, and Ontario became the second Canadian province to protect the rights of gays and lesbians in housing, employment, membership in professional associations, and so forth. Over the next decade, most other Canadian provinces followed suit, and the Canadian Human Rights Act (the federal human rights statute) was also successfully amended to include protection on the basis of sexual orientation.

COMITÉ D'URGENCE ANTI-RÉPRESSION HOMOSEXUELLE/ EMERGENCY COMMITTEE AGAINST THE REPRESSION OF HOMOSEXUALS (ECARH). The ECARH was formed by 16 French gay and lesbian organizations in the late 1970s to advance the political interests of gays and lesbians in an atmosphere of increasing intolerance. Although France had expunged sodomy statutes (q.v.) from its law codes in 1791, the post-World War II period was characterized by a crackdown on gays and lesbians. The so-called Pétain-de Gaulle law, which dated from the Nazi occupation, established a higher age of consent for homosexuals than for heterosexuals. This was used to intimidate not only adults seeking relations with minors but all homosexuals under the age of 21 as well. Discriminatory public indecency laws punished public displays of affection by gays and lesbians more harshly than those of their heterosexual counterparts. Furthermore, postwar French society was uncharacteristically homophobic, and gay culture was effectively repressed.

The ECARH was not the first to oppose the growing animosity toward gays and lesbians in France. André Baudry's journal *Arcadie* and the Front Homosexuel d'Action Révolutionnaire (Revolutionary Homosexual Action Front [RHAF-F]) (qq.v.) both attempted to defend the rights of gays and lesbians. But the RHAF-F ceased to exist in 1973, and Baudry and his followers were perceived to be too apolitical to effectively lead the struggle.

Among the ECARH's notable accomplishments was the publication of its journal *Homophonies* and the inception of *Gay Pied*. *Gay Pied* was founded in 1979 by a group of gay men attached to the ECARH, and it quickly became the most important new gay publication in the 1980s. Both outlasted the ECARH. *Homophonies* remained in print until 1986; *Gay Pied*, until 1992.

The ECARH's success was attributable to its platform of equal rights and its cultivation of support within the political Left, particularly the Socialist Party. The ECARH supported the candidacy of François Mitterrand in the 1981 elections, and his success brought with it a commitment to eliminate discrimination against gays and lesbians. The Pétain-de Gaulle law was rescinded in 1982 and, thus, the discriminatory age of consent laws.

ECARH's success was its own undoing. After 1982, provincial organizations affiliated with the ECARH dwindled and its membership began a steady decline, which continued until the disappearance of its journal *Homophonies*. There is no organization similar to the ECARH in France today, although there are numerous regional social organizations serving the interests of gays and lesbians.

COMMITTEE FOR HOMOSEXUAL EQUALITY (CHE). The predecessor of Great Britain's Committee for Homosexual Equality (CHE) was the North-Western Committee of the Homosexual Law Reform Society (HLRS) (q.v.). The most radical of the HLRS's subsidiary organizations, the North-Western Committee was dissatisfied with the direction the HLRS was taking after the enactment of the 1967 Sexual Offenses Act (q.v.). The principal objective of the HLRS had been the decriminalization of adult male homosexuality. The Sexual Offenses Act had accomplished this, at least in England and in Wales, and the HLRS seemed unwilling to take on more innovative tasks to further the gay and lesbian movement. Thus, the North-Western Committee evolved into an independent organization and, in 1969, became known as the Committee for Homosexual Equality. Based in Manchester, the organization changed its name to the Campaign for Homosexual Equality (CHE) in 1971. For a brief time in the early 1970s the CHE joined with the Scottish Minorities Group (SMG) and the Union for Sexual Freedom in Ireland (USFI) in the National Federation of Homophile Organizations (NFHO) (qq.v.).

Whereas the HLRS had devoted its energies to legal reform, the CHE was motivated by the need to advance the social and cultural interests of gays and lesbians as well as legal reform. The CHE promoted the idea of "Esquire" clubs, social clubs that would serve as meeting places for gays and lesbians, sponsored dances and other social events around the country, and for a brief time even had a travel service.

Beyond organizing social events, the CHE engaged in a number of other activities. In 1971, the CHE launched Friend, a counseling service that eventually offered counseling to isolated gays and lesbians on a nationwide basis. In 1971 it inaugurated its own magazine, *Lunch*, and shortly thereafter its own newspaper, *Out*. In 1973 Icebreakers, a London telephone service, was initiated to facilitate the interaction of gays and lesbians. The telephone service was supplemented by regular meetings to bring individuals together in a supportive atmosphere. In 1974 the CHE sponsored a group interested in providing a social outlet for older gays and lesbians known as the August Trust.

Although the NFHO disintegrated in 1973, the CHE continued to work with the SMG and USFI, promoting a draft bill to rectify the remaining legal injustices pertaining to gay men in Great Britain. Among the items proposed in this draft bill was a reduction in the age of consent to 16. The 1967 Sexual Offenses Act had made the age of consent 21. Furthermore, because the Sexual Offenses Act excluded Scotland and Northern Ireland, they were still governed by the provisions of the buggery statute (the Act of 25 Henry VIII, c.6, as amended in 1861) as well as by the Labouchère Amendment (qq.v.). The draft bill proposed bringing the laws of Scotland and Northern Ireland in line with England's. It also proposed that homosexual relations in the armed services be decriminalized and that the definition of privacy in the Sexual Offenses Act be liberalized. Thus far, the only provision of the draft bill that has been enacted is the extension of the Sexual Offenses Act to Scotland and Northern Ireland.

The CHE became the largest gay and lesbian rights organization in Britain. But, as was true of other gay and lesbian rights organizations during the 1970s, its activities appealed mostly to gay men. Law reform was strictly a gay male issue in that sexual relations between women had never been criminalized in Great Britain and, with a few exceptions, the CHE did not openly embrace other issues or activities of great interest to lesbians. Consequently, the membership of the CHE declined as lesbians devoted more and more of their energies to the women's movement.

The CHE also became increasingly factionalized and ineffective in the face of the challenges posed by AIDS and the conservative backlash against gay rights in the 1980s. The 1980s proved to be a difficult time for gay rights organizing. The Gay Liberation Front (q.v.) had come and gone in the early 1970s. So had the NFHO. In 1980 the Albany Trust (q.v.) ceased to exist owing to lack of funds, and the Sexual Law Reform Society (formerly HLRS) barely escaped the same fate. The CHE was also underfunded and understaffed as many of its members became preoccupied with specific issues such as defending the *Gay News* from blasphemy charges in the British courts. In 1988, over the protests of the CHE, the British Parliament adopted Clause 28 (q.v.), a provision designed to undermine the educational activities of organizations such as the CHE.

By the end of the 1980s the gay rights movement in Britain had become highly decentralized as the CHE was surpassed in size by some of the special interest groups it had spawned. Nevertheless, the CHE has remained active in the struggle for gay and lesbian rights. In 1990, the CHE supported the Stonewall Group (q.v.) in its efforts to end discrimination against lesbians and gay men in the member states of the European Community (EC). Although the EC has failed to amend its social charter to incorporate protections for lesbians and gay men, the CHE has collaborated with other British and European groups to advocate the principle of nondiscrimination on the basis of sexual orientation.

COMMITTEE ON HOMOSEXUAL OFFENSES AND PROSTITUTION, REPORT OF (1957). Established on 26 August 1954 by the British home secretary, the Committee on Homosexual Offenses and Prostitution became commonly known as the Wolfenden Committee after its chair, Sir John Wolfenden, vice-chancellor of Reading University. The 15 committee members included clergy, educators, lawyers, prison administrators, physicians, and members of Parliament. Its report was published three years later in September 1957. Part I of the report concerned prostitution; part II dealt with homosexuality.

Public pressure to reevaluate the rationality of British law pertaining to homosexual offenses mounted after World War II. For reasons that are not entirely clear, prosecutions for homosexual offenses increased markedly after the war. Moreover, the defection of Guy Burgess and Donald Maclean to the Soviet Union in 1951 resulted in a purge of homosexuals from the British foreign service and from the military. Burgess and Maclean were homosexuals, and their defection to the USSR constituted a major security breach. The United States urged the British to follow the example of President Harry Truman's Loyalty and Security Program and President Dwight Eisenhower's Executive Order 10450. Both labeled homosexuals as security risks and were used to remove homosexuals from the U.S. federal service. Great Britain followed suit.

Great Britain also experienced a number of highly publicized prosecutions of well-known public figures, members of Parliament, authors, and so forth. Thus the impact of the law on the lives of British citizens became more understandable, and the questionable tactics of the police in obtaining convictions became the object of criticism in the press and in Parliament. Finally, the Church of England Moral Welfare Council's investigation of the issue, *The Problem of Homosexuality*, culminated with an appeal for legal reform in 1954.

The Wolfenden Committee heard testimony from a wide variety of individuals and institutions over the three years of its existence. The Wolfenden Report criticized the prevalent notions that homosexuality led to moral decay, that male homosexuals inevitably preyed on boys, that the damage to family life warranted criminalizing the practice, and that decriminalization would inevitably lead to unbridled moral license.

Instead, the report emphasized the value of privacy. The committee concluded that the law should not be used to regulate sexual morals between consenting adults as long as the behavior occurred in private and that it should be restricted to the maintenance of public order and decency and the protection of individuals from exploitation. Thus, although the report advocated the decriminalization of private homosexual activity, it also advocated strengthening prohibitions against public displays of homosexuality and sex with minors, and it recommended raising the age of consent from 16 to 21. Further recommendations included a statutory limit of 12 months on the prosecution of consensual homosexual infractions, a requirement that the attorney general or the director of public prosecutions approve the indictment of anyone under the age of 21, and the reduction of the crime of buggery to a misdemeanor. The report concluded by calling for an investigation of the etiology of homosexuality. The Wolfenden Report set the stage for the liberalization of British law pertaining to male homosexuality. Although reform would not come for another decade, it was the recommendations of the Wolfenden Committee that provided the framework for the final adoption of the 1967 Sexual Offenses Act (q.v.).

COUNCIL ON RELIGION AND THE HOMOSEXUAL (CRH). Founded in San Francisco in December 1964, the CRH pioneered an interfaith coalition between heterosexuals and gays and lesbians in the Bay Area during the 1960s. Its first president was the Reverend Ted McIlvenna.

Sponsored by the Glide Memorial Methodist Church, a meeting between gay and lesbian rights leaders and Protestant ministers from around the United States took place in May 1964. The aim of the four-day meeting was to develop lines of communication and cooperation among ministers and the gay and lesbian rights movement.

One outcome of the meeting was the formation, in December, of the CRH. The CRH attracted the support of many gay and lesbian rights advocates, including Harry Hay, the founder of the Mattachine Society (qq.v.), and Del Martin and Phyllis Lyon, founders of the Daughters of Bilitis. The initial goal of the CRH was to promote the civil rights (q.v.) of gays and lesbians.

The disruption of a fundraising dance on New Year's Eve by the San Francisco police catapulted the CRH into prominence in the Bay Area. At a news conference on 2 January 1965, the CRH decried the wanton disregard of individual rights and police harassment at the fundraiser. Charges against several individuals, including three sympathetic attorneys, were thrown out of court. This was an important victory for gay and lesbian rights advocates in San Francisco who had complained for years about the routine police harassment of gays and lesbians in the Bay Area. By legitimizing the charges of police harassment, the CRH drew public attention to the problem. Its report, *A Brief of Injustices*, contributed to the eventual reform of police practices. Together with the Society for Individual Rights (q.v.) the CRH brought a militancy to the movement that was theretofore unknown in San Francisco.

In addition to the San Francisco chapter of the CRH, chapters formed in other large cities, including Los Angeles, Dallas, Washington, Philadelphia, and New York. Their activities included interfaith dialogues on homosexuality, legal actions on behalf of the civil rights of gays and lesbians, and the provision of meeting places for gay and lesbian activities. In 1971 the First National Conference on Religion and the Homosexual was held in New York City.

Although the CRH soon disappeared, its approach to gay and lesbian issues was embraced by at least one Protestant denomination, the United Church of Christ, and it inspired the creation of organizations such as the Universal Fellowship of Metropolitan Community Churches. *See also* Metropolitan Community Church.

CULTUUR-EN-ONTSPANNINGS CENTRUM/CULTURE AND RECREATIONAL CENTER (CRC). The CRC was founded in the Netherlands in 1946 by Bob Angelo (q.v.) and others associated with *Levensrecht* (Right to Live), a prewar homosexual magazine. Its national office was established in Amsterdam, but other branches soon opened in such cities as The Hague and Rotterdam. Throughout its existence, the CRC has engaged in a wide variety of activities. It has provided a social outlet for Dutch gays and lesbians, published a variety of newsmagazines, been instrumental in developing international gay and lesbian organizations, and fought for the civil rights (q.v.) of gays and lesbians in the Netherlands. It has been legally incorporated since 1973 and has been the recipient of government subsidies ever since.

As the name implies, the CRC sought to provide gays and lesbians with opportunities for interaction missing in the wider community. The CRC initiated discussion groups for gays and lesbians to facilitate their coming out and their subsequent adjustment and integration into Dutch society. The CRC also provided recreational opportunities. The opportunity for gays and lesbians to meet others and socialize in a safe and wholesome environment was a novelty in postwar Europe. At a time when dancing was almost universally prohibited, at least for men, the CRC provided both dance floors and bars for its members.

Unlike many other homosexual rights groups, the CRC fostered the conviction that homosexuals were neither reprobates nor mentally ill. It promoted the idea that society should accept gays and lesbians and that gays and lesbians should be integrated into society at large.

During its existence, the CRC has published a number of periodicals intended for its members as well as a wider audience. In addition to *Levensrecht*, which circulated between 1946 and 1949, it has also published *Vriendschap* (Friendship), *Dialoog* (Dialogue), *Informatie Bulletin Dialoog* (Information Bulletin Dialogue), and *Sek*, as well as a number of publications produced exclusively for its membership. Its current monthly newsmagazine is *XL*. Together with the publications of its various chapters, the national office of the CRC has provided a reliable source of information for the Dutch gay and lesbian community since its founding in 1948.

Another objective of the CRC has been the creation of an organization to spearhead international cooperation among gay and lesbian groups. In 1951 the CRC founded the International Committee for Sexual Equality (ICSE), in which organizations from a number of Western European countries as well as the United States participated. During the 1950s the CRC was the most well-organized gay and lesbian organization in the world. Outside of the Netherlands, however, the gay and lesbian movement was very ineffectual. The organizational and financial problems that beset postwar groups led to the discontinuation of the ICSE in 1960. In 1978 the dream of the CRC was realized when discussions between the Campaign for Homosexual Equality (q.v.), a British group, and the CRC led to the formation of the International Gay Association (q.v.), the first effective international organization of gays and lesbians in the world.

The CRC also began promoting an equal rights agenda for gays and lesbians in the Netherlands immediately after World War II. Like its predecessor, the Nederlandsch Wetenschappelijk-Humanitair Komitee (Dutch Scientific-Humanitarian Committee [DSHC]) (q.v.), the CRC focused on education and building alliances with influential political, religious, medical, and social work professionals.

When the Nazi imposition of criminal penalties for homosexual male sodomy during the 1940–1945 German occupation was repealed after the war, the CRC focused on the repeal of Article 248bis. Applicable to both gays and lesbians, the repeal of this discriminatory age of consent law had been the principal goal of the DSHC since its enactment in 1911. Like the DSHC, the CRC argued that there was no rational basis for 248bis, which raised the age of consent for homosexual relations to 21 while leaving the corresponding heterosexual age of consent at 16. After 60 years of efforts by both the DSHC and the CRC, the government finally repealed 248bis in 1971 but not before some 5,000 individuals had been incarcerated for violations of the statute.

Renamed Nederlandse Vereniging tot Integratie van Homoseksualiteit COC (Netherlands Association for the Integration of Homosexuality COC [NAIH COC]), it has also played a key role in the 20-year struggle to enact antidiscrimination ordinances protecting gays and lesbians. Although Article 1 of the Dutch Constitution has prohibited discrimination on the basis of sexual orientation since 1983, specific statutory prohibitions did not exist until the passage of statutes in 1992 and 1993. In 1992 the Dutch Penal Code was revised to include prohibitions against discrimination on the basis of sexual orientation. This included provisions prohibiting incitement to commit harm as well as libel. The General Equal Treatment Act, adopted in 1993, prohibits discrimination against individuals in the private sector on the basis of their sexual orientation. These reforms follow, in general terms, the Norwegian reforms of 1981.

The NAIH COC's most recent political agenda included lobbying for the passage of a partners registration act similar to the Danish Registered Partnership Act (q.v.). A government commission reported its findings and recommendations to the Parliament in August 1997 and, shortly thereafter, enacted a statute granting gays and lesbians marriage (q.v.) rights.

The organization continues to serve as a quasi-public social service agency and, in conjunction with academic institutions, has organized scholarly conferences of gay and lesbian writers in addition to its political activities. Today there are many organizations serving the needs of gays and lesbians in the Netherlands, but the NAIH COC remains the only national gay and lesbian organization providing a full range of services to its members. It has roughly 50 branches throughout the country. The NAIH COC celebrated its 50th anniversary in 1996, making it the world's oldest gay and lesbian rights organization.

D

DANISH REGISTERED PARTNERSHIP ACT (1989). The Danish Registered Partnership Act was enacted five years after the Danish Parliament (Folketing) established a commission on gay and lesbian discrimination. The commission was set up to study the desirability of emulating the 1981 Norwegian antidiscrimination statutes protecting the civil rights (q.v.) of gays and lesbians. The commission's report resulted in the enactment of Article 289, an equal access public accommodations law protecting the rights of lesbians and gay men, and Article 266a, a hate crimes bill protecting individuals on the basis of their sexual orientation. Both became law in 1987.

Another recommendation of the commission was the recognition of the validity of same-sex marriages (q.v.), a longtime goal of the Danish national gay and lesbian organization, the Landsforeningen for Bøsser og Lesbiske (National Organization of Gays and Lesbians) (NOGL) (q.v.). The first legislation of its kind in the world, the Danish Registered Partnership Act provides gays and lesbians the right to register their relationships with civil authorities. This registration process is tantamount to a civil marriage and entitles gay and lesbian couples to all the privileges of marriage, with the exception of the right of joint adoption of children and the right to a church ceremony. One of the partners must be a Danish citizen.

The Danish Registered Partnership Act was enacted on 26 May 1989, two years after its proposal in the Folketing. The first partners to register were Axel Axgil (q.v.), the founder of the NOGL, and his partner Eigil Axgil, on 1 October 1989. Since that time thousands of Danes have registered their partnerships. This Danish statute has become a model piece of civil rights legislation pertaining to gays and lesbians. Similar legislation has been enacted in Greenland, Hungary, Iceland, Norway, the Netherlands, and Sweden and is now under consideration in Finland, Portugal, Spain, and in the state of Hawaii.

DEFENSE OF MARRIAGE ACT (DOMA). The DOMA was introduced into the U.S. Congress in 1996 in response to the Hawaii Supreme Court's decision in the case of *Baehr v. Lewin* (q.v.) (now *Baehr v. Miike*). After the DOMA passed both houses of the U.S. Congress by overwhelming margins, President Clinton signed it into law on 21 September 1996. The president's action was condemned by gay and lesbian rights leaders around the country such as Elizabeth Birch, the executive director of the Human Rights Campaign (q.v), who called the statute a violation of the "states' traditional jurisdiction over marriage." (*New York Times* 22 September 1996, 13.).

The introduction of the DOMA anticipates the eventuality of gay and lesbian marriages (q.v.) in the state of Hawaii. Despite the Full Faith and Credit clause of the U.S. Constitution, which requires states to recognize the validity of contracts concluded in other states, many U.S. states have enacted statutes prohibiting the legal recognition of such unions. The DOMA provides a federal imprimatur for such state action.

The DOMA also prohibits all agencies, bureaus, and departments of the federal government from recognizing the legality of gay or lesbian marriages in their rules and regulations. Thus, for example, spouses of gay and lesbian employees of the federal government would not qualify for spousal benefits, gays and lesbians would not be permitted to file joint income tax returns, the marital status of gays and lesbians would not be recognized by the Immigration and Naturalization Service, and so forth. Because the DOMA is virtually unprecedented in U.S. law, and because of the Full Faith and Credit clause of the U.S. Constitution, the prospect of the DOMA surviving a constitutional challenge in U.S. federal courts is problematic.

DER EIGENE (**THE SPECIAL**). A literary and artistic magazine published by Adolf Brand, a cofounder of the Gemeinschaft der Eigenen (The Community of the Special [COS]) (qq.v.). *Der Eigene* became the voice of the COS between 1903 and 1931 and contributed to the success of this prominent German homosexual rights organization.

Der Eigene was the first magazine devoted to homosexual art and culture in the world. Originating in 1896 as an anarchist journal, *Monatsschrift für Kunst und Leben* (Monthly Journal for Art and Life), Brand changed the focus of the magazine in 1898. Published intermittently until its demise in 1931, *Der Eigene* focused on literary, artistic, and philosophical essays on male homosexual history and culture. It also featured polemical attacks on Paragraph 175 (q.v.) (the article in the German law code that criminalized homosexual relations between men) as well as against the ideological adversaries of the COS.

Contributors to *Der Eigene* traced the origins of love between men to the idealization of pedagogical eros in the works of Plato, to the reinvigoration of male friendships during the Renaissance, and to its roots in German culture. They touted the cultural superiority of love between men and between men and boys in comparison with heterosexuality. Writers such as Brand and Benedict Friedländer (q.v.), a cofounder of the COS, were especially critical of the German sexologist Magnus Hirschfeld, the leader of the Wissenschaftlich-humanitäres Komitee (The Scientific-Humanitarian Committee [SHC]) (q.v.) and publisher of the *Jahrbuch für sexuelle Zwischenstufen* (Yearbook for Sexual Intermediates), because of his advocacy of biological explanations of homosexuality. Especially offensive to Brand and Friedländer was the close relationship between Hirschfeld's explanations of homosexuality and Karl Heinrich Ulrichs's "third-sex" theory (qq.v.), the idea that male homosexuals were little more than women trapped in male bodies.

Der Eigene also functioned as the format for the program of the COS. Unlike the SHC, the COS was not preoccupied with legal reform. The abolition of Paragraph 175 was, relatively speaking, only a minor aspect of its program. The COS was more concerned with the restoration of the values of ancient Greece and the Renaissance, and it campaigned for a restoration of masculine virtues that it deemed necessary to the attainment of a high German culture. *Der Eigene* provided the forum for Brand, Friedländer, and others to espouse the values of the COS and promote its activities.

The emphasis on the superiority of masculine virtues and love between men was often accompanied by a deprecation of feminism. This limited the appeal of *Der Eigene* as well as that of the COS, as did Brand's conviction on a morals charge for publishing photographs of nude male youths in 1903. Magnus Hirschfeld's journal, the *Jahrbuch*, and the SHC, by contrast, adopted the mantel of scientific respectability and openly appealed to women through advocacy of the women's rights movement. Thus, *Der Eigene* never attained the eminence of its chief competitor.

Der Eigene ceased publication entirely in 1931, although Brand continued to advocate his ideas through other publications until 1933 when the activities of the COS were banned by the Nazi Party.

DET NORSKE FORBUNDET AV 1948 / THE NORWEGIAN ALLIANCE OF 1948 (NA / 1948). A National Federation of Norwegian gay and lesbian rights groups, the NA/48 is the primary gay and lesbian rights organization in Norway.

Homosexual relations are not illegal under Norwegian law and, since 1972, the age of consent for heterosexual and homosexual relations has been 16. Together with the Fellesraadet for Homofile Organisasjoner i Norge (Joint Council for Homophile Organizations in Norway [JCHON]), another federation of Norwegian gay and lesbian rights groups, the NA/1948 lobbied the Norwegian parliament (Storting) to pass an antidiscrimination statute protecting the rights of gays and lesbians. Their efforts were rewarded in 1981 when the Storting passed a comprehensive civil rights (q.v.) statute, the first nationwide antidiscrimination statute protecting the rights of gays and lesbians in the world.

The 1981 statute prohibits two forms of discrimination based on homosexual orientation. Section 135a is a "hate crimes" code that provides for up to two years imprisonment for inciting "hatred, persecution or contempt" against homosexuality. Section 349a is a "public accommodations" code prohibiting discrimination against homosexuals in the provision of goods and services in the private sector. Norway's civil rights initiative was the model for Denmark's civil rights ordinances of 1987.

The most recent initiative of NA/1948 has been the enactment of a domestic partnership law similar to the Danish Registered Partnership Act (q.v.), a proposal that was recently adopted by the Storting. In 1995, Denmark, Norway, and Sweden concluded an international treaty that provides for the mutual recognition of registered partnerships among the three Scandinavian countries.

DEUTSCHER FREUNDSCHAFTSVERBAND / GERMAN FRIENDSHIP ASSOCIATION (GFA). Founded in 1919 by Hans Kahnert, the GFA was the largest homosexual organization in Germany. It sought to appeal to those who felt alienated from the two principal German homosexual rights organizations, the Wissenschaftlich-humanitäres Komitee (Scientific Humanitarian Committee [SHC]) and the Gemeinschaft der Eigenen (Community of the Special [COS]) (qq.v.). The constituency of the SHC consisted primarily of doctors, scientists, lawyers, and other professionals whereas the advocacy of pedophile relationships limited the appeal of the COS to those who were enamored by the cult of masculinity and the cultural ideals of ancient Greece and Renaissance Italy.

The GFA catered to those who were primarily interested in socializing with other homosexuals and who were not interested in scientific or literary endeavors pertaining to homosexuality. It sponsored social events, maintained a center in Berlin, and published *Die Freundschaft* (Friendship), a weekly newspaper. It became very popular and had chapters throughout Germany. It was the GFA that inspired Henry Gerber to form the first homosexual rights organization in North America, the Society for Human Rights (qq.v.).

Although the GFA formed a brief political coalition with the SHC and the COS known as the Aktionsausschuss (Action Committee) (q.v.), it was never successful as a political organization. Dissension over the increasing political involvement of the organization led to its withdrawal from the coalition after only three years, in 1923, when it also ironically changed its name to the Bund für Menschenrechte (League for Human Rights).

DON'T ASK, DON'T TELL. Common parlance for U.S. President Bill Clinton's 29 January 1993 recruitment directive ordering the Pentagon to lift its ban on the enlistment of gays and lesbians in the armed services.

Prior to World War II, although the act of sodomy committed by service personnel was grounds for court-martial and imprisonment, there was no ban on the recruitment of homosexual men or women. Between 1941 and 1943 the Selective Service and the armed services instituted new procedures to deal with homosexuality. Psychiatric screening became increasingly commonplace, one objective of which was the exclusion of homosexuals from military service. Dishonorable discharges also became increasingly common, replacing the cumbersome process of courts-martial except in cases of rape.

During the 50-year ban on homosexuals in the U.S. military, it is estimated that over 80,000 gay men and lesbians were discharged from the military, most with less than honorable discharges. The election of Bill Clinton in 1992 proffered hope that this long nightmare for gay and lesbian service personnel was over. Clinton had publicly stated his opposition to the ban on numerous occasions and had openly embraced the idea of civil rights (q.v.) for gays and lesbians.

The inability of President Clinton to reverse the ban on homosexuals in the military in 1993 was a great setback to gays and lesbians in the United States. Facing stiff opposition from the Joint Chiefs of Staff and the Senate Armed Services Committee Clinton compromised. The compromise retains courts-martial for violence in the commission of sodomy and discharge from military service for acknowledged gays and lesbians. It differs from previous policy only in that the services may not inquire into an individual's sexual orientation, either in the recruitment process or after enlistment ("don't ask"), unless the individual's sexual orientation becomes manifest ("don't tell").

Discharges of gays and lesbians from the U.S. armed services remain at very high levels, at a time when many other nations have embraced the right of gays and lesbians to enlist for military service (q.v.). The U.S. Supreme Court will probably review the constitutionality of the "don't ask, don't tell" policy in the near future.

DORIAN SOCIETY (DS). The first gay and lesbian rights organization in New Zealand, the DS took up the cause of legal reform in 1964 after a man was severely beaten by a gang of youths in Christchurch. It was widely regarded to have been a case of gay bashing. The victim's death and the subsequent acquittal of the perpetrators led the DS to establish a legal taskforce to make recommendations concerning the reform of New Zealand's sodomy statutes (q.v.). In the 22-year reform battle the DS, subsequently renamed the New Zealand Homosexual Law Reform Society (NZHLRS), played an important role.

New Zealand's annexation by England in 1840 led to the imposition of British law on New Zealand, including English laws pertaining to homosexual relations. Because of the common legal tradition, the movement for law reform in New Zealand has borne a strong resemblance to its counterpart in England.

The English "buggery" statute, the Act of 25 Henry VIII, c.6 (q.v.), became the law of New Zealand in 1840 and remained so until the Offenses against the Person Act was passed in 1867. Similar to the English Offenses against the Person Act of 1861, New Zealand's 1867 statute also reduced the penalties for anal intercourse. Whereas the Act of 25 Henry VIII, c.6, had prescribed death and the confiscation of all property, the Offenses against the Person Act in both England and New Zealand reduced the penalties to 10 years to life imprisonment.

Likewise, the 1885 enactment of the Labouchère Amendment (q.v.) in England, led to the enactment of similar legislation in New Zealand in the form of Part XIII of the Criminal Code Act of 1893. Like the Labouchère Amendment, the act criminalized all homosexual acts between males, as well as the attempt to procure homosexual relations, whether such occurred in private or not. The penalties of the New Zealand Criminal Code Act, however, were harsher than their English counterparts. Life imprisonment with hard labor and flogging was the prescribed penalty for commission of buggery. Although the provisions for flogging and hard labor were deleted in 1941 and 1954, respectively, other provisions of the 1893 statute remained unchanged until 1961.

The 1961 Crimes Act introduced a new schedule of penalties for homosexual relations and extended its provisions to lesbian relationships. This was a departure from the British tradition where sexual acts between women had never been an object of the criminal law. Consensual and nonconsensual relations between males carried the punishment of five to seven years in prison. Consensual or nonconsensual relations between a woman over 16 with a female under 16 carried the penalty of seven years' imprisonment as did a nonconsensual assault of one woman against another.

The NZHLRS initiated the campaign to reform New Zealand's antihomosexual laws by calling for the establishment of a committee similar to the Committee on Homosexual Offenses and Prostitution (Wolfenden Committee) (q.v.) in Britain. Its objective was the enactment of a law similar to the Sexual Offenses Act (q.v.), which had decriminalized homosexual relations in England in 1967.

Eighteen years of organizing and parliamentary initiatives took place between the establishment of New Zealand's committee in 1968 and the eventual enactment of a reform bill. The NZHLRS, together with such groups as the National Gay Rights Coalition of New

Zealand, the Auckland Gay Task Force, and the Lesbian and Gay Rights Resource Center, cooperated with sympathetic heterosexual citizens groups and members of Parliament until sufficient votes existed to pass a reform bill. Introduced by Fran Wilde in 1985, the reform bill was enacted in 1986. Known as the Homosexual Law Reform Act, its provisions were more liberal than the British 1967 Sexual Offenses Act, the statute that had originally inspired the reformers. Since its passage consensual homosexual relationships between individuals over the age of 16 have been legal. Most recently, in 1993, New Zealand enacted a nationwide human rights law protecting the rights of gays and lesbians.

DYSON, A. E. (1928–   ). A. E. (Tony) Dyson was the founder of the Homosexual Law Reform Society (HLRS) (q.v.) in May 1958 in Great Britain. The Albany Trust (AT) (q.v.), a charitable counterpart to the HLRS, was formed soon after, with Dyson as one of its trustees. Dyson founded the HLRS to educate the public about homosexuality and to pressure the British government to adopt the recommendations of the Report of the Committee on Homosexual Offenses and Prostitution (the Wolfenden Report) (q.v.), which would decriminalize private homosexual acts between adult men. Dyson accepted the role of vice-chair, in deference to Kenneth Walker, a well-known sexologist and psychiatrist, who became the first chair of the HLRS. Although Tony Dyson resigned his position of leadership with the HLRS in 1960, he remained actively involved with the HLRS and the AT. In 1967 one of Dyson's major objectives was accomplished when the Sexual Offenses Act (q.v.) decriminalized private homosexual relations between adult men in England and Wales.

E

EAST COAST HOMOPHILE ORGANIZATIONS (ECHO). *See* EASTERN REGIONAL CONFERENCE OF HOMOPHILE ORGANIZATIONS (ERCHO).

EASTERN REGIONAL CONFERENCE OF HOMOPHILE ORGANIZATIONS (ERCHO). In 1963, the New York Daughters of Bilitis and New York Mattachine, Washington Mattachine, and the Janus Society founded the East Coast Homophile Organizations (ECHO), the first regional association of homosexual organizations in the United States. In 1966 ECHO, together with homophile groups throughout the United States, founded the North American Conference of Homophile Organizations (NACHO) (q.v.), a nationwide federation of homosexual organizations. ECHO was superseded by the Eastern Regional Conference of Homophile Organizations (ERCHO).

ERCHO provided a modicum of regional coordination and leadership in the aftermath of the 1961 breakup of the Mattachine Society's (q.v.) national organization. One of its most noteworthy accomplishments was the demonstrations it organized in 1965 at the Pentagon, Civil Service Commission, State Department, and White House. Organized primarily by Franklin Kameny (q.v.), the principal figure in the Washington Mattachine Society, the purpose of the picketing was to protest the ban on hiring homosexuals by the U.S. federal government. This was the first gay and lesbian rights demonstration in the nation's capital.

Such protest activities as these caused considerable dissension in ERCHO between those who favored challenging discriminatory practices through the courts and those who favored more direct action. But this was only a portent of things to come. The emergence of the Gay Liberation Front (GLF) (q.v.) in 1969 would prove to be the undoing of ERCHO. At the November 1969 general meeting of ERCHO, representatives of the GLF criticized the politics of the older and more conservative membership. The GLF not only stood for more militant strategies, it also advocated building alliances with other groups, such as the antiwar movement and the Black Panthers, in a broad-based coalition of revolutionary organizations. The mainstays of ERCHO disagreed with the GLF, asserting that ERCHO should focus on gay and lesbian rights and should not dissipate its limited resources on tangential causes of little significance to homosexuals. They also felt that more moderate political strategies would have a greater long-run impact than those advocated by the GLF. The dissension over the influence of the GLF at the convention left the organization hopelessly divided, and it disintegrated before its next regularly scheduled meeting in 1970.

ELLIS, HAVELOCK (1859–1939). Born Henry Havelock Ellis, he became one of England's foremost sexologists and sex reformers. Ellis wrote widely on a variety of subjects, from socialism to women's rights to eugenics but he is probably best known for his publications on the psychology of sex and for his prominent role in the formation of the British Society for the Study of Sex Psychology (BSSP) and the World League for Sexual Reform (WLSR) (qq.v.). The first to use the term homosexual in English, he made significant contributions to the reform of attitudes toward homosexuality.

Havelock Ellis was influenced by H. M. Hyndman, the founder of the Social Democratic Federation, a Marxist organization, and the author of *England for All*, a popular distillation of socialist principles.

Ellis was acquainted as well with Eleanor Marx who was active in socialist organizing long after the death of her father, Karl, and Edward Aveling, Eleanor's companion, who was best known for his English translation of *Capital*. Ellis helped to found the Fellowship for a New Life, a socialist organization, where he met Edward Carpenter (q.v.) with whom he developed a lifelong professional relationship, and Edith Lees, his future wife. He was also acquainted through correspondence with John Addington Symonds (q.v.), who later coauthored *Sexual Inversion* with Ellis and who played a major role in forming Ellis's attitudes toward homosexuality. It was Symonds who initiated the correspondence.

The collaboration between Ellis and Symonds began in 1892, a few years after Symonds had read *The New Spirit*, a book by Ellis that contained an essay on Walt Whitman (q.v.). The collaboration was cut short by Symonds's death in 1893. Nevertheless, Ellis went ahead with the project and published it as a coauthored work with a German publishing house in 1896. A year later *Sexual Inversion* was published in England with all references to Symonds expunged at the behest of Symonds's family. *Sexual Inversion* immediately became embroiled in a prosecution. Although Ellis was not the subject of the prosecution, *Sexual Inversion* was labeled a scandalous and lewd book by the prosecutors, who sought to topple a small sexual reform group, the Legitimation League, for the sale and distribution of the book. Ellis's subsequent works in his *Studies in the Psychology of Sex* series were printed in the United States.

In contrast to prevailing Victorian attitudes toward homosexuality, Ellis and Symonds made a case for its acceptability by referencing the widespread frequency of the practice in all cultures throughout history. This aspect of *Sexual Inversion* was probably due mostly to Symonds's historical research. Unlike 19th-century Britain, they noted, not all cultures condemned homosexuality, and some had even revered it. Similarly, according to the authors, because many persons renowned for their contributions to civilization had been homosexual, homosexuality had been falsely labeled a degenerative illness. From their perspective it was no more than a normal variation in the sexual instinct.

Like Magnus Hirschfeld (q.v.), Ellis and Symonds concentrated on the congenital dimension of sexual orientation. Ellis ultimately came to agree with Richard von Krafft-Ebing, the eminent Viennese psychiatrist, and others that some cases could be explained by environmental influences, a condition he labeled homosexuality, but he continued to insist that true inversion was mostly a condition beyond the control of the individual. Following Hirschfeld's pioneering work, Ellis sought to distinguish inversion from transvestism, further reinforcing the essential normality of the true invert. He even sought to dissociate inversion from buggery and effeminacy. It was the law that was out of step with nature, he said, not the invert.

Sexual Inversion also broached the topic of lesbianism, which distinguishes this work from many others of the day. Ellis was acquainted with a number of lesbians owing to the influence of his wife, Edith, who was herself a lesbian. He vigorously defended the publication of Radclyffe Hall's *The Well of Loneliness*, and thus the rights of all lesbians, in a preface to the novel. Comparatively speaking, however, the amount of space devoted to lesbians in Ellis's work is much less than that devoted to male homosexuals, and the insights are much more dated.

Ellis's professional association with Edward Carpenter was a long and mutually fulfilling one. Their common interests included socialism, women's rights, the rights of homosexuals, and a commitment to other sexual reforms such as birth control and the reform of marriage laws. Edward Carpenter was not only a friend and associate of Havelock Ellis, he became a close friend of Edith Ellis and her circle of female friends. Carpenter and Ellis were the principal figures behind the creation of the BSSP in 1914, and both were instrumental in the formation of the WLSR in 1921.

Ellis's contribution to the homosexual rights movement was confined to his various publications and his participation in the BSSP and WLSR. He was not an outgoing man and not a political organizer, but he was convinced that before discriminatory statutes could be expunged from the law public attitudes had to change, and this could only occur through the scientific study of sexuality. Although many of his ideas about homosexuality and feminism are old-fashioned, his contribution to understanding human sexuality was remarkable.

EMPLOYMENT NON-DISCRIMINATION ACT (ENDA). Proposed legislation in the U.S. Congress that would prohibit discrimination on the basis of sexual orientation in the workplace. The enactment of the ENDA is a high priority of the National Gay and Lesbian Task Force and the Human Rights Campaign (qq.v.).

On 10 September 1996, the same day that the U.S. Senate overwhelmingly voted in favor of the Defense of Marriage Act (DOMA) (q.v.), the Senate narrowly defeated the ENDA with a final vote of 50 to 49. This narrow defeat garnered more votes in support of a federal civil rights (q.v.) statute protecting gays and lesbians than any bill, including HR-14752, the first such legislation introduced by Representatives Bella Abzug and Ed Koch in 1974.

Although gays and lesbians enjoy various degrees of civil rights protection in nine states and roughly 150 cities and counties, the prospects for passage of the ENDA are remote. Although the vote in the Senate was close and President Clinton has endorsed its passage, there were insufficient cosponsors of the ENDA in the House of Representatives to bring it to a floor vote during the 105th Congress.

ENGELSCHMAN, NIEK. *See* ANGELO, BOB.

EREN, IBRAHIM. Turkey's most prominent gay rights leader and a leader of the Turkish Radical Green Party.

Although Turkish law does not prohibit gay or lesbian sexual relations, the Turkish government is highly intolerant of homosexuality and the police highly repressive. The police have raided gay bars, forced gays to submit to venereal disease testing, and have engaged in beatings and torture. The publication of Arslan Yüzgün's *Homosexuality in Turkey: Yesterday, Today* was the object of government censorship in the late 1980s. *Yesil Baris*, the Turkish Radical Green Party's newspaper, came under attack in 1989 after publishing a series on lesbians and gays. Among other charges, the publishers were accused of "slandering the state" because of one reference to the alleged homosexuality of modern Turkey's founding father, Kemal Atatürk.

Ibrahim Eren has been jailed on at least two occasions for his association with the gay and lesbian cause. In 1989, Eren called a press conference at his New Byzantine Cultural Center to condemn police attacks on transvestites in Istanbul. Following the press conference, he was arrested for violating Turkey's penal code, which prohibits unlawful public assemblies, and jailed for three months. A year later, he was wrongfully accused of promoting homosexual prostitution at his place of business, a sauna in Istanbul. Badly beaten, he again served two weeks in jail.

Turkish society remains highly repressive despite the efforts of gay and lesbian rights leaders such as Ibrahim Eren. In 1991 police again raided the residences of transvestites in Istanbul, arresting and torturing a number of the occupants, and in 1993 an international conference of gay and lesbian rights advocates in Istanbul was suppressed by the police.

EUROPE. The birthplace of the gay rights movement. As early as the 1860s, individuals such as Karl Heinrich Ulrichs and Karl Maria Kertbeny (qq.v.) protested sodomy statutes (q.v.) such as Paragraph 175 (q.v.) of the German Imperial Legal Code. These protests represent the first recorded instances of resistance to the subordination of homosexuals to the legal and social hegemony of heterosexuality.

Europe is also the site of some of the earliest literary and scientific publications on the subject of homosexuality, the first homosexual rights organizations in the world, as well as the first organizations devoted to the study of sexuality. Early scientific and literary works, such as *The Riddle of "Man-Manly" Love* by Karl Heinrich Ulrichs, and the writings of prominent British authors such as Sir Richard Burton, Edward Carpenter, Havelock Ellis, and John Addington Symonds (qq.v.) had a profound international impact on the development of a humane understanding of the subject of same-sex love.

The founders of the first homosexual rights organizations were, themselves, scientists and literati. Magnus Hirschfeld (q.v.), the acknowledged leader of the Wissenschaftlich-humanitäres Komitee (Scientific-Humanitarian Committee) (q.v.), authored numerous articles and books, many of which dealt with the subject of homosexuality. Likewise, Adolph Brand and Benedict Friedländer (qq.v.), co-founders of the Gemeinschaft der Eigenen (Community of the Special) (q.v.), published many essays as well as book-length works on love between men and man-boy love.

The first institutes devoted to the study of sexuality were also of European origin. The British Society for the Study of Sex Psychology (BSSP) (q.v.), founded in 1914, and the Institut für Sexualwissenschaft (Institute for Sexual Science [ISS]) (q.v.), founded five years later in Berlin, conducted research on sexually transmitted diseases, birth control, and so forth, and promoted women's rights and the rights of homosexuals through systematic studies of sexuality. The organizations frequently collaborated in their research and participated in the annual conferences of the World League for Sexual Reform (WLSR) (q.v.).

If World War I interrupted the progress of homosexual rights organizations and the progress in the scientific study of sexuality, World War II brought an abrupt end to both endeavors. Not a single homosexual rights organization, or the BSSP, the ISS, or the WLSR survived the war. Furthermore, the imprisonment and extermination of tens of thousands of "pink triangles" (q.v.) in German prison camps represented a tremendous setback to the cause of homosexual rights.

Nevertheless, shortly after the cessation of hostilities, homosexual rights organizations began to reappear in Europe at approximately the same time as the first homosexual rights organizations appeared in North America (q.v.). The first to emerge, in 1946, was the Dutch organization Cultuur-en-Ontspannings Centrum (Culture and Recreational Center), followed by the Danish group Landsforeningen for Bøsser og Lesbiske (National Organization of Gays and Lesbians) in 1948, the French group Arcadie (1953), and, in Britain, the Homosexual Law Reform Society (1958) (qq.v.). Groups such as these provided social and recreational venues for gay men and lesbians and renewed the effort to eliminate sodomy statutes as well as age of consent laws (q.v.).

Although Stonewall (q.v.) was an American event it had profound repercussions in Europe. Just as it had in the United States and Canada, Stonewall transformed the gay and lesbian rights movement in Europe into a mass movement and, comparatively speaking, a more highly politicized movement. The number of gay and lesbian organizations increased rapidly, and the work of securing civil rights for gays and lesbians began in earnest. Today, European countries such as Denmark, France, Norway, the Netherlands, and Sweden can claim to have either paved the way for the integration of gays and lesbians into military service (q.v.), or to have been the first to enact nationwide statutes protecting the civil rights (q.v.) of gays and lesbians, or to have been leaders in the trend to broaden the legal definition of marriage (q.v.) to include gays and lesbians. Although the progress of gay and lesbian rights has been more pronounced in Western Europe than in Eastern Europe, the recent dissolution of the Soviet Union has resulted in the abolition of sodomy statutes in many Eastern European countries formerly under the influence of the USSR and the emergence of the first gay and lesbian organizations such as the Sexual Minorities Association and the Latvian Association for Sexual Equality (qq.v.) Hungary recently became the first Eastern European country to grant gays and lesbians the right to marry, a goal promoted by Szivarvany (Rainbow) (q.v.).

Progress toward the formation of the European Union (EU) has also presented gays and lesbians an opportunity to assert their interests in the ongoing EU deliberations pertaining to civil rights. Groups such as the Stonewall Group and the International Lesbian and Gay Association (qq.v.) have been actively involved in this endeavor. If gays and lesbians are able to achieve full civil rights in the EU, it will constitute the movement's greatest achievement in the arena of international law.

F

FRENTE HOMOSEXUAL DE ACCIÓN REVOLUCIONARIA/ REVOLUTIONARY HOMOSEXUAL ACTION FRONT (RHAF–M).

The RHAF–M, the Grupo Lambda de Liberación Homosexual (Lambda Homosexual Liberation Group [LHLG]) (q.v.), and Oikabeth were the first politically active gay and lesbian groups to emerge in Mexico. Previous groups such as the Frente de Liberación Homosexual de Mexico (Homosexual Liberation Front of Mexico [HLFM]) (q.v.) had been much more circumspect about publicizing their existence.

The RHAF–M was inspired by the example of the Gay Liberation Front (GLF) (q.v.) in the United States and in Great Britain. The GLF espoused not only gay and lesbian liberation but also racial equality and socialist and feminist principles. Like the GLF, the RHAF–M was a coalition of groups. Although it espoused a feminist ideology, its membership was predominantly male, and lesbians found other groups, such as Oikabeth, more suitable to their purposes.

The RHAF–M emerged on the stage of leftist politics in Mexico in a most dramatic fashion. On 26 July 1978, at the annual march commemorating the Cuban Revolution, the members marched in protest of the treatment of gays and lesbians in Cuba. In October, the same year, the RHAF–M participated in a demonstration marking the tenth anniversary of the 1968 student massacre in Tlatelolco.

Reminiscent of the GLF's confrontational tactics in New York City, the RHAF–M protested police harassment of gays in Mexico City by staging a sit-in at police headquarters in 1980. RHAF–M also published its own newspaper, *Nuestro Cuerpo* (Our Body). So initially successful were the RHAF–M, LHLG, and Oikabeth that the Partido Revolucionario de los Trabajadores (PRT) (Revolutionary Workers' Party) incorporated homosexual rights into its party platform during the 1982 election campaign and backed the candidacies of gays and lesbians such as Max Mejía and Claudia Hinojosa.

The 1982 elections, however, proved to be the high-water mark of the gay and lesbian movement in Mexico and thus of the RHAF–M. Many PRT supporters were unwilling to be associated with the gay and lesbian agenda, and the RHAF–M experienced increasing difficulties recruiting members because of its socialist ideology. By 1988, the issue of gay and lesbian rights had been eliminated from the PRT's platform. Furthermore, beyond public demonstrations, the RHAF–M was unable to mobilize gays and lesbians to tackle the more practical chore of reforming specific discriminatory practices. The RHAF–M disappeared from the scene in 1984 shortly after disrupting a Mexico City Gay Pride Day march in an effort to call attention to the "death" of the original goals of the movement.

Although the RHAF–M no longer exists, Colectivo Sol, a small group composed of former RHAF–M activists, has recently engaged in AIDS-related activities and has begun to develop a gay and lesbian archives in Mexico City. Furthermore, other Mexico City organizations such as Guerrilla Gay and Circulo Cultural Gay have recently begun operations as have numerous organizations in other Mexican metropolitan areas.

FRENTE DE LIBERACIÓN HOMOSEXUAL DE MEXICO/HO-MOSEXUAL LIBERATION FRONT OF MEXICO (HLFM). Along with other organizations such as El Grupo de Martes and Grupo de Domingos the HLFM was founded in the early 1970s in Mexico City. Fashioned after Gay Liberation Front (GLF) (q.v.) organizations in the United States and in England, the HLFM was composed of both men and women and was the most significant of the initial homosexual rights organizations in Mexico. Like its counterparts in the North America and Europe (qq.v.), it was dedicated to eliminating sexism, in addition to the persecution of gays and lesbians, which the founders felt were inextricably interconnected.

One of the main accomplishments of this short-lived group was the publication of its research on homosexuality and Mexican law. Before the publication of the HLFM's research, information on this subject was not widely available. The HLFM's report revealed that, unlike the laws of the United States, Mexican law contained no criminal penalties for private, consensual homosexual relations between adults. This was because of the lasting impact of the Napoleonic Code on Mexican law, dating from the French occupation of Mexico in the mid-1860s.

Mexican law, however, was found to contain public indecency and censorship statutes that had implications for gays and lesbians. Public indecency statutes gave wide discretionary powers to the police to arrest individuals for lewd behavior, and censorship laws gave judges the power to censor written materials which they deemed immoral. Public indecency statutes (*el reglamento de policía*) were used, for example, to detain gays and lesbians who were guilty of nothing more than congregating for social or political purposes. Censorship laws (*la ley de imprenta*) gave judges the power to prohibit the circulation of gay and lesbian newspapers and magazines and to imprison anyone found guilty of distributing such information to minors.

From its inception, the HLFM was beset with organizational difficulties, and the group quickly factionalized and ceased to exist after only a year of organizing. However, the HLFM was only the harbinger of things to come. Shortly after its demise, groups such as the Frente Homosexual de Acción Revolucionaria (Revolutionary Homosexual Action Front) and the Grupo Lambda de Liberación Homosexual (Lambda Homosexual Liberation Group) (qq.v.) began to organize in a much more public and effective way in Mexico City.

FREUD, SIGMUND (1856–1939). *See* MEDICAL MODEL OF HOMOSEXUALITY.

FRIEDLÄNDER, BENEDICT (1866–1908). A cofounder of the Gemeinschaft der Eigenen (Community of the Special [COS]) (q.v.)

with Adolf Brand (q.v.) and Wilhelm Jansen in 1902. Friedländer is remembered for his sharp differences with Magnus Hirschfeld and the Wissenschaftlich-humanitäres Komitee (Scientific-Humanitarian Committee [SHC]) (qq.v.), and for his advocacy of a Hellenistic model of homosexual relationships between men.

Although Friedländer was a member of the SHC until 1906 when he resigned, he was openly critical of the committee's scientific interpretation of homosexuality. Friedländer was deeply influenced by the 1900 publication of *Lieblingminne und Freundesliebe in der Weltlitteratur* (Chivalric affection and comrade love in world literature), a literary anthology that encompassed homoerotic prose and verse from ancient Greece through the 19th century. The veneration of masculine aesthetics and homoeroticism evident in the pages of this anthology had, according to Friedländer, been sullied by Magnus Hirschfeld and the SHC through the espousal of Hirschfeld's version of Karl Heinrich Ulrichs's "third sex" theory (qq.v.).

Friedländer was convinced of the ethical superiority of male homoerotic friendships and was appalled by the thought that a male homosexual could be portrayed as an invert, a woman trapped in a man's body. He was married, but he had also participated in the nudist movement where he said his appreciation for male eros was awakened. Friedländer advocated a German form of the ancient Hellenistic practice of bisexuality, the erotic friendship between married men and boys.

His views were set forth in 1904 in his *Renaissance des Eros Uranios* (Renaissance of Eros Uranios), published only four years before his death. Friedländer's advocacy of both homosexuality and pedophilia limited the popularity of his philosophy. His attempt to attract members away from the SHC with his resignation in 1906 failed, as did his aspirations that the COS would displace the SHC as the principal homosexual rights organization in Germany.

FRONT HOMOSEXUEL D'ACTION RÉVOLUTIONNAIRE/ REVOLUTIONARY HOMOSEXUAL ACTION FRONT– FRANCE (RHAF–F). Inspired by the May 1968 protests in Paris, the Comité d'Action Pédérastique Révolutionnaire (Revolutionary Pederastic Action Committee) was founded at the Sorbonne. This short-lived confrontational group preceded the equally confrontational Gay Liberation Front (q.v.) organizations in the United States and Britain Similarly inspired, the RHAF–F was founded on 10 March 1971, after lesbians and gay men disrupted a psychoanalytical discussion in Paris on the condescending topic of "l'homosexualité, ce douloureux problème"("homosexuality, this painful problem"). The RHAF–F's disruption of a 1 May demonstration by the Confédération Général du Travail (General Confederation of Labor), with open displays of homosexuality, announced the birth of a new phase in gay and lesbian politics in France. The RHAF–F's most prominent spokesperson was Guy Hocquenghem.

The RHAF–F, like its counterparts in the United States and Britain, attempted to weave the struggle for racial justice, feminism, gay rights, and the class struggle into a single movement. Because each movement sought self-determination for heretofore marginalized individuals, the RHAF–F envisioned a broad-based coalition of groups working for the emancipation of all from repressive institutions.

Integral to each movement was the liberation of the individual from ideologies that were counterproductive to self-determination. In the case of gays and lesbians, the medical model of homosexuality (q.v.) came under attack for psychiatry's classification of homosexuality as a mental illness.

Unlike earlier homosexual reform movements such as the Wissen-schaftlich-humanitäres Komitee (Scientific-Humanitarian Committee [SHC]) in Germany or the British Society for the Study of Sex Psychology (BSSP) (qq.v.) in Britain, the RHAF–F was critical of psychiatry for perpetuating the repression of gays and lesbians. But unlike the overt rejection of psychiatry by the GLF, the RHAF–F focused on the reinterpretation of psychiatric models of sexual orientation and gender.

Hocquenghem was instrumental in developing the theoretical basis of this critique in his *Homosexual Desire*, first published in France in 1972. Using such diverse sources as Louis Althusser's interpretation of Marxism, the semiotics of Jacques Lacan, Michel Foucault's histories of sexuality, and the work of Gilles Deleuze and Félix Guattari, Hocquenghem sought to recover the subversive implications of Freud's psychoanalytical theory. Written in the same spirit as Herbert Marcuse's *Eros and Civilization*, Hocquenghem's *Homosexual Desire* contended that homosexual male sodomy was not marginalized because it was a perversion of nature but because of the privileged nature of heterosexual patriarchal relations in the power structure of bourgeois civilization. In this regard Hocquenghem saw the practice of homosexuality as subversive to capitalism and thus implicitly communistic. The RHAF–F's political perspective was also spelled out in the pages of its journals *L'Antinorm* and *Le Fléau*.

The RHAF–F, as well as the more established Arcadie (q.v.), fought the introduction into French law of criminal penalties for homosexual conduct. Homosexuality had not been the object of criminal law in France for more than 150 years when, in 1942, Marshal Pétain introduced discriminatory penalties for homosexual relationships with anyone under 21, male or female. Prior to 1942, the age of consent for homosexuals and heterosexuals alike had been 16. Beginning in 1942, homosexual relations with anyone under the age of 21, regardless of the age of the parties involved, was penalized with prison sentences of up to three years. Charles de Gaulle's government reaffirmed the Vichy ordinance in 1945. In 1960, the French government, again under de Gaulle, adopted discriminatory penalties for homosexual indecent exposure. Whereas the penalty for both heterosexual and homosexual indecent exposure had been the same, homosexual indecent exposure was now subject to greater penalties than corresponding heterosexual conduct.

Hocquenghem saw these discriminatory ordinances as evidence of the latent moral fascism of modern civilization and worked to achieve equality under the law for gays and lesbians. But the RHAF–F and Hocquenghem stood for much more than the principle of legal equality. For the RHAF–F, gay and lesbian activism had the potential to undermine the very social norms, and thus the power structure, that subtends the modern patriarchal family structure.

The RHAF–F dissolved in 1973 and was followed by the Groupe de Libération Homosexuelle (Homosexual Liberation Group) and the Comité d'Urgence Anti-Répression Homosexuelle (Emergency Committee against the Repression of Homosexuals) (qq.v), organizations that ultimately rejected the countercultural emphasis of the RHAF–F and developed the idea of civil rights (q.v.) as the mainstay of the gay and lesbian liberation movement in France.

FUTUR. See ARCADIE.

G

GAY ACTIVISTS ALLIANCE (GAA). Founded in New York City in December 1969, the GAA arose out of frustrations with the Gay Liberation Front (GLF) (q.v.). The leadership of the GAA, such as Jim Owles, Kay Tobin, and Marty Robinson, who had been active in the GLF, became disillusioned with the GLF owing to its lack of organization and its affiliation with other left-wing groups such as the Black Panthers and the antiwar movement. They felt that this affiliation drained energy from the homosexual rights cause, and many of the groups that the GLF sought affiliation with were blatantly anti-gay. Although the tactics of the GAA were no less confrontational, the GAA was committed to the single issue of gay and lesbian liberation and was structured on more conventional lines.

Like the Mattachine Society of New York (MSNY), the GAA undertook legal actions, but unlike the MSNY it was not preoccupied with pursuing reform through the courts. The GAA saw itself as a political organization. The membership felt that genuine reform would only come if gays and lesbians exercised their political muscle.

Much time and energy was devoted to electoral politics. Candidates for election, whether in primary or general elections, were questioned about their positions on a wide variety of issues from civil rights (q.v.) to police behavior. Pressure was brought to bear on elected officials from city council members and the mayor to state legislators, the governor, and federal officials. Often the pressure took the form of direct confrontations (zaps) in public meetings, on the streets, or in their offices.

The GAA, like the GLF, also engaged in a variety of other direct actions. For example, in March 1970 the GAA picketed the sixth police precinct station after the false arrest of 167 patrons of a Greenwich Village gay bar and brought legal action against the New York City police on their behalf. They pressured the *New York Post* to desist from its habitual negative stereotyping and put-downs of gays and lesbians. The GAA participated as well in the protests against New York University's refusal to allow gay and lesbian groups to use its facilities. Along with other East Coast groups, the GAA participated in the first Christopher Street Liberation Day Committee, which organized the first annual pride march commemorating the anniversary of the Stonewall (q.v.) riots on 28 June 1970. The march has become an annual event in New York City as well as other cities around the world.

At the heart of GAA politics were five demands: (1) the repeal of New York State's sodomy and solicitation laws; (2) an end to police entrapment of gay men; (3) an end to police harassment of gay bars and an investigation into corruption in the New York State Liquor Authority; (4) a law protecting gays and lesbians against discrimination in employment; and (5) an end to the bonding company practice of denying bonds to gays and lesbians (by refusing to bond gays and lesbians, bonding companies had the power to exclude them from jobs requiring bonding).

Although the GAA ceased operations in 1974, shortly after its community center was destroyed by fire, activists associated with the GAA founded the National Gay Task Force (q.v.) (renamed the National Gay and Lesbian Task Force), a leading contemporary gay and lesbian rights organization in the United States.

GAY AID IDENTIFICATION DEVELOPMENT AND ENRICH-MENT (GAIDE). With the possible exception of the South African gay liberation movement activities on the campus of the University of Natal, GAIDE was the first gay and lesbian organization to emerge in South Africa since the demise of the Homosexual Law Reform Fund (HLRF) (q.v.) in 1969. The South African gay liberation movement collapsed almost before it began under intense pressure from the police in 1972. GAIDE was considerably more successful, perhaps because of its apolitical character.

Founded in Durban, South Africa, in 1976 by Bobby Erasmus, GAIDE was organized primarily as a social outlet for gays and lesbians. It also provided a range of social support services, such as information and peer counseling, and published a monthly newsletter. Like the HLRF, GAIDE was all white but, unlike the HLRF, a significant proportion of the membership were lesbians.

Bobby Erasmus's emigration in 1978 precipitated the collapse of GAIDE, but it became a model for other gay and lesbian social clubs, and its newsletter was emulated by other groups around the country. The eventual development of politically active gay and lesbian rights groups in South Africa, such as the Gay Association of South Africa (q.v.), owed much to the social support networks developed by groups such as GAIDE and its successors.

GAY AND LESBIAN ASSOCIATION OF CUBA (GLAC). Formed in July 1994, GLAC was the first gay and lesbian organization to emerge in Cuba. Short lived, it has been superseded by the Grupo de Acción por la Libertad de Expresión de la Elección Sexual (Action Group for the Liberty of Expression of Sexual Choice [AGLESC]).

The formation of the GLAC in 1994 was, in itself, testimony to the changing climate of opinion concerning homosexuality in Cuba and, more specifically, in the Communist Party of Cuba. Although homosexuals are still excluded from membership in the party, the persecution of gays and lesbians has decreased over the last two decades.

Prior to the adoption of the 1979 penal code, homosexual relations between consenting adults in private were considered a criminal offense. In 1979, private consensual homosexual relations were decriminalized. However, other provisions of the prerevolutionary legal code remained. The 1979 law retained the prerevolutionary public indecency provisions pertaining to homosexuality. Similar to the 1967 British Sexual Offenses Act (q.v.), the 1979 law defined private to mean not only occuring in nonpublic venues but also sexual acts occuring between no more than two parties. Third parties to a sexual act could expose the participants to charges of "public ostentation." Furthermore, it was illegal to solicit another for homosexual relations, to engage in habitual homosexual relations, or to flaunt one's homosexuality in public. Age of consent laws (q.v.) in the 1979 code also discriminated against homosexuals.

A 1987 revision of the penal code eliminated the aspect of the 1979 law pertaining to "public ostentation," but it retained penalties of up to 12 months for other offenses against public decency. The 1987 revision of the penal code also did not eliminate the discriminatory age of consent laws. The age of consent for homosexual relations (male or female) remained 16, whereas the corresponding age of consent for heterosexual relations was 12. Penalties for homosexual relations with anyone under 14 remained very harsh, potentially including the death penalty. The 1987 code also contains articles prohibiting anyone convicted of such sexual crimes, even those involving adults, of having any position of authority over children, such as teaching.

Cuban homosexuals have also been the subject of harsh, repressive tactics by the Cuban Communist Party. Between 1965 and 1968, the Cuban government set up rehabilitation camps, Military Units to Aid Production camps, designed to discipline "unrevolutionary" individuals. Although estimates vary, a large proportion of those sent to hard labor camps were Cuban homosexuals who were deemed unworthy of military service (q.v.) because of their immoral lifestyle. In the late 1960s homosexuals were purged from universities and the arts, and, in 1971, the National Congress on Education and Culture adopted a series of antihomosexual measures, including a provision prohibiting homosexuals from representing Cuba in international cultural events. Most recently, the Cuban policy of quarantining people with AIDS has provoked criticism from international AIDS organizations.

The Military Units to Aid Production camps were disbanded in 1968 because of criticism from Cuban as well as international human rights advocates, and, in 1975, the Cuban Supreme Court nullified Resolución Número 3 of the Consejo de Cultura, the resolution that mandated the purge of homosexuals in universities and the arts. Nevertheless, the high proportion of homosexuals in the 1980 Mariel boat lift, and again in the 1994 refugee crisis, is a reminder that although official repression of homosexuality is at a low ebb, traditional attitudes toward homosexuality have remained firmly entrenched in Cuba.

It was in this atmosphere that GLAC was created by a handful of gay and lesbian activists in Havana in 1994. Its manifesto, although recognizing the decline in official repression, called upon Cuban gays and lesbians to fight against all forms of discrimination against gays and lesbians, including the discrimination against people with AIDS. The group's successor, the AGLESC, is committed to obtaining official recognition from the government as the representative of Cuba's gay and lesbian population. If official recognition is granted, it would represent a historic first step toward the recognition of Cuban homosexuals as legitimate citizens.

GAY AND LESBIAN ORGANIZATION OF THE WITWATERSRAND (GLOW). Founded in 1989 by Simon Nkoli (q.v.), Linda Ngcobo, and others, GLOW, together with the Organization of Lesbian and Gay Activists (OLGA), championed the struggle to politicize gay and lesbian rights issues within the antiapartheid movement in South Africa. OLGA evolved out of the original Cape Town activist organization, Lesbians and Gays against Oppression (LAGO). LAGO was formed in 1986, and roughly a year later changed its name to OLGA. OLGA was joined two years later by GLOW and, since 1989, the two groups have become the principal organizations responsible for advancing the rights of gays and lesbians within the African National Congress (ANC) and other progressive South African political parties.

The impetus to form GLOW was the imprisonment of the gay antiapartheid activist Simon Nkoli. Nkoli was arrested in 1984 for his participation in a rent boycott demonstration and was subsequently prosecuted for murder. Nkoli was a member of the Gay Association of South Africa (GASA) (q.v.). The GASA's unwillingness to support Nkoli's cause and its unwillingness to join the antiapartheid struggle led Nkoli to form GLOW after his acquittal.

Like the GASA, GLOW served as a social outlet for its members. But, unlike the GASA, GLOW was a truly interracial organization. It was more overtly political and did not envision itself as a single-issue organization. Reflecting Nkoli's background as an antiapartheid activist as well as a gay rights supporter, GLOW sought to advance the interests of gays and lesbians within the broader movement for racial justice.

As a member of the ANC, Nkoli brought GLOW's influence to bear on the development of the ANC's Freedom Charter. Consequently, the ANC's draft Bill of Rights, which was adopted in 1990, included a specific provision proposing that discrimination on the basis of sexual orientation be unlawful. Furthermore, the ANC publicly supported the 1991 Gay Pride March organized by GLOW in Johannesburg, and its *Policy Guidelines For a Democratic South Africa* (adopted in 1992) made explicit references to the rights of lesbians and gays.

The ANC's silence during Winnie Mandela's 1991 trial and thereafter, however, cast into doubt the ANC's commitment to the principle of gay and lesbian rights. Winnie Mandela was a high-ranking official of the ANC at the time of her arrest on kidnapping and assault charges. Mandela and her codefendants claimed that they were rescuing four young men from the sexual abuse of the Reverend Paul Verryn, a Methodist minister in charge of a manor house where the boys lived. Mandela's supporters' equation of homosexuality with child abuse, despite Verryn's acquittal of child abuse charges in a trial court, was attacked by GLOW as a deliberate attempt to use homophobia in an effort to win her acquittal.

Although Winnie Mandela was found guilty on a variety of assault and kidnapping charges, imprisoned, and fined, the prison sentence was overturned on appeal in 1993. Despite her resignation from positions of leadership in the ANC in 1992, her supporters' public pronouncements before, during, and after the trial (claiming that homosexuality was un-African and a legacy of apartheid) polarized the membership of the ANC on the question of gay rights.

GLOW fought within the ANC to rectify the damage done to the interests of gays and lesbians by the Winnie Mandela trial. Its efforts were rewarded in 1994 when the ANC backed the inclusion of gay and lesbian rights in the interim constitution of South Africa. The prohibition against discrimination on the basis of sexual orientation was one of the first such constitutional provisions in the world. The adoption of South Africa's permanent constitution in 1996 retained the antidiscriminatory language contained in the interim constitution. Although GLOW no longer exists, its contribution to South Africa's gay and lesbian movement and to the international gay and lesbian rights movement was profound.

GAY ASSOCIATION OF SOUTH AFRICA (GASA). Founded in Johannesburg, South Africa, in 1982, the GASA was the first nationwide gay and lesbian rights organization in South Africa since the Homosexual Law Reform Fund (q.v.) ceased activities in the late 1960s. Created through the combined efforts of three gay and lesbian groups, Lambda, the Azanian Men's Organization (AMO), and Unité, GASA quickly spawned chapters in the major cities of South Africa and asserted a public presence uncharacteristic of previous lesbian and gay organizations.

Of the three groups that united to form GASA, only one had a political agenda. The AMO and Unité were supper clubs. Lambda, the most overt political group, was formed in 1981 in response to the increasingly frequent police raids of gay social events that year. Together they formed the GASA to provide social outlets for gays and lesbians and to combat police harassment.

Like the AMO and Unité, the GASA's political agenda was secondary to its social functions. It initiated a counseling service, the

Gay Advice Bureau, and published *Link/Skakel,* a newsletter eventually renamed *Exit.* GASA sponsored numerous public gatherings and parties at bars that catered to gay people. The GASA also spawned a number of affiliates, such as student groups on university campuses, Christian and Jewish associations, and the Transvaal Organization for Gay Sport (TOGS).

As with its predecessor organizations, the GASA's members were predominately white, male, and middle class. Attempts to attract lesbians and black South Africans to the organization were only marginally successful. Lesbians felt that the GASA was more interested in promoting social outlets for men than for women and that it was insensitive to women's issues. Blacks felt alienated from the GASA, which sought no role in the antiapartheid struggle and often sponsored events at establishments that refused to serve blacks. Antiapartheid activist Simon Nkoli (q.v.) attempted to integrate the GASA in 1983, but the lack of interest in the unique needs of black gays and lesbians led Nkoli to form the Saturday Group, a group devoted to serving the black gay and lesbian population. Similar difficulties plagued the GASA's efforts to attract working class gays and lesbians who felt uncomfortable in the predominantly white, middle-class environment characteristic of GASA events.

The GASA disintegrated as a national organization in 1986 due in large measure to internal conflicts between those who sought to transform the GASA into a forthright political organization and those who were content with the group's social activities. The arrest and detention of Simon Nkoli in 1984, and his subsequent indictment on murder charges in 1986, created an impasse within the organization. The inability of the GASA to marshal its membership in his defense caused the group's expulsion from the International Lesbian and Gay Association (q.v.) later that year. It dissolved shortly thereafter.

Despite its relatively short life span the GASA left a permanent imprint on the gay liberation movement in South Africa. Some of its regional affiliates, such as GASA 6010 and GASA Natal Coast survived the downfall of the national organization and continued to provide vital services such as AIDS counseling and education. *Exit* became an independent entity and became the principal publication serving South African gays and lesbians. The Gay Advice Bureau and TOGS continue to function as autonomous entities.

New organizations with more overt political agendas and a commitment to racial and sexual democracy, such as the Gay and Lesbian Organization of the Witwatersrand (q.v.) and the Organization of Lesbian and Gay Activists, have replaced the GASA at the forefront of the struggle for gay and lesbian equality in South Africa.

GAY COUNSELING SERVICE of NSW: *See* CAMPAIGN AGAINST MORAL PERSECUTION.

GAY LIBERATION FRONT (GLF). Unlike those of other gay and lesbian organizations, the activities of the GLF were not confined to a single country. Soon after its founding, GLF organizations quickly spread abroad with major centers in the United States and Great Britain.

United States

The Gay Liberation Front (GLF) originated in New York City in the days and weeks following the police raid on the Stonewall (q.v.) Inn on 27 July and the ensuing riots on 28 and 29 July 1969. The weekend confrontations between the police and gays and lesbians inspired a new enthusiasm for political action and created a rare opportunity for organizing a theretofore apolitical population. The GLF developed out of the perceived inability of existing homosexual rights organizations, the Mattachine Society of New York (MSNY) and the New York chapter of the Daughters of Bilitis (NYDOB), in particular, to address issues of concern to younger and more militant gays and lesbians. Shortly after Stonewall, the MSNY began to organize gays and lesbians in the Greenwich Village area under the banner of the Mattachine Action Committee. The NYMS originated as a chapter of the Mattachine Society (MS) (q.v.), becoming an independent organization after the dissolution of the national organization in the early 1960s. Although the Mattachine Action Committee worked out of the MSNY's offices, it quickly developed a high degree of independence from the MSNY. The MSNY had a policy of involving itself only in actions relevant to gays and lesbians, whereas the Mattachine Action Committee proposed coalitions with other left-wing groups such as the Black Panthers and was in favor of adopting a much more militant political posture. This precipitated a split between the Mattachine Action Committee and the MSNY. Although a second action committee developed in the MSNY, it quickly disbanded because of a lack of enthusiasm.

On 31 July, at a meeting called by members of the Mattachine Action Committee and sympathizers, a new, more vigorous, more combative organization, the Gay Liberation Front (GLF) was founded. What set the GLF apart from older, more established rights organizations was its membership. The GLF attracted student radicals, many of whom had gained their political experience in the civil rights (q.v.) movement, the Students for a Democratic Society, or in antiwar mobilizations. The GLF also attracted those whose ideas were formed in the counterculture, and lesbians brought ideas from the burgeoning women's movement. Many who were attracted to the GLF, however, were still primarily interested in a single-issue organization but one that was divorced from the more staid and established organizations. From the outset the tenor of the GLF was quite different from that of its predecessors. Symbolized by its appropriation of the word *gay* in place of *homosexual*, the GLF asserted a pride in being gay and lesbian.

The GLF sponsored a wide variety of activities, including dances on college campuses as an alternative to the gay bar scene, which had become increasingly unattractive to many younger gays and lesbians. The GLF also mounted a campaign against the *Village Voice*, which had refused to print ads promoting GLF activities on the grounds that *gay* was an offensive word even though it regularly used such words as *fag*, *queer*, and *dyke*. A 12 September 1969 demonstration outside the *Village Voice* resulted in a change in the paper's policy whereby they agreed that the paper would no longer censor classified ads and that it would no longer object to the use of the word *gay* in its pages. By the end of the year, the GLF began publishing its own newspaper, *Come Out*, and there were GLF organizations developing in Berkeley, Chicago, Los Angeles, Minneapolis, and elsewhere. The GLF participated in the Christopher Street Liberation Day Committee, which organized the first annual march on 28 June 1970, celebrating the anniversary of the Stonewall riots. The march has become an annual event in New York City and in cities around the world.

Internal divisiveness soon undermined the initial successes of the GLF. Reflecting its heterogeneous constituency and its penchant for participatory democracy, differences of opinion developed over the goals and strategies of the GLF. This was first apparent when cells, specialized subgroups, developed under the umbrella of the GLF. One of the earliest and most successful was the Red Butterfly Cell, a contingent of Marxist-Leninists interested in applying socialist theory in the gay and lesbian rights struggle. The Red Butterfly Cell began publishing its own newspaper, *Gay Flames*, in September 1970. Beyond the proliferation of cells, many left the GLF and founded other groups. The Gay Activists Alliance (GAA) (q.v.), a more structured and more narrowly focused single-issue gay and lesbian rights organization, was one offshoot of the GLF. Another, the Radicalesbians, was founded to compensate for the GLF's lack of sensitivity to lesbian issues. The Street Transvestite Action Revolutionaries (STAR) and Transsexuals and Transvestites (TAT) were also spinoffs of the GLF in New York; the Transvestite Transsexual Action Organization (TAO) also developed in Los Angeles. Members of STAR, TAT, and TAO felt that the GLF did not welcome the participation of either transvestites or transsexuals, despite the role that they had played in the Stonewall riots and subsequent gay and lesbian rights demonstrations. Third World Gay Revolution (TWGR), an organization of nonwhite gays and lesbians, espoused a socialist philosophy as well as a philosophy of sexual self-determination. Gay Youth evolved to serve the interests of younger gays and lesbians and soon was active around the country from Ann Arbor to Tampa.

By the end of 1970, the GLF was indeed little more than a loose coalition, and in the ensuing months it disappeared as an independent organization. However, it wrought an enormous amount of change in its short existence and changed the entire character of the gay and lesbian liberation movement. It was now a mass movement.

Great Britain

Aside from the numerous GLF groups that developed around the United States, a GLF organization soon developed in Great Britain. The British GLF was founded in London by Bob Mellors and Aubrey Walter in 1970. They had become acquainted with one another in the United States earlier that year and returned home impressed by the emergence of the GLF there. Mellors and Walter concluded that the time was ripe for such an organization in England. The London School of Economics was chosen to be the site of the first meeting in the autumn, although the initial popularity of the GLF soon forced it to find alternative sites.

There were many similarities between the philosophies, goals, and strategies of the British and U.S. GLFs. Like its American counterpart, the London GLF was very critical of existing organizations serving the gay and lesbian community, most notably the Committee for Homosexual Equality (CHE) and the Albany Trust (AT), an auxiliary of the Homosexual Law Reform Society (HLRS) (qq.v.). The CHE itself had evolved out of the frustrations of the North-Western Committee of the HLRS concerning the future direction of the HLRS. Although the HLRS was largely responsible for the enactment of the Sexual Offenses Act (q.v.), which decriminalized private homosexual relations between adult males, the North-Western Committee felt that the parent organization lacked new ideas and leadership. The CHE was founded to provide that leadership.

However, the social and political milieu of the late 1960s and early 1970s was changing almost as fast in Britain as it was in the United States. As in the United States, the examples of direct political action provided by the civil rights movement, the antiwar movement, and the women's liberation movement had an enormous impact on the gay and lesbian rights movement. Despite its radical origins, the CHE found itself in the same predicament as the Mattachine Society (q.v.) and the Daughters of Bilitis in the United States. The AT, if anything, was viewed with even greater distrust. Both the CHE and the AT were perceived as too timid, too closeted, and too "liberal" to meet the challenges of the 1970s.

Thus, the rise of the GLF in Britain, as well as in the United States, reflected the impatience of many gays and lesbians with the politics of established gay and lesbian rights organizations, and particularly the view that these organizations sought little more than social and political tolerance and were overly bureaucratized and legalistic. The GLF emphasized a very different strategy. The emphasis on "coming out" was designed to combat the negative self-image foisted on gays and lesbians by both liberals and conservatives and to broaden the political base for future organizing.

Consequently, the GLF inaugurated a new stage in the gay and lesbian liberation movement in Britain, a much more visible, assertive, and mass-action phase. Its activities included sit-ins at commercial establishments that refused service to gays and lesbians, attacks on psychiatry for its complicity with the oppression of gays and lesbians, the development of social alternatives to the commercialization of the gay ghetto, gay pride events, marches, and demonstrations.

Two notable GLF initiatives involved attempts to broaden the focus of gay and lesbian politics beyond the specific legal issues of direct concern to gays and lesbians. The first was an attempt to embrace the politics and the philosophy of feminism. The feminist critique of patriarchy provided a framework for understanding the artificiality of traditional gender roles and therefore afforded an opportunity for identifying the elements common to the discrimination against women as well as gays and lesbians. For a time, a common front between the women's movement and the gay and lesbian movement seemed a possibility. The GLF participated, for example, in the activities surrounding International Women's Day in 1971 and again in 1973. Another initiative involved an attempt to embrace the goals of the labor movement. Many who were attracted to the GLF were socialists who felt that gays and lesbians ought to reach out to other oppressed groups and form broad political coalitions. The GLF participated in a number of labor initiatives, including the demonstrations in 1970 and 1971 against the Industrial Relations Act, which labor felt undermined the rights of workers.

Ultimately, however, these initiatives did not produce the effects intended by the GLF. Despite the feminist rhetoric of many gay men, the GLF was still perceived by lesbians to be male identified. Lesbians increasingly found more and more support in the women's movement and withdrew much of their energy from the GLF. Furthermore, the labor movement was never enthusiastic about the participation of the GLF in their activities, and not many gays and lesbians were interested in the politics of the labor movement.

These failures, together with the lack of organizational structure, brought about the GLF's demise in 1972. After 1972 only offshoots of the parent London organization survived, some in London itself, and some in other cities such as Manchester. But as its American counterpart had done in the United States, the British GLF changed the face of the gay and lesbian movement in Great Britain. It too was now out of the closet.

GAY RIGHTS NATIONAL LOBBY. *See* HUMAN RIGHTS CAMPAIGN FUND.

GEMEINSCHAFT DER EIGENEN/COMMUNITY OF THE SPECIAL (COS). Founded on 1 May 1902, by Adolf Brand, Benedict Friedländer (qq.v.), and Wilhelm Jansen, the COS became one of the most influential homosexual rights organizations in Germany. Adolf Brand published *Der Eigene* (The Special) (q.v.), a magazine devoted to literary, artistic, and cultural aspects of masculinity, the centerpiece of the COS's organizational efforts. Benedict Friedländer, the principal architect of the COS until his death in 1908, had been active in the nudist movement as a young adult, an activity he credited with awakening his interest in male eros. He authored *Renaissance des Eros Uranios* (Renaissance of Eros Uranios) in 1904, where he set forward the ideas that animated the COS. Wilhelm Jansen was a cofounder not only of the community but of the Jungwandervogel, an organization devoted to friendship between men and boys.

Unlike the Wissenschaftlich-humanitäres Komitee (Scientific-Humanitarian Committee [SHC]) (q.v.), the COS had no affinity for Karl Heinrich Ulrichs's "third sex" theory (qq.v.). To the contrary, the COS was critical of the biological theories propounded by the SHC, arguing that the biological emphasis of the SHC inculcated the idea that homosexuality was a medical phenomenon and that male homosexuals were inverts, women trapped in male bodies. The COS asserted that male homosexuals were neither congenital inverts nor effeminate and that erotic friendships between men was a legitimate alternative to the culture of heterosexuality.

More specifically, the COS sought to reinvigorate the sexual norms of classical Greece and Renaissance Italy, which had been all but obliterated by the rise of Christianity in Europe (q.v.). Erotic friendships between adult married men and boys were customary in ancient Greece and became fashionable once again during the Italian Renaissance. The COS touted the superiority of pedophile relationships, although its public pronouncements never advocated sexual relationships between men and boys but, rather, platonic friendships. Because of its emphasis on the virtues of male camaraderie the COS, unlike the SHC, was an all-male organization and never sought to enlist women in the struggle for homosexual rights in Germany.

Despite its differences with the SHC, the COS did enter into a brief coalition with the SHC and the Deutscher Freundschaftsverband (German Friendship Association [GFA]) (q.v.), a third prominent homosexual organization, between 1920 and 1923. The Aktionsausschuss (Action Committee) (q.v.) disintegrated because of GFA's withdrawal from the coalition in 1923.

The COS's activities came to an abrupt end in 1933 owing to the rise of the Nazi Party. Adolph Brand died in 1945, and the COS did not resume its activities after the defeat of Germany in World War II.

GERBER, HENRY (1892–1972). Founder of the Society for Human Rights (SHR) (q.v.), the first homosexual rights organization in the United States. A German immigrant, Gerber served in the United States Army after World War I. Stationed in Koblenz between 1920 and 1923, he became aware of the German homosexual emancipation movement through several German homosexual publications. Based on his understanding of the German movement, Gerber embarked on a plan to initiate a homosexual rights movement in the United States after his return home. With six of his friends, he incorporated the SHR in Chicago on 10 December 1924 as a nonprofit organization. The name of the organization was borrowed from the Bund für Menschenrechte (League for Human Rights), a German homosexual rights organization. Gerber succeeded in publishing two issues of the group's newsletter, *Friendship and Freedom*, shortly before the officers of the organization were arrested on morals charges. Gerber and the other officers of the organization were briefly incarcerated, and Gerber lost his job as a postal employee before the court dismissed the charges against them. This police action effectively brought about an early end to the SHR only months after its incorporation.

Despite losing his job, Gerber continued his advocacy of homosexual rights through a number of articles published in German and American publications. These included a 1928 article in *Blätter für Menschenrecht* (Journal of Human Rights) criticizing the censorship of Radclyffe Hall's *Well of Loneliness* in England; a 1932 article in *The Modern Thinker* (under the pen name of Parisex), entitled "In

Defense of Homosexuality"; and a number of essays in a 1934 issue of *Chanticleer*. In 1962, *One* (q.v.) published an account of the SHR by Henry Gerber.

Gerber's views were influenced by prominent European advocates for homosexual rights, including Edward Carpenter, Havelock Ellis, and Magnus Hirschfeld (qq.v.). He was a lifelong opponent of what he referred to as heterosexual propaganda, whether it took the form of self-loathing novels, psychiatric classifications of homosexuality as a mental illness, laws that criminalized homosexual relations, or the condemnation of homosexuality by religious zealots. Long before anyone else, Gerber stood almost alone in his advocacy of homosexual rights in the United States until the emergence of the modern homosexual rights movement after World War II.

GREY, ANTONY (A. E. G. WRIGHT) (1928–). Antony Grey was a principal figure in the Homosexual Law Reform Society (HLRS) and the Albany Trust (AT) (qq.v.). He was instrumental in securing the passage of the 1967 Sexual Offenses Act (q.v.), and he was the first and only chair of the National Federation of Homophile Organizations (NFHO) (q.v.), a short-lived coalition of gay and lesbian rights groups in Britain.

While a student at Cambridge University, he developed a keen understanding of the discrimination faced by homosexuals and he resolved to become involved in the reform of British attitudes on the subject. The publication in 1957 of the Report of the Committee on Homosexual Offenses and Prostitution (q.v.), better known as the Wolfenden Report, provided the occasion. The Wolfenden Report proposed the decriminalization of homosexual relations between adult males in private. In 1957, British law was governed by the Act of 25 Henry VIII, c. 6, as amended in 1861, and the Labouchère Amendment to the 1885 Criminal Law Amendment Act (qq.v.). Both statutes contained harsh penalties for males engaged in homosexual relations, whether in public or in private.

In 1958, 10 years after his graduation from Cambridge, Grey met A. E. Dyson (q.v.), the founder of the HLRS. Dyson conceived the HLRS to be the spearhead of the legal reforms called for by the Wolfenden Report, and he recruited Grey and others to work toward that goal. Grey's activities with the HLRS and its close relative, the AT, were many and varied. He engaged in numerous public debates, arranged meetings with social work agencies, churches, sympathetic members of Parliament, and facilitated contacts with homophile organizations abroad. For a time he served as treasurer of the HLRS.

In 1962 Grey was appointed to head the HLRS, and in 1963 he accepted the offer to simultaneously head both the HLRS and the

AT. The effort to implement the recommendations of the Wolfenden Report culminated in 1967 with the passage of the Sexual Offenses Act. Antony Grey is widely regarded as the prime mover of this reform in British law. Although the reforms created by this statute were more modest than Grey had wished, the act did institutionalize the central recommendation of the Wolfenden Report (the decriminalization of private homosexual relations between adult males).

Since 1967, Grey has remained active in the gay and lesbian liberation movement. That year, at the invitation of the Erickson Foundation and One Inc. (q.v.), he traveled in the United States on a lecture tour explaining the changes in British law. Although he resigned his position with both the HLRS and the AT in 1970, within a year he had reassumed the leadership of the AT, which he held until 1977. In 1977, he became chair of the Albany Society, a charitable organization affiliated with the AT that has initiated a number of AIDS projects in Great Britain. Under his leadership the Albany Society created the All-Party Parliamentary Group on AIDS (APPGA). Grey remains active in promoting gay and lesbian rights and in AIDS education and counseling.

GROUPE DE LIBÉRATION HOMOSEXUELLE/HOMOSEXUAL LIBERATION GROUP (HLG).

Founded in the aftermath of the demise of the Front Homosexuel d'Action Révolutionnaire (Revolutionary Homosexual Action Front–France [RHAF–F]) (q.v.) in 1973, the HLG forged a new direction in French gay and lesbian politics. Initially torn between the countercultural ideology of "antinormalcy" characteristic of the RHAF–F and a more pragmatic civil rights (q.v.) approach, the HLG eventually turned in the direction of greater pragmatism.

The factionalism that characterized the early days of the organization was eventually resolved in favor of the GLH–Politique et Quotidien (HLG–Politics and Everyday Life [HLG–PEL]) wing of the HLG. It developed a base of local groups, cooperated with other social movements in organizing events of mutual interest, organized gay rights demonstrations in Paris, and even ran candidates for local and national offices.

The HLG–PEL was a forerunner of the civil rights approach of the Comité d'Urgence Anti-Répression Homosexuelle (Emergency Committee against the Repression of Homosexuals [ECARH]) (q.v.), a strategy that eventually succeeded with the election of François Mitterrand in 1981. It was also instrumental in the origins of the most influential French gay publication of the 1980s, *Gay Pied*. Members of the ECARH, many formerly associated with HLG–PEL, founded the journal in 1979. *Gay Pied* provided a national forum for gay politics during a critical period in the battle for gay rights in France.

GRUPO DE ACCIÓN POR LA LIBERTAD DE EXPRESIÓN DE LA ELECCIÓN SEXUAL/ACTION GROUP FOR THE LIBERTY OF EXPRESSION OF SEXUAL CHOICE. *See* GAY AND LESBIAN ASSOCIATION OF CUBA.

GRUPO DE ORGULLO HOMOSEXUAL DE LIBERACIÓN/ GROUP PRIDE FOR HOMOSEXUAL LIBERATION (GPHL). The origins of the GPHL can be traced to the growing influence of Mexican gay and lesbian groups in socialist party circles during the late 1970s and early 1980s. In Mexico City, for example, organizations such as the Grupo Lambda de Liberación Homosexual (Lambda Homosexual Liberation Group [LHLG]) and the Frente Homosexual de Acción Revolucionaria (Revolutionary Homosexual Action Front [RHAF–M]) (qq.v.) espoused a socialist feminist ideology and became active in socialist party politics. As a result, the Partido Revolucionario de los Trabajadores (PRT) nominated gay and lesbian candidates from Mexico City for the 1982 elections to the Chamber of Deputies.

During the early 1980s the gay and lesbian community in Guadalajara also became highly active. The Committee of Lesbians and Homosexuals in Support of Rosario Ibarra was formed to support the candidacy of the PRT's presidential candidate. Like its Mexico City counterparts, it too embraced socialist party politics. In return, two candidates from Guadalajara, Lupita Garcia de Alba and Pedro Preciado (q.v.), were nominated by the PRT. Their candidacies were largely a reflection of the organizational skills of Pedro Preciado.

However, the 1982 elections were a debacle for the gay and lesbian movement in Mexico. None of the gay or lesbian candidates were elected, most gays and lesbians proved unwilling to support a socialist party, and the PRT found that their endorsement of gay and lesbian rights was out of step with the wishes of the rank and file of the party. As a result, the PRT quickly divorced itself from the gay and lesbian movement, and groups such as the RHAF and LHLG soon folded.

This was not the case with the gay and lesbian movement in Guadalajara. In the highly repressive atmosphere following the 1982 elections in Guadalajara, the GPHL was founded and grew in support and efficacy. Under the leadership of Preciado, it attacked police corruption and harassment and won the right to open a disco, using the profits to run a community center catering to the needs of gays and lesbians. Among other things, the center provided a hotline, legal services, and AIDS information and education. For a time it published its own newsletters, *Crisálida* and *Las Maracas*, and produced its own radio program, *Ruta 41.*

A major setback was the closure of the disco after the 1988 elections brought a conservative mayor to power. This, in turn, forced the GPHL to find new quarters and to limit many of its activities. Another setback was the cancellation of the annual conference of the International Lesbian and Gay Association (ILGA) (q.v.) scheduled for Guadalajara in 1991. Despite the efforts of the GPHL and a lesbian organization, the Grupo Lésbico Patlatonalli, the conference was canceled due to intense pressure from highly entrenched church, business, and political leaders. The ILGA met instead in Acapulco.

The future of the GPHL in the conservative stronghold of Guadalajara is uncertain, particularly given the 1994 elections, which resulted in the election of a member of the ultraconservative National Action Party to the mayor's office. However, the GPHL is widely regarded as the most successful gay and lesbian rights organization in Mexico, and it continues to function in Guadalajara.

GRUPO LAMBDA DE LIBERACIÓN HOMOSEXUAL / LAMBDA HOMOSEXUAL LIBERATION GROUP (LHLG). Founded in the late 1970s, the LHLG was allied with a number of left-wing groups in Mexico. It was the cofounder of the Frente Nacional por la Liberación y los Derechos de las Mujeres (National Front for the Liberation and Rights of Women), and it was an active participant in the Frente Nacional Contra la Represión (National Front against Repression). Like the Frente Homosexual de Acción Revolucionaria (Revolutionary Homosexual Action Front [RHAF]) (q.v.), it was linked with the Partido Revolucionario de los Trabajadores (PRT) during the election campaign of 1982. Lambda published its own newspaper, *Nuevo Ambiente.*

Thus the LHLG had extensive ties with the Mexican Left. The National Front against Repression was the largest coalition of Left groups, and the LHLG's participation enabled it to introduce gay and lesbian issues into the more traditional socialist concerns of the Left. This, to some degree, was responsible for the PRT's decision to endorse gay and lesbian rights and gay and lesbian candidates during the 1982 election campaign. As a founding member of the National Front for the Liberation and Rights of Women, the LHLG challenged feminists to incorporate lesbian concerns into the platform of the women's movement. Its ties to the women's movement also resulted in its own leadership structure being evenly balanced between gays and lesbians and a strong commitment to lesbian concerns.

Like the RHAF and Oikabeth, a lesbian group, the LHLG did not survive the mid-1980s. The PRT's inclusion of gay and lesbian issues in its 1982 election campaign backfired, as its own membership proved unwilling to tolerate gays and lesbians in its midst. At the same time, gays and lesbians who were predominantly middle class showed no interest in being associated with socialist political parties. As Mexico sank into a deep depression, sexual politics was eclipsed by a preoccupation with economic issues, and the LHLG collapsed.

After the eclipse of the LHLG, some of its former members founded a legal aid and medical service known as Cálamo. Cálamo was still active in the early 1990s, engaging in such activities as AIDS fundraising and legal counseling.

In the 1990s, the impetus created by groups such as the LHLG has resulted in the proliferation of gay and lesbian groups around the country. Over 50 such groups can now be found in such cities as Cuernavaca, Culiacán, Monterrey, Oaxaca, and Tijuana.

GUÉRIN, DANIEL (1904–1988). French historian, socialist, member of the antifascist Popular Front, and gay rights activist.

Daniel Guérin was exposed from an early age to left-wing publications and the politics of the Left by his father, Marcel. He read Marx, Trotsky, and Gandhi and was also exposed to the writings of Charles Fourier and Pierre Joseph Proudhon, who influenced not only his conception of liberty but also his understanding of sexuality and its relationship to politics. Another significant influence on Guérin was the eminent British sexologist Havelock Ellis (q.v.).

Like his father who was his confidant, Daniel Guérin was sexually attracted to both men and women, and, like his father, he married in spite of his habitual sexual liaisons with men. When Daniel was young, he and his father became mutually aware of each other's homosexual inclinations, and, following the advice of his father, Daniel concealed his sexuality for many years.

Beginning in the mid-1920s, Guérin became actively involved in a wide range of left-wing political activities. Even before his participation in the Popular Front, he was an active supporter of La Révolution Prolétarienne (Proletarian Revolution), a syndicalist organization. Voyages to Indochina and the Middle East between 1927 and 1930 made him an outspoken opponent of colonialism and an activist in the French working-class movement. Guérin was acquainted with Leon Trotsky, whom he met in France during Trotsky's visit in 1933. Although Guérin shared many of Trotsky's visions concerning the promise of socialism, his political philosophy was less collectivist, and this often brought him into conflict with Trotsky and other leaders of the international communist movement. His ideas have been set forth in many publications, such as *Fascisme et grand capital*, *La Lutte des classes sous la première république: 1793–1797*, and *Le mouvement ouvrier aux États-Unis.*

It was not until the 1950s that Guérin was moved to politicize his sexuality. Following a three-year visit to the United States with his wife, he returned to France alone and immersed himself in the gay subculture. What he found was a much more highly restrictive legal environment than had existed prior to the war. In 1942, the Vichy government began a campaign against gays and lesbians by raising the age of consent for homosexual intercourse. Article 334 of the French penal code imposed a penalty of six months to three years and fines up to 50,000 francs for homosexual relations with anyone between the ages of 15 and 21 (the applicable age of consent for heterosexual intercourse remained 16). The law applied equally to lesbians and gay men, and neither the age of the individuals nor consent was a defense. After liberation in 1945 these changes to French law were reaffirmed by the de Gaulle administration in the form of Article 331. It was this discriminatory age of consent law (q.v.) that was responsible for Guérin's first public pronouncements on homosexuality. *Arcadie* (q.v.), André Baudry's gay rights journal, and its affiliated organization attracted his attention. Beginning in the mid-1950s Guérin became increasingly associated with the organization's activities and began to publish his own views on gay rights.

In his 1957 article for *L'Express*, "La Répression de l'homosexualité en France" (The Repression of Homosexuality in France) Guérin wrote of the repression of homosexuality as one aspect of a regime of sexual conservatism enveloping France. Sexual asceticism, the inequality of women, the attempt to resurrect the patriarchal family structure, and the renewed repression of homosexuality were, from his point of view, inextricably linked. And Guérin did not spare the puritanical attitudes of the socialist Left whose disavowal of homosexuality he found inexcusable.

It was the events of 1968 that afforded Guérin the opportunity to merge his interest in socialism with his gay rights activism. The association of sexual liberation with the traditional economic and political demands of the working class separated the student/worker uprisings of 1968 from others in French history. With the founding of the Front Homosexuel d'Action Révolutionnaire (Revolutionary Homosexual Action Front [RHAF–F]) (q.v.) in 1971, Guérin shifted his loyalties from the reformist aspirations of Arcadie to the revolutionary vision of the RHAF–F, an organization with goals similar to the Gay Liberation Front (q.v.). Not only did the RHAF stand for the alliance between gays and lesbians and other oppressed groups, it also espoused the potential of gays and lesbians to transform traditional gender roles and class boundaries.

Although the RHAF was shortlived, Guérin remained active in gay and lesbian politics and continued to promote many of the ideas nurtured by the RHAF in books such as *Homosexualité et révolution* until his death in 1988.

H

HAIRE, NORMAN (1892–1952). Born in Australia, Norman Haire emigrated to England where he became a permanent resident in 1919. Haire was a gynecologist and obstetrician who studied at the Institut für Sexualwissenschaft (Institute for Sexual Science [ISS]) (q.v.) in Berlin and who became one of the most prominent British sexologists. His published works often appeared under his pseudonym, Wykeham Terris.

Haire was a leading figure in the British Society for the Study of Sex Psychology (BSSP) (q.v.); the Sex Education Society, of which he was president for many years; and the World League for Sexual Reform (WLSR) (q.v.). He served as chair of the British chapter of the WLSR, under whose auspices the 1929 meeting of the WLSR took place in London, and later as chair of the international organization.

Although Haire's specialization was birth control, he supported homosexual law reform both at home as well as abroad. The BSSP, the Sex Education Society, and the WLSR devoted a substantial amount of time and energy to the reform of outmoded laws and attitudes concerning homosexuality.

Along with J. H. Leunbach, Norman Haire was the copresident of the WLSR during the rise of fascism in Germany in the 1930s. The threat of German fascism to individual freedom, including individual sexual expression and sex research, was graphically illustrated by the Nazi closure of the ISS and the German homosexual rights group, the Wissenschaftlich-humanitäres Komitee (Scientific-Humanitarian Committee) (q.v.). This led many to argue that the WLSR should become actively involved in attempts to combat the rise of Nazism. Despite his affiliation with the ISS, Haire opposed this viewpoint, arguing that the WLSR should restrict itself to the pursuit of a scientific understanding of sexuality. Leunbach, on the other hand, was sympathetic with those who felt that combating Nazism was consistent with the scientific study of sexuality. The inability of Haire and Leunbach to resolve this split resulted in the dissolution of the World League in 1935.

After the war, Haire helped resuscitate the Sex Education Society with which he had been associated in the 1930s. He was both the president of the Sex Education Society and, in 1948, the founder and editor of the *Journal of Sex Education*. Though independent of the society, it published the proceedings of the society's meetings. Although homosexual issues were only one of its concerns, the Sex Education Society and the *Journal of Sex Education* provided an important outlet for research on homosexuality until Haire's death in 1952 precipitated the collapse of both institutions.

HAY, HENRY (HARRY) JR. (1912–   ). Harry Hay was the principal founder of both the Mattachine Society (MS) (q.v.), the most prominent pre-Stonewall (q.v.) gay rights organization in the United States, and the Radical Faeries. He is also the author of published and unpublished essays in the field of gay and lesbian studies.

Hay's idea for an organization to represent the interests of homophiles, a name he preferred to homosexuals, crystallized in the summer of 1948. Although he was married at the time to a woman he had met in left-wing political circles and with whom he had two adopted children, Hay never overcame his desire for close male companionship. Hay had been sexually active with men from the age of 14 and had publicly come out at Stanford University where he was a student from 1930 to 1932. His eventual divorce in 1951, which ended a marriage of 13 years to Anita Platky, was sparked by his homophile interests as well as a strong romantic interest in Rudi Gernreich, an aspiring fashion designer.

Hay's initial idea was to press for the incorporation of a right to privacy plank in the platform of the Progressive Party. He had been active for many years in left-wing political causes, including the Communist Party of the United States of America (CPUSA), and he was inspired by the prospects of a left of center party in the 1948 November presidential elections. Hay felt that the candidacy of Henry Wallace, the standard-bearer of the Progressive Party and advocate of grassroots political activity and socially progressive causes, represented an opportunity for homophiles to advance their interests.

In an era when homophile liaisons were almost universally illegal in the United States, because of the existence of state sodomy statutes (q.v.), gay men were routinely entrapped by the police. The ensuing criminal penalties and public humiliation often resulted in dire consequences for those who fell victim to such police schemes. Hay correctly understood that the right to privacy in consensual sexual activities was essential if homophiles were ever to have equal rights (a demand that remains at the core of the contemporary gay, lesbian, and bisexual rights movement).

Although the incorporation of a right to privacy plank in the platform of the Progressive Party never came to fruition, Hay continued to pursue a related idea, that of forming an organization of homophiles. He first called it the International Bachelors Fraternal Order for Peace and Social Justice, although it was commonly referred to as Bachelors for Wallace and, subsequently, Bachelors Anonymous.

It was not until mid-1950 that Hay succeeded in finding others who were similarly motivated. Together with Rudi Gernreich, Robert Hull, and Charles Rowland, Harry Hay presided over the first discussions of the Society of Fools, as the founders referred to themselves. The four founders were soon joined by Dale Jennings, Konrad Stevens, and James Gruber. In the spring of 1951 the organization adopted the name "Mattachine Society" (MS) (q.v.) and began a campaign to attract a wider audience.

The initial success of the early MS increased its public visibility and proved to be Hay's undoing. Hay's long association with the CPUSA and other left-wing causes became a political problem for the organization in the anticommunist hysteria of the early 1950s. In 1953, Hay was identified as a Marxist teacher in a Los Angeles newspaper. In the same year MS's attorney, Fred Snyder, was identified as an uncooperative witness before the House Un-American Activities Committee (HUAC) by a syndicated columnist for the *Los Angeles Daily Mirror*. The rank and file of the MS became increasingly concerned about the association of the organization with communism and called for a convention to draft a democratic constitution.

The convention in April 1953 resulted in Hay's and the other founders' ouster and left Hay with no role in the organization he had founded. Furthermore, many of his former leftist politicos became alienated from Hay because of his association with the homophile movement. To further compound his personal situation, a former student identified Hay as a Marxist teacher in testimony before the HUAC. The committee's decision to subpoena Hay and the notoriety of his testimony in June 1955 further damaged his reputation among homophile activists and led to an uncharacteristic withdrawal from homophile organizing for roughly 10 years.

Although he was active as the chair of the first gay pride parade in Los Angeles in 1966, a protest against Defense Department treatment of homosexuals organized by the North American Congress of Homophile Organizations (NACHO), in the Council on Religion and the Homosexual, and the Gay Liberation Front (GLF) (qq.v.), it was not until he was inspired to create the Radical Faeries (RF) that Hay once again became absorbed in organizing gays.

After years of theorizing about gay spirituality and the possibility of gay community in speeches and position papers, Harry Hay, with John Burnside, Don Kilhefner, and Mitch Walker organized the first gathering of the RF on Labor Day weekend 1979. It attracted more than 200 men. A second meeting in August 1980 attracted almost twice as many participants. Conceived as an alternative to the stifling conformity of heterosexuality and the anomie of established gay culture, RF members saw themselves as a countercultural and spiritual association as opposed to an overtly political organization, although Hay continued to be active in a wide variety of political causes and urged Faeries to become similarly involved.

Hay felt that the founding of the RF was an opportunity to explore and develop gay consciousness, a fundamentally different worldview from that of heterosexuality. This "gay window" was not based on subject-object thinking or competitiveness but subject-subject thinking, equality, sharing, and loving. He urged gays and lesbians to resist the temptation to assimilate into heterosexual culture.

Differences of opinion between the founders, however, led to a split in the organization. In June 1981, Kilhefner and Walker resigned from the RF and formed a rival organization (Treeroots). Based upon Jungian psychology, Treeroots offered an alternative spiritual root to gayness and attracted a wide audience among gay men in the Los Angeles area during the 1980s.

Meanwhile the RF continued to meet annually and, in 1987, acquired property in Oregon as a permanent site for future gatherings. Hay has remained active in the RF as well as innumerable other causes, such as the Rainbow Coalition and the Native American rights movement, in recent years.

HETEROSEXUALITY. *See* KERTBENY, KARL MARIA.

HIRSCHFELD, MAGNUS (1868–1935). German physician, sex researcher, author, and political activist, Hirschfeld was a pioneer in the field of sex research. He published numerous works on the subject of human sexuality, including innovative works on homosexuality such as *Berlins Drittes Geschlecht*, *Sappho und Sokrates*, and *Die Homosexualität des Mannes und des Weibes*. Influenced by the "third sex" theory of Karl Heinrich Ulrichs (qq.v.), Hirschfeld argued that homosexuality was rooted in human biology and therefore was as natural as heterosexuality. He is also responsible for coining the term *transvestite*, and for distinguishing transvestism from homosexuality.

Hirschfeld is best known as the cofounder of the first homosexual rights organization in the world. The Wissenschaftlich-humanitäres Komitee (Scientific-Humanitarian Committee [SHC]) (q.v.) was founded on 15 May 1897 in Berlin by Hirschfeld, Max Spohr, Erik Oberg, and Franz Josef von Bülow. It quickly became the chief advocate of homosexual emancipation in Germany and throughout the world. The SHC was responsible for publishing numerous books on the subject of homosexuality as well as a journal, *Jahrbuch für sexuelle Zwischenstufen* (Yearbook for Sexual Intermediates). It was responsible, as well, for initiating the campaign to repeal Paragraph 175 (q.v.) of the German legal code, which criminalized male homosexual conduct.

Hirschfeld was also responsible for the creation of the Institut für Sexualwissenschaft (Institute for Sexual Science [ISS]) in 1919 (q.v.). Renowned as a center for sex research, education, and counseling, the ISS produced the first film depicting the plight of the homosexual. *Anders als die Andern* (Different from the Others) featured Magnus Hirschfeld advocating social tolerance and legal reform of punitive laws.

The birth of the World League for Sexual Reform (WLSR) (q.v.) in 1921 was also due to the efforts of Hirschfeld. Created at the conclusion of the First Congress for Sexual Reform at the ISS in September, the WLSR held four subsequent conferences in 1928, 1929, 1930, and 1932 before it disbanded in 1935.

On several occasions Hirschfeld was the subject of physical attacks for his role in the homosexual emancipation movement. In 1920, an address by Hirschfeld in Berlin was interrupted by an attack. In 1921, an obituary appeared in a Munich newspaper mistakenly announcing the death of Hirschfeld after a beating by anti-Semites. And, in 1923, in Vienna, another speech by Hirschfeld was interrupted by an armed assault on the meeting. Although Hirschfeld was unharmed, members of the audience were injured.

On 6 May 1933, the building that housed the SHC, ISS, and WLSR was ransacked by students at the College of Physical Exercise and by the Sturmabteilung (SA). Items confiscated by the SA included medical records, scientific research, books, and journals, as well as the publications of Hirschfeld and other leading authorities on sexuality.

The contents of the building were burned along with the works of other prominent sexologists such as Sigmund Freud, Havelock Ellis (q.v.), and Albert Moll in a public demonstration on 10 May 1933. Hirschfeld was in Paris at the conclusion of a worldwide lecture tour at the time and never returned to Germany.

HOCQUENGHEM, GUY. See FRONT HOMOSEXUEL D'ACTION RÉVOLUTIONNAIRE.

HOMEROS LAMBDA (HOMEROS HOMOSZEXUÁLISOK SZABADIDÖS ÉS EGÉSZÉGVÉDÖ EGYESÜLETE [HOMO-SEXUAL ASSOCIATION FOR LEISURE AND HEALTH PROTECTION]). The Homosexual Association for Leisure and Health Protection, also known as Homeros Lambda (HL), was the first officially sanctioned gay and lesbian organization in Hungary, as well as in all of Eastern Europe. The application for official recognition was made in 1987 and approved in 1988.

Under the communist regime of the Hungarian People's Republic, gay and lesbian sexual relations were decriminalized in 1961. Nevertheless, antihomosexual attitudes remained prevalent. The recognition of HL by the government resulted in greater publicity of gay and lesbian issues and a more open attitude toward homosexuality. In 1989, HL hosted the third annual conference of gay and lesbian rights groups from Eastern Europe. Participants from Hungary, Czechoslovakia, East Germany, Poland, and Yugoslavia gathered at a new gay center in Budapest to coordinate the activities of gay and lesbian rights groups in the newly independent countries.

HL also initiated legal proceedings before the Constitutional Court of Hungary to legalize common-law marriages (q.v.) between same-sex couples, an initiative that ultimately led to the court's decision, in March 1995, that forbidding gays and lesbians to marry was unconstitutional. Although HL ceased operations shortly thereafter because of internal problems, its activities were taken up by other gay and lesbian rights organizations such as Szivarvany (Rainbow) (q.v.).

HOMOSEXUAL LAW REFORM FUND (HLRF). Founded in Johannesburg and Pretoria, South Africa, in 1968, the HLRF fought Prime Minister Verwoerd's attempt to criminalize adult homosexual intercourse. Although penalties for cross-dressing, solicitation, and public indecency could be found in the criminal code, and although sodomy was illegal in common law, private homosexual relations between adults had never been forbidden by statute. Verwoerd's proposal would have amended South Africa's Immorality Act to include criminal penalties for homosexual relations between adults in private. Sexual relations between women, in addition to those between men, would have been prohibited by statute with a maximum sentence of three years in prison.

The HLRF was composed primarily of white, middle-class professionals. The overwhelming majority of activists were male, and blacks were not permitted. It was a single-issue organization devoted to blocking the enactment of the aforementioned amendments to the Immorality Act. Toward this end, the HLRF retained attorneys to represent the interests of gay men and lesbians before a Select Committee of Parliament that had been designated to hear evidence pertaining to the proposed legislation. Although Parliament accepted the recommendations of the Select Committee to raise the age of consent for male homosexual relations from 16 to 19 and to narrow the definition of *private* to occasions where no more than two persons were present, the HLRF was successful in preventing the enactment of the centerpiece of Verwoerd's legislative initiative.

The defeat of the proposal to criminalize adult homosexual relations in private brought a quick end, in 1969, to the first gay rights organization in the history of South Africa. Although there were many informal networks of lesbians and gay men in South Africa following the demise of the HLRF, it was not until the inception of a group named Gay Aid Identification Development and Enrichment (q.v.), in 1976, that another formal organization catering to the needs of the gay community emerged.

HOMOSEXUAL LAW REFORM SOCIETY (HLRS). Founded in 1958 by A. E. Dyson (q.v.), lecturer at the University of Wales, this British organization took up the cause of legal reform after the publication of the Report of the Committee on Homosexual Offenses and Prostitution (q.v.), better known as the Wolfenden Report. The first chair was Kenneth Macfarlane Walker, a sexologist affiliated with the British Social Hygiene Council and the British Social Biology Council; Dyson held the position of vice-chair. The HLRS also included an Honorary Committee composed of prominent persons. The Albany Trust (AT) (q.v.) was affiliated with the HLRS. In addition to the HLRS's newsletter, *Spectrum*, the AT published *Man and Society*, a journal devoted to the discussion of a wide variety of sex reform issues. Some years later, it began yet another journal, *At Work*. In addition to its fund-raising activities, the AT engaged in educational, counseling, and research activities. The HLRS fostered the repeal of existing legislation that criminalized adult male homosexuality, the Act of 25 Henry VIII, c.6 and the Labouchère Amendment (qq.v.). At its very outset, the HLRS published two letters in *The Times* protesting the failure of Parliament to act on the recommendations of the Wolfenden Report pertaining to homosexuality. On 7 March 1958, 33 highly respected individuals including Bertrand Russell, Isaiah Berlin, Lord Attlee, and Barbara Wootton signed the initial letter objecting to the inhumanity of the government's policy. A second letter in April urging the government to implement the conclusions of the Wolfenden Report, was signed by 15 prominent married women, including Lady Adrian, the wife of the vice-chancellor of Cambridge University.

The HLRS published a number of leaflets and pamphlets designed to have an impact on Parliament. These included *Homosexuality and the Law*, *Christian Society and the Homosexual*, *The Homosexual and Venereal Disease*, and *Some Questions and Answers about Homosexuality*.

The HLRS also sponsored innumerable speeches, debates, and letters to members of Parliament in their effort to decriminalize adult male homosexual relations. Nine years after the formation of the HLRS, Parliament enacted the Sexual Offenses Act (q.v.) in July 1967. The Sexual Offenses Act decriminalized private, consensual, adult male homosexuality. In his speech to the House of Lords praising the Lords for assenting to the new statute, Lord Arran, a long-time supporter of the HLRS, acknowledged the tireless efforts of the secretary of the HLRS, Antony Grey (q.v.), as chiefly responsible for its enactment. The Sexual Offenses Act became law on 27 July 1967.

After the HLRS attained its limited legal objectives, its support decreased steadily, and it was soon overwhelmed by the rise of the Gay Liberation Front (q.v.) in the early 1970s. In the wake of law reform the North-Western Committee, the most radical of its local support organizations, separated from the society and launched a more militant organization, the Committee for Homosexual Equality (q.v.). The HLRS changed its name to the Sexual Law Reform Society (SLRS) in 1970 and continued its counseling and public education activities.

The SLRS's primary objective through the 1970s and 1980s was the liberalization of the 1967 statute. In 1970, a working party of the SLRS was convened to draft revisions to the 1967 Sexual Offenses Act. Its final report was rendered in 1974. Its recommendations called for the abolition of age of consent laws (q.v.), the liberalization of obscenity laws, and the elimination of sexual offenses as a separate and distinct category of British law. The report also criticized the remaining inequities pertaining to homosexual offenses that persisted despite the enactment of the Sexual Offenses Act. The report met with a storm of public protest and parliamentary intransigence. Only that part of the report calling for the extension of the Sexual Offenses Act to Scotland and Northern Ireland was eventually adopted by Parliament.

HOMOSEXUALITY. *See* KERTBENY, KARL MARIA.

HOMOSEXUELLE ARBEITSGRUPPEN DER SCHWEIZ/ SWISS HOMOSEXUAL WORKING GROUPS (SHWG). A national organization of Swiss gay male groups, the SHWG, as well as a nationwide gay and lesbian group, Schweizerische Organisation der Homophilen (Swiss Organization of Homophiles [SOH]), campaigned for over a decade against articles in Switzerland's penal code that discriminated against gays and lesbians.

Prior to 1992, the age of consent for homosexual relations was 20, even though the corresponding age of consent for heterosexual relations was 16. Similarly, although heterosexual prostitution was legal, homosexual prostitution was not. Responding to public pressure chiefly from organizations such as the SHWG, SOH, and other gay and lesbian groups such as the Pink Cross, a government proposal to reform Switzerland's sexual offenses statutes was ratified by voters in a 1992 referendum.

The reform equalized the age of consent for heterosexuals and homosexuals (16 years) and decriminalized homosexual prostitution. Additionally, homosexual acts committed while in the armed services were decriminalized.

Most recently petitions have been presented to the Swiss Parliament urging the adoption of a domestic partnership statute similar to the Danish Registered Partnership Act (q.v.).

HOMOSEXUELLE INTERESSEN-GEMEINSCHAFT BERLIN/ HOMOSEXUAL INTEREST GROUP BERLIN (HIB). Sometimes also refered to as Homosexuelleninitiative Berlin, the HIB was the first gay and lesbian rights group to publicly emerge in the German Democratic Republic (GDR). Its prospects were thwarted in 1973 when the government refused to grant its petition for legal recognition. Legal recognition in the GDR, among other things, conferred rights upon organizations, such as the right to use meeting spaces and publicity. Without legal recognition, the HIB failed to develop as a formal organization and was banned by the authorities in 1978.

Most gay and lesbian organizations in the GDR, therefore, evolved under the auspices of the Lutheran/Evangelical Church because of its autonomy from the state. The church provided meeting spaces as well as support for groups in a number of East German cities at a time when it was impossible for gays and lesbians to organize officially.

The official repression of gays and lesbians began to change in 1985 with the first of three state-sponsored conferences on homosexuality. The conferences had the effect of altering the attitude of the GDR toward gays and lesbians. In an abrupt turnaround, the GDR sanctioned the creation of gay and lesbian groups affiliated with communist youth organizations, giving rise to positive discussions of homosexuality in the mass media.

The church-sponsored network of gay and lesbian organizations became the backbone for the formation of a nationwide federation of groups in 1990, the Schwulenverband der DDR (q.v.), an organization composed of both secular as well as religious gay and lesbian groups. At the time of the merger of East and West Germany, the Schwulenverband was engaged in negotiations with the East German Parliament concerning the enactment of a comprehensive package of antidiscrimination ordinances. Negotiations were terminated because of the reunification of East and West Germany.

HOSI WIEN (HOSI VIENNA [HV]). Homosexuelle Initiative (HOSI) was founded in Vienna in 1979 and can now be found in major Austrian cities. HOSI Vienna (HV) is the most prominent HOSI group, and serves as the organization's headquarters.

Prior to 1971, both lesbian and gay male sexual relations were punishable as criminal offenses in Austria. This changed in 1971 when homosexual relations were legalized. Nevertheless, Section 220 of the Austrian penal code continued to make advocacy of homosexuality a crime, and 221 criminalized membership in organizations that promote "homosexual lewdness," thereby creating an offense to the public. Furthermore, Article 209, the provision that establishes the age of consent for sexual relations, discriminates against gay men. It fixes the age of consent for heterosexual and lesbian relations at 14 while the corresponding age of consent for gay men is 18. Violations of 209 are punishable with prison sentences between six months and five years, and the statute has been vigorously enforced.

In 1990 the directors of the Viennese gay and lesbian rights group HV were prosecuted under section 220. Copies of two gay magazines, *Tabu* and *Lambda-Nachrichten* (Lambda Report), featuring gay-positive stories and advertisements, were sent to secondary schools by the youth group of HV in 1988. The conviction of the directors of the organization resulted in the introduction of legislation to repeal both Sections 220 and 221.

In 1995 Austria's gay and lesbian groups, including HV, as well as other concerned organizations, formed Platform against Article 209 to fight for the repeal of the discriminatory age of consent laws in Austria.

The battle to overturn Articles 209, 220, and 221 is not yet complete. Despite the growing influence of the Austrian gay and lesbian movement, increasingly conservative governments have refused to act on their demands to end discrimination against gays and lesbians in Austrian law.

The first gay, lesbian, bisexual, transgendered pride march took place in Vienna on 29 June 1996.

HOUSMAN, LAURENCE (1865–1959). Author and illustrator Laurence Housman was a member of the Order of Chaeronea, a secret society of British homosexual activists, the British Society for the Study of Sex Psychology (BSSP) (qq.v.), and a men's support group of the Women's Social and Political Union.

Housman was acquainted with Oscar Wilde, the noted author and playwright, and Edward Carpenter (qq.v.), the prolific and outspoken proponent of gay and lesbian rights and first president of the BSSP. Oscar Wilde's trials and subsequent imprisonment had a deep effect on Housman. The outcome of this scandal may have been the event that precipitated the creation of the Order of Chaeronea. In any case, from the mid-1890s until his death, Housman committed himself to the cause of legal reform.

Housman and Carpenter shared an interest in feminist issues as well as gay and lesbian issues, and it was Carpenter who was responsible for involving Housman in the BSSP. He found in the BSSP an outlet for his advocacy of women's suffrage as well as an outlet for his advocacy of gay and lesbian rights, which he advanced through papers and publications. He also performed numerous administrative duties as chair of the BSSP. Through the activities of Housman and others associated with the BSSP, the impetus for reform of British attitudes and law pertaining to homosexuality was kept alive until their work was interrupted by World War II.

HUMAN RIGHTS CAMPAIGN FUND (HRCF). Founded in 1980, it was renamed the Human Rights Campaign (HRC) in 1996. The HRCF evolved out of the Gay Rights National Lobby (GRNL), the first nationwide U.S. lobby for gay and lesbian rights, founded by Steve Endean in 1978. Two years later Endean and others on the board of directors of the GRNL founded the HRCF, the first gay and lesbian political action committee in the United States. The GRNL and HRCF coexisted as separate organizations until 1986 when the GRNL was subsumed by the HRCF.

In 1997, the HRC claimed more than 175,000 members and an annual revenue in excess of $7,000,000, making it the largest gay and lesbian rights organization as well as one of the wealthiest Political Action Committees in the country. The HRC makes financial contributions to congressional candidates, provides officeholders with information pertaining to gay and lesbian issues, lobbies for gay and lesbian civil rights (q.v.), procures funding for HIV/AIDS research, and opposes antigay legislative initiatives. The HRC lobbying efforts were instrumental in the passage of such legislation as the Americans with Disabilities Act, the Ryan White Comprehensive AIDS Resources Emergency Care Act, and the Hate Crimes Statistics Act. The HRC also contributed financial resources to gay and lesbian litigants in *Romer v. Evans* (q.v.), helping to defeat Colorado Amendment no. 2 in the U.S. Supreme Court. Most recently, the HRC lobbied unsuccessfully to defeat the Defense of Marriage Act (q.v.) in the U.S. Congress and is currently lobbying for passage of the Employment Non-Discrimination Act (q.v.).

The HRC is a cosponsor of the forthcoming "Millennium March on Washington for Equality," the fourth national gay, lesbian, bisexual march on Washington, D.C. March organizers plan to stress the need for federal legislation protecting the rights of gays and lesbians.

I

INSTITUT FÜR SEXUALWISSENSCHAFT/INSTITUTE FOR SEXUAL SCIENCE (ISS). Founded on 1 July 1919 in Berlin by Magnus Hirschfeld (q.v.), the institute was housed in a building purchased by Hirschfeld for the purpose of facilitating research and education pertaining to human sexuality. Housed in the same building was the Wissenschaftlich-humanitäres Komitee (Scientific-Humanitarian Committee [SHC]) and, after 1921, the offices of the World League for Sexual Reform (WLSR) (qq.v.).

The ISS served as a depository for biological, sociological, and ethnological research. Various services such as venereal disease tests, marriage counseling, sex education, and psychiatric counseling were available. The library was estimated to contain 20,000 books as well as a collection of 35,000 photographs. The first research institute of its kind, it was visited by thousands of individuals, including some of the most prominent scientists in the field of sexual science. The First Congress for Sexual Reform was held at the ISS in September 1921, which led to the development of the WLSR.

The ISS, together with the SHC and other nongay organizations interested in the reform of Germany's sexual crime codes, was a participant in the Kartell für Reform des Sexualstrafrechts (Coalition for Reform of the Sexual Crimes Code). Among its objectives was the elimination of Paragraph 175 (q.v.), which criminalized consensual sexual relations between adult men. The coalition fell apart in 1930 with its goals unfulfilled. Shortly after the narrow parliamentary victory of the Nazi Party in the elections of 5 March 1933, the Nazis began a campaign to rid Berlin of objectional (un-German) publications. On 6 May 1933, the ISS was attacked first by students from a nearby college and later in the day by the Sturmabteilung (SA). Most of the contents of the building, including a bust of Hirschfeld, were carried away and subsequently burned in a demonstration on 10 May. Hirschfeld was in Paris at the time and witnessed the destruction of the ISS in French newsreels.

INTERNATIONAL BACHELORS FRATERNAL ORDER FOR PEACE AND SOCIAL JUSTICE (BACHELORS ANONYMOUS). *See* HAY, HENRY (HARRY) JR.

INTERNATIONAL GAY ASSOCIATION. Founded in 1978 as the International Gay Association (IGA), the organization became known as the International Lesbian and Gay Association (ILGA) in 1986. Now in its 21st year of activities, the ILGA is the oldest international organization of gays and lesbians in existence.

An international organization of lesbians and gay men has long been a priority of the lesbian and gay movement. Magnus Hirschfeld's Wissenschaftlich-humanitäres Komitee (Scientific-Humanitarian Committee) (qq.v.) fostered numerous international contacts and acquired an international reputation before its suppression by the Nazis in 1933. The World League for Sexual Reform (q.v.), although not a homosexual rights organization per se, provided an international forum for those interested in promoting the interests of homosexuals during the 1920s and early 1930s. In the immediate postwar era, the International Committee for Sexual Equality, a European organization, organized international conferences on homosexuality between 1951 and 1959. And, in 1974, the Scottish Minorities Group organized a large international conference on gays and lesbians in Edinburgh. But it was not until the founding of the IGA that a permanent international organization came into being.

The IGA originated from discussions between the Dutch Cultuuren-Ontspannings Centrum (Center for Culture and Recreation) and the British Campaign for Homosexual Equality (CHE) (qq.v.) in 1978. At a subsequent international conference hosted by the CHE in 1978 in Coventry, England, the IGA was founded.

Since its founding, the ILGA has organized numerous international conferences throughout the world and serves as a clearinghouse for the exchange of information about gay and lesbian issues. The ILGA publishes a bulletin for its members, informing them of ILGA actions. Every five years, it publishes the *ILGA Pink Book*, which, among other items, contains a worldwide country survey of gay and lesbian rights. The *ILGA Euroletter* can be found on the World Wide Web (http://www.ilga.org/).

The ILGA also plans political initiatives. It was very active, for example, in persuading Amnesty International to recognize those imprisoned because of their sexual orientation as "prisoners of conscience" and in the successful campaign to delete homosexuality as a mental illness from the World Health Organization's International Classification of Diseases. In recent years, the ILGA has spoken out against discrimination perpetrated against people with AIDS and, in 1993, initiated the International Gay and Lesbian Human Rights Commission (IGLHRC) (q.v.), an arm of the ILGA devoted to advancing the international human rights of gays, lesbians, bisexuals, transgendered people, and people with AIDS.

INTERNATIONAL GAY AND LESBIAN HUMAN RIGHTS COMMISSION (IGLHRC). Founded in San Francisco in 1991 as a nonprofit Action Secretariat of the International Lesbian and Gay Association (ILGA) (q.v.), the IGLHRC's purpose is to advance the international human rights of gays, lesbians, bisexuals, transgendered people, and people with AIDS. Julie Dorf was named its first executive director.

The IGLHRC monitors and documents human rights abuses around the world, advocates and lobbies on behalf of sexual minorities, provides technical assistance to grassroots organizations, and engages in a variety of educational activities. It has provided legal assistance to hundreds of gays and lesbians seeking asylum from persecution and, in 1995, staged the International Tribunal on Human Rights Violations against Sexual Minorities, an event that drew attention to the plight of sexual minorities around the world. Among its other accomplishments was the 1994 revision of U.S. policy on political asylum, which theretofore had excluded sexual orientation as a legitimate petition for asylum.

Among its numerous publications is a report to the United Nations Fourth World Conference on Women detailing human rights abuses against lesbians in 31 countries and a report summarizing the proceedings of the aforementioned international tribunal on human rights violations.

INTERNATIONAL LESBIAN AND GAY ASSOCIATION (ILGA). *See* INTERNATIONAL GAY ASSOCIATION.

INTERNATIONAL LESBIAN AND GAY ASSOCIATION–JAPAN (ILGA–J). Although the advent of the gay liberation movement in Japan is a relatively recent phenomenon, homosexual practices were not uncommon among Buddhist monks and the Japanese samurai prior to the 20th century. There are no laws that prohibit homosexual relations, and the Buddhist religion does not condemn the practice. Thus, unlike in Western nations, there has been little state regulation of sexual practices between men in private and therefore less impetus to form gay and lesbian rights groups.

Nevertheless, the social pressure to conform, related primarily to family and work, has made living a gay lifestyle very difficult at a time when Western gay and lesbian culture has made its presence felt in Japan. Thus, the gay and lesbian movement gradually began to take form in Japan in the 1980s. ILGA–J was created by Teishiro Minami in 1986. Based in Tokyo, ILGA–J sponsors social activities, discussion groups, and AIDS awareness and has been active in promoting annual conferences of Asian Lesbians and Gays. ILGA–J is indirectly responsible for the existence of OCCUR, a gay youth group, which split from the parent organization several years after the ILGA–J was founded. The two groups cooperate on items of mutual concern. Although the organization is nominally open to lesbians, most of the membership is male.

INTERNATIONAL LESBIAN AND GAY ASSOCIATION–PORTUGAL (ILGA–P). Founded in Lisbon, the ILGA–P is the first nationwide lesbian and gay organization in Portugal. It is a fully independent organization and is a member of the International Lesbian and Gay Association (q.v.). Its first chair was Goncalo Dumas Diniz.

Portuguese law does not define homosexual relations as a criminal offense, and discrimination in the workplace against individuals because of their "social condition" is technically illegal. Furthermore, the Portuguese armed services does not prohibit the enlistment of gays and lesbians, and it is not uncommon for service personnel to be open about their sexual orientation.

Nevertheless, there is a strong social stigma against gays and lesbians in this predominantly Catholic country, and discrimination against individuals in the workplace because of their sexual orientation does occur. Thus the ILGA–P's immediate goals include educating the populace about the nature of homosexuality, providing a social space for gays and lesbians to associate, and organizing gays and lesbians in the struggle for equal rights. The ILGA–P participated in the World AIDS Day activities in Lisbon in 1995.

The ILGA–P's most immediate political objective has been the revision of Article 13 of the Portuguese Constitution to specifically preclude discrimination on the basis of sexual orientation. On 28 March 1996 the ILGA–P presented its proposal for constitutional reform to parliament. Most of the major political parties agreed to discuss the proposal with representatives of the ILGA–P, but the outcome of the parliamentary debates is uncertain.

Other parliamentary objectives of the ILGA–P are the introduction of a registered partnership act, similar to the Danish Registered Partnership Act (q.v.) and the elimination of the remaining inequities in Portuguese law pertaining to lesbians and gay men, such as Article 175, which establishes a higher age of consent for homosexual intercourse than for heterosexual intercourse.

INTERNATIONAL NETWORK OF LESBIAN AND GAY OFFICIALS (INLGO). An organization founded in Minneapolis, Minnesota, in 1985 as a nonprofit organization to further the repeal of laws that discriminate against lesbians and gays, to promote education and research on the subject of sexual orientation, and to encourage lesbians and gays to become actively involved in public activities.

The INLGO's 13 founders, municipal- and state-elected officeholders in the United States, include Harry Britt (San Francisco, California, supervisor), Karen Clark (Minnesota state representative), John Heilman (West Hollywood, California, mayor), and Kathleen Nichols (Dane County, Wisconsin, supervisor).

Since inception, the INLGO has sponsored a yearly conference to aid and assist openly gay and lesbian candidates and elected and appointed public officials from around the world. The conference focuses on, for example, teaching organizing skills and sponsoring discussions of social and political issues relevant to the lesbian and gay community. The objective is to use the knowledge and experience of seasoned officials to assist individuals interested in becoming politically involved at the local, state, or national level.

IVES, GEORGE CECIL (1867–1941). Author, criminologist, Fellow of the Zoological Society, and member of the Order of Chaeronea and the British Society for the Study of Sex Psychology (BSSP) (qq.v.).

George Cecil Ives was acquainted with Oscar Wilde (q.v.) and Lord Alfred Douglas and was deeply saddened by the outcome of the Oscar Wilde trials which resulted in Wilde's imprisonment. It was perhaps his visits to Wilde in prison that prompted him to become involved with a group of gay men in the Order of Chaeronea, a secret society of homosexual activists. Ives is regarded to have been the chief figure in this group, which dates from the mid-1890s.

Ives was also acquainted with Edward Carpenter (q.v.), a leading proponent of homosexual rights and president of the BSSP with which Ives was actively involved. Among Ives's other responsibilities, he developed a library for the use of BSSP members.

He was familiar with leaders of the German homosexual emancipation movement such as Magnus Hirschfeld and Adolph Brand (qq.v.). Ives's communications with Brand no doubt also brought him into contact with the Gemeinschaft der Eigenen (Community of the Special [COS]) (q.v.), because of Brand's association with that organization. Whether there were any formal links between the COS and the Order of Chaeronea is uncertain.

Ives was not outspoken in his defense of homosexual rights, but his leadership of the Order of Chaeronea and his participation in the BSSP helped advance the cause of legal reform in Britain.

K

KALININ, ROMAN (1966–   ). At 24 years of age, Roman Kalinin became cochair (with Yevgenia Debryanskaya) of the Moscow Union of Lesbians and Homosexuals (MULH). MULH was formed in 1990 after disagreements within the ranks of the first gay and lesbian rights organization in the USSR, the Sexual Minorities Association (q.v.), led to its dissolution. The association's newspaper, *Tema*, continued to be published under MULH. Kalinin was named the exclusive editor of the newspaper, the first gay and lesbian publication in the USSR.

Under the leadership of Kalinin and Debryanskaya, MULH's organizational style resembled that of the Gay Liberation Front (GLF) (q.v.). Eschewing bureaucratic formalities, MULH engaged in numerous protest demonstrations demanding human rights for gays and lesbians, particularly the repeal of Article 121.1 (q.v.) of the USSR's legal code, which criminalized adult male homosexuality. Kalinin's brash and courageous leadership earned him an international reputation among gays and lesbians. During his 1991 visit to San Francisco, for example, he met with city officials, including the mayor, who designated his arrival in the city "Roman Kalinin Day." The *Advocate* named Roman Kalinin "man of the year" in 1991.

Kalinin became the subject of an attack in the communist press after an interview in *Karetny ryad* in which he was quoted as defending bestiality, pedophilia, and necrophilia. The interview became a pretext to attack not only the gay and lesbian rights movement but also the Mossovet (Moscow City Council) and the entire democratic reform movement for their lax attitude concerning sexual perversion. The established communist press such as *Pravda* and *Tass* capitalized on the story by reprinting it and editorializing against Kalinin and the Mossovet. Despite the fact that *Karetny ryad* published a retraction after losing a civil suit brought against the paper by the Mossovet, the publicity generated by the story damaged the fledgling gay and lesbian movement in the Soviet Union.

Kalinin was further embarrassed when he announced his candidacy for the presidency of Russia. It was soon discovered that Kalinin was too young to qualify, and he had to withdraw from the race. This discredited Kalinin not only in the eyes of the general public but in the eyes of other influential gays and lesbians. However, one of Kalinin's objectives was accomplished when the newly independent republics of Armenia, Estonia, Latvia, Moldova, and the Ukraine repealed their criminal laws pertaining to homosexual sex and when President Boris Yeltsin followed suit in 1993 by repealing Article 121.1.

Despite recent changes in the criminal law, the future of the gay and lesbian movement in the Russian Federation is very tenuous. Kalinin's leadership was instrumental in forging the movement, but his leadership style also alienated more traditional gay and lesbian leaders. Cooperation between organizations has also been unpredictable during this period of economic hardship and political instability, thus rendering the prospects of the gay and lesbian movement in the Russian Federation highly problematic.

KAMENY, FRANK (1925–). An astronomer, cofounder of the Washington, D.C., Mattachine Society, and longtime gay rights activist who championed the reform of the U.S. Civil Service Code.

Kameny received his Ph.D. from Harvard University in 1956. After one year as a faculty member at Georgetown University, he accepted a position as a civilian employee with the U.S. Army Map Service. In 1957 he was dismissed on the grounds that he was a homosexual. Kameny's dismissal precipitated a struggle to reform the U.S. Civil Service Code as well as the policies of other U.S. government agencies that discriminated against gays and lesbians and thrust Kameny into a leadership role in the emerging homosexual rights movement in the United States.

The appeal of his dismissal from the U.S. Army, between 1958 and 1961, culminated in the denial of a writ of certiorari by the U.S. Supreme Court in March 1961. This unsuccessful effort to overturn his dismissal in the federal courts, however, transformed Kameny into a lifelong gay rights activist. In November 1961 Kameny and Jack Nichols cofounded the Washington, D.C., chapter of the Mattachine Society (MS) (q.v.). The Mattachine Society of Washington, D.C. (MSW), became independent shortly after the dissolution of the national structure of the MS. Today it remains a registered nonprofit corporation in Washington, D.C.

Aside from the reform of the U.S. Civil Service Code, the objectives of the MSW included reforming the policy of denying security clearances to gays and lesbians and the policy of excluding gays and lesbians from the uniformed military. In 1963, MSW, under Kameny's leadership, together with the Janus Society of Philadelphia, the New York Mattachine Society (MSNY), and the New York Daughters of Bilitis (NYDOB), formed a regional association known as the East Coast Homophile Organizations (ECHO) (q.v.) to coordinate the activities of gay rights groups. Kameny was also instrumental in the formation of the first national association of homophile organizations in 1966, the North American Conference of Homophile Organizations (NACHO) (q.v.).

In 1975, Kameny's long battle with the Civil Service Commission came to an end when the commission reversed its previous policy of denying gays and lesbians the right of employment in the civil service. President Clinton widened this policy to include the entire federal workforce. Similarly, the Clinton administration ended the policy of routinely denying security clearances on the grounds of sexual orientation. The reform of the ban on gays and lesbians in the uniformed military, however, has yet to be fully accomplished. *See also* Don't Ask, Don't Tell.

Perhaps Kameny's most notable achievement was his successful crusade against the American Psychiatric Association's (APA) classification of homosexuality as a mental illness. Kameny argued that the label of mental illness was an almost insuperable obstacle to achieving civil rights (q.v.) for gays and lesbians. He was opposed not only by many practicing psychiatrists and psychologists but also by the more conservative leaders of homophile organizations. Together with other gay and lesbian activists, such as Del Martin, and sympathetic psychiatric professionals, Kameny was vindicated in 1974 when the APA declassified homosexuality as a mental illness in its *Diagnostic and Statistical Manual of Psychiatric Disorders.*

Now in his 70s, Kameny remains active in the gay and lesbian rights movement.

KERTBENY, KARL MARIA (1824–1882). Born Karl Maria Benkert, he is remembered as the originator of the terms *heterosexuality* (*Heterosexualität*) and *homosexuality* (*Homosexualität*). Kertbeny used these terms in an 1868 letter to Karl Heinrich Ulrichs (q.v.). Kertbeny is also remembered as the author of pamphlets critical of Paragraph 143 of the Prussian legal code. Published in 1869, these pamphlets, in which Kertbeny criticized the legal proscription of adult male homosexuality, mark the first public use of the term *homosexuality*. Although credit for the two pamphlets cannot be established with certitude because they were published anonymously, he has been presumed to be the author since Magnus Hirschfeld's (q.v.) 1905 reprint of the first pamphlet in the *Jahrbuch für sexuelle Zwischenstufen* (Yearbook for Sexual Intermediates).

Kertbeny was born in Vienna and grew up in Hungary. In the literature on the 19th-century homosexual rights movement in Germany it is often assumed that Kertbeny was a pseudonym, Benkert being his real name. This would not appear to be the case. On 22 February 1848, Karl Maria Benkert officially changed his name to Karl Maria Kertbeny.

Kertbeny was aware of the work of Karl Heinrich Ulrichs on urnings and Ulrichs's protests against Prussian laws pertaining to homosexuals. Along with Ulrichs, Kertbeny's own protests against the criminal punishments contained in Paragraph 143 of the Prussian legal code rank among the very first public utterances in defense of homosexual love. But the ideas he expressed in his pamphlets were considerably different from Ulrichs's theories.

Kertbeny remained unconvinced of Ulrichs's explanation of the origins of same-sex love. He did not set forth an alternative explanation but was content in insisting that his own homosexual desire was completely normal and that science could not explain homosexuality. Kertbeny's insistence that he spoke not as a woman but as a man can be seen as the core of his distaste for Ulrichs's concept of *urning*, a womanly soul trapped in the body of a man, and of his desire to develop an alternative terminology.

Kertbeny's term *homosexuality* did not become the standard referent for same-sex desire for many years. Because of the increasing attention devoted to same-sex desire in psychiatric and legal literature there was no shortage of terminology to describe the behavior. Ulrichs's *urning*, Johann Ludwig Casper's *päderast*, Carl von Westphal's *contrary sexual feeling*, Tamassia's and Ellis's *invert*, as well as other referents were among the more commonly used terms. *Homosexuality* was used only intermittently between 1869 and the turn of the 20th century. Perhaps its eventual popularity can be attributed in part to its use in Richard von Krafft-Ebing's 1886 publication *Psychopathia Sexualis*, a work that quickly became a standard psychiatric reference source on sexual disorders, and to Sigmund Freud's use of the term in his early works on sexual orientation. Nevertheless, a variety of terms remained in use until roughly World War II when *homosexuality* eventually superseded the alternatives as standard nomenclature.

L

LABOUCHÈRE AMENDMENT (1886). The "Outrages on Public Decency" amendment to the British Criminal Law Amendment Act of 1885, commonly known as the Labouchère Amendment, after its sponsor Henry Labouchère.

Unlike the Act of 25 Henry VIII, c.6 (q.v.), the Labouchère Amendment criminalized all homosexual acts between males whether they occurred in private or in public. Furthermore, it criminalized the procurement or the attempt to procure a male for the purpose of engaging in homosexual acts. Consent was no defense, and it was applicable to minors as well as adults. The maximum penalty was two years at hard labor. It was enacted into law on 1 January 1886 and became the model for similar legislation in New Zealand and in Canada. It was the Labouchère Amendment that was utilized by prosecutors in the infamous prosecution of the famous British playwright Oscar Wilde (q.v.). An attempt to extend the provisions of the law to lesbians was defeated in Parliament in 1921.

The Labouchère Amendment together with the notorious "buggery" statute of 1533 (the Act of 25 Henry VIII, c.6) became the principal targets of the homosexual emancipation movement in Britain. The Homosexual Law Reform Society (HLRS) (q.v.) led the drive to repeal the provisions of both statutes following the publication of the 1957 Report of the Committee on Homosexual Offenses and Prostitution (q.v.) commonly referred to as the Wolfenden Report, which recommended the decriminalization of private consensual homosexual activity between adults. The long-awaited reform occurred a decade after the Wolfenden Report in the form of the Sexual Offenses Act of 1967 (q.v.).

LAMBDA GROUPS ASSOCIATION OF POLAND (LGAP). The Lambda Groups Association of Poland (LGAP) is a nationwide federation of lesbian and gay organizations and publications. It was founded in 1989 and accorded legal recognition in 1990. Members of the LGAP include ETAP, (the first gay and lesbian group in Poland, founded in 1986 in Wroclaw), Filo (founded in Gdansk), Warzawski Ruch Homoseksualny (Warsaw Homosexual Movement), as well as a number of other groups from smaller cities.

Homosexuality has not been an object of the criminal law since 1932 when Poland enacted its first unified national legal code. The prohibitions against male and female homosexuality were repealed, and a common age of consent for heterosexual and homosexual intercourse was established at 15 years of age. The Napoleonic Code was the inspiration for this highly progressive legal reform, a reform advocated by well-known Polish sexologists such as Andrzej Mikulski during the 1920s.

Consequently, the LGAP has focused its attention on improving the social acceptability of gays and lesbians. Most importantly,

LGAP has worked to end the police practice of maintaining files on gays and lesbians and to end police harassment of gay establishments. Other objectives have included working with the media to ensure objective coverage of gays and lesbians, AIDS education and prevention, and the protection of the rights of gays and lesbians.

Poland is in the process of adopting a new constitution. The LGAP has worked toward including antidiscrimination provisions pertaining to lesbians and gays. Despite the opposition of the Catholic Church and former President Lech Walesa, the Constitutional Committee recommended the inclusion of sexual orientation as a protected category in the human rights clause of its draft constitution. The defeat of Walesa for president by the former head of the Constitutional Commission, Aleksander Kwasnieski, has raised the hopes of gays and lesbians that the Parliament of Poland will accept the recommendations of the Constitutional Commission.

LAMBDA LEGAL DEFENSE AND EDUCATION FUND (LLDEF). Founded in the United States in 1973, the LLDEF is the most prominent nationwide legal defense organization devoted to securing the legal rights of gays and lesbians. Other national associations in the United States include Gay and Lesbian Advocates and Defenders, the National Lesbian and Gay Law Association, and the National Gay and Lesbian Rights Project of the American Civil Liberties Union.

The LLDEF's application for incorporation as a nonprofit organization was denied by a New York state court in 1972. The LLDEF appealed the decision and, in 1973, the New York state high court reversed the decision. The LLDEF has grown steadily ever since. Based initially in New York City, the LLDEF now also has offices in Los Angeles and Chicago.

Among the issues litigated by the LLDEF are workplace, housing, and public accommodations discrimination complaints, domestic partner benefits, state sodomy statutes (q.v.), and marriage (q.v.) rights. The LLDEF has also been actively engaged in HIV/AIDS discrimination cases. In addition it has represented litigants challenging their dismissal from the U.S. military for their homosexuality. LLDEF has participated in many landmark U.S. cases, including *Bowers v. Hardwick*, *Romer v. Evans*, and *Baehr v. Lewin* (now *Baehr v. Miike*) (qq.v.).

LAMBDA PRAHA/LAMBDA PRAGUE (LP). The first public gay and lesbian rights organization in the former Czechoslovakia began operations in 1988 before the overthrow of the communist regime. Czechoslovakia had decriminalized lesbian and gay male sexual relations many years before, in 1961, and was more tolerant of homosexuality than most other Eastern European countries. State-run newspapers and television often featured stories of gays and lesbians, and gay bars and discos were tolerated. Informal private gay and lesbian organizations operated throughout the 1980s, but Lambda Praha remains significant as the first gay and lesbian organization to operate publicly.

One of the chief demands of LP after the overthrow of the communist government in 1989 was the equalization of the age of consent laws for homosexuals and heterosexuals. Despite the fact that homosexual relations had been legal since 1961, the age of consent for homosexuals remained fixed at 18, three years older than for heterosexuals. Legislation was introduced into the new democratically elected Czech and Slovak Federal Republican Parliament shortly after meetings with representatives of LP and subsequently enacted into law in 1990. The age of consent is now 15 for both homosexuals and heterosexuals. Criminal penalties for male prostitution were also repealed. Further demands of LP were the enactment of domestic partnership laws and asylum (q.v.) for gays and lesbians fleeing persecution, struggles that have been carried on since the dissolution of Czechoslovakia.

Gay and lesbian groups have now emerged in major cities in the independent Czech republic (Czechia), including the formation of a nationwide federation of gay and lesbian groups known as SOHO. *Lambda*, the first gay and lesbian publication, provides national and international news to the gay and lesbian community. Ganymedes, a gay and lesbian organization in the Republic of Slovakia, has recently begun operations and, in 1992, hosted a conference of the International Lesbian and Gay Association's (q.v.) youth organization.

LAMPIÃO. The first national gay and lesbian newspaper in Brazil, *Lampião* published monthly editions for three years before it closed in 1981.

The proposal to publish a newspaper serving the gay and lesbian community arose out of discussions in 1977 between a group of writers concerning a forthcoming anthology of Latin American gay literature. These discussions led to the formation of a writers' collective and the publication of the first edition of *Lampião* in April 1978.

Published in Rio de Janeiro, *Lampião* was not affiliated with any political ideology or political party. It acquired the reputation of publishing sexually explicit articles and quickly became the focus of intense criticism from both right-wing and left-wing groups who were offended by the paper's iconoclastic coverage of gays' and lesbians' lives.

The newspaper also became the object of an investigation by the federal police on the grounds that it had offended public morality. Although Brazil has no sodomy statutes (q.v.) with which to regulate sexual behavior, it does have criminal statutes pertaining to public indecency as well as censorship laws that have been used to regulate gays and lesbians. It was such a censorship law, the Press Law, that the federal police used to detain and interrogate the editors of *Lampião*. The charges were ultimately dropped for lack of evidence.

Lampião's undoing was the result of internecine struggles within the emerging gay and lesbian movement in Brazil. As early as 1980, the editors of *Lampião* objected to the efforts of the Left to co-opt the energy of gay and lesbian organizations by encouraging their integration into existing party bureaucracies. Trotskyists were particularly effective in this regard. The most successful gay and lesbian organization in the early 1980s, Somos (q.v.), was taken over by Trotskyists and made a section of the Worker's Party. *Lampião*'s opposition to this trend resulted in its isolation from many gay and lesbian activists in Brazil and a decline in its circulation. The ensuing financial difficulties resulted in quarrels among the editorial staff and, eventually, the paper's closure. Its last edition was published in July 1981.

Despite its short life span, *Lampião* was very influential in the origins of the gay and lesbian movement in Brazil. It originated at the same time as Somos, and its nationwide circulation created opportunities for organizing and networking at the very dawn of the gay and lesbian movement in Brazil.

LANDSFORENINGEN FOR BØSSER OG LESBISKE / NATIONAL ORGANIZATION OF GAYS AND LESBIANS (NOGL). Founded in 1948 by Axel Axgil (q.v.) in Ålborg Denmark, the National Organization of Gays and Lesbians has become Denmark's exclusive nationwide organization representing gays and lesbians.

One of the NOGL's objectives was the enactment of a civil rights (q.v.) statute emulating the 1981 Norwegian antidiscrimination statute, the first national legislation protecting the rights of lesbians and gay men. In 1987, Article 289, an equal-access public accommodations law, and Article 266a, a hate crimes bill, were enacted. Both provide civil rights protections to lesbians and gay men. In 1996, the Danish Parliament, the Folketing, enacted further civil rights protections for gays and lesbians. As of 1 July 1996 it became illegal to discriminate against individuals in the private labor market on the basis of sexual orientation.

Another chief priority of the NOGL since its inception was the enactment of a partnership law in Denmark. In 1987 a same-sex partnership law was introduced into the Folketing, which provided that the domestic partners of gays and lesbians be accorded all the privileges accorded to heterosexual married couples except the right to adopt children and the right to a church ceremony. A further stipulation was that one of the partners be a Danish citizen. The provision prohibiting gays and lesbians from adopting children, even stepchildren from previous marriages, divided the NOGL. Nevertheless, by a razor-thin margin, the NOGL decided to support the bill and the Folketing passed the Danish Registered Partnership Act (q.v.) on 26 May 1989.

The NOGL currently operates out of a building in the heart of Copenhagen. In addition to serving as the headquarters of the NOGL, it also functions as a gay and lesbian community center. Office space for other gay and lesbian organizations, a radio station, AIDS education, a coffeehouse, a disco, as well as meeting rooms, are included in the center.

At the top of the NOGL's agenda is a campaign to amend the Danish Registered Partnership Act to allow married gays and lesbians to adopt children.

LATIN AMERICA. Although there is evidence of scientific and medical literature on the subject of homosexuality as well as evidence of informal networks of gays and lesbians prior to Stonewall (q.v.), the gay and lesbian liberation movement in Latin America appears to have been ignited by press reports of the emergence of the Gay Liberation Front (q.v.) in New York City in 1969.

The situation of gays and lesbians in Latin America is bleak. Although, unlike in North America and Europe (qq.v.), sodomy statutes (q.v.) exist in only a few countries such as Chile, Cuba, Ecuador, and Nicaragua, many countries repress homosexuality through the use of "public indecency" or "public morality" statutes, and censorship laws are often invoked to restrict the circulation of information. Strong social taboos also inhibit gay and lesbian relationships, and gays, lesbians, and bisexuals have been the victims of extrajudicial violence in countries such as Brazil and Colombia. Nevertheless, the gay and lesbian movement now has a tenuous foothold throughout much of the region.

As early as the 1970s, groups such as the Frente de Liberación Homosexual de Mexico (q.v.) became active in Mexico City. Other groups soon emerged, both in Mexico City as well as in Guadalajara, where the Grupo de Orgullo Homosexual de Liberación (q.v.) began organizing in 1982. Although Mexican gay and lesbian groups have yet to achieve the civil rights (q.v.) successes of their North American counterparts, they have spawned many gay, lesbian, and bisexual organizations throughout Mexico and have established their presence in the Mexican political arena.

By the late 1970s groups in other Latin American countries had also begun to emerge. In Brazil, for example, Somos (q.v.) began recruiting members in 1977, at about the same time the first national gay and lesbian magazine, *Lampião* (q.v.), appeared. In 1980 the first nationwide congress of homosexual groups was staged and although Somos disappeared shortly thereafter, Brazil (like Mexico) now boasts many gay and lesbian groups. Unlike Mexico, however, in Brazil some progress has been achieved in achieving civil rights protections for gays and lesbians, and a Brazilian gay and lesbian partnership law, similar to the Danish Registered Partnership Act (q.v.) is under active consideration in the Brazilian legislature.

Antidiscrimination laws protecting gays and lesbians have also recently been passed in Buenos Aires and Rosario, Argentina. The Rosario legislation, drafted by the Collectivo Arco Iris (Rainbow Collective), took effect in December 1997.

Gay and lesbian rights groups have also begun to emerge elsewhere in Latin America, such as the Comunidad Homosexual Argentina, the Colectivo Gay Universitario in Costa Rica, and the Moviemento Homosexual de Lima in Peru. Gay and lesbian rights have even become a topic of public discussion in Cuba where gays and lesbians have suffered under the harsh repression of the state. Nevertheless, the first gay and lesbian group, the Gay and Lesbian Association of Cuba (GLAC) (q.v.) formed in 1994. The GLAC soon gave way to a successor, but it may have opened the door for a discussion of gay and lesbian issues and the eventual liberalization of Cuba's historic antihomosexual laws.

Much progress has been made in Latin America since the appearance of the first gay and lesbian rights groups in the early 1970s, but social attitudes toward homosexuals remain very intolerant and discriminatory, and few laws exist that protect homosexuals from discrimination or persecution.

LATVIAN ASSOCIATION FOR SEXUAL EQUALITY (LASE).
Founded in 1990 after the fall of the Communist regime in Latvia, the LASE petitioned the government of Latvia to repeal the criminal penalties for sexual relations between men, to eliminate differences in age of consent laws (q.v.) between heterosexuals and homosexuals, to enact antidiscrimination legislation, and to provide for AIDS education and prevention. Article 124 of the Latvian criminal code, which criminalized sexual relations between men, was imposed on Latvia after its takeover by the Soviet Union in 1940. In 1991, the

Latvian parliament took the first step toward eliminating legal distinctions between heterosexuals and homosexuals when it voted to repeal Article 124. Although homosexual relations are not as widely accepted in Latvia as in Western Europe, the activities of organizations such as the LASE are working to redress the damage done to gays and lesbians by decades of Soviet rule.

LIND, EARL, pseud. (1874–?). Together with Xavier Mayne (q.v.), Earl Lind was one of the first American writers to defend homosexuality in print.

Lind's *Autobiography of an Androgyne*, published in 1918, sets forth arguments in defense of the homosexual lifestyle and challenges Americans to integrate homosexuals into society. His sequel, *The Female Impersonators*, which he published under the name of Ralph Werther, discusses the sexual underground in New York City, particularly male transvestism. Earl Lind/Ralph Werther was also known as Jennie June.

Lind was born into an affluent family in the New York City area. College educated, he decided at an early age to expose his lifestyle in the sexual underground to enlighten the general public and garner sympathy for the plight of individuals such as himself. Perhaps indicative of the antipathy toward homosexuality in the United States at the dawn of the 20th century, Lind searched 18 years in vain for a publisher of his autobiography. Considered too controversial for the general reading public, it was eventually published by *The Medico-Legal Journal* and sold exclusively to professionals such as lawyers and physicians.

Lind was familiar with the term *urning*, commonly used to refer to homosexuals at the turn of the century and coined by Karl Heinrich Ulrichs (q.v.). Lind apparently became aware of the term through the works of sexologists such as Richard von Krafft-Ebing and Havelock Ellis (q.v.). Even though the condition described by Ulrichs (a womanly soul trapped in the body of a man) is a precise account of his own self-description (a *"fille de joie"*), Lind incorrectly assumed that the term referred to "active" inverts such as Oscar Wilde (q.v.), men who sought effeminate youths as their sexual companions. Thus, Lind, who was "passive," preferred to use the term *androgyne* in reference to his sexual preference.

Although his published works received scant public recognition, they contain important insights into the homosexual underground in New York City and such European capitals as Berlin, London, and Paris. His autobiography also contains a detailed account of his personal anguish, including his expulsion from the university as a graduate student and his unsuccessful attempts to reverse his sexual preference through electroshock, drug therapy, hypnotism, and, eventually, castration. The *Autobiography of an Androgyne* also contains one of the earliest appeals for social justice by an American author.

M

MARRIAGE. In addition to other civil rights (q.v.) struggles, gays and lesbians have campaigned for the right to enter into legally binding marriage contracts. Although gay couples and lesbian couples have historically engaged in commitment ceremonies conducted by lay as well as ordained ministers, it was not until the enactment of the 1989 Danish Registered Partnership Act (q.v.), that civil marriages between gay men or lesbians were recognized by a sovereign state. The movement to extend the right of civil marriage to gays and lesbians quickly spread to other Scandinavian countries as well as to Greenland and Iceland. An unanticipated development was the extension of the right to civil marriages for gays and lesbians in Hungary in 1996. In 1998, the Netherlands became the most recent country to provide the benefits of a registered partnership act to gays and lesbians. *See also* Det Norske Forbundet av 1948; Riksförbundet för Sexuellt Likaberättigande; Samtökin 78; Szivarvany.

Even where the right of gay and lesbian civil marriage has been enacted into law, however, gays and lesbians do not enjoy the full rights of their heterosexual counterparts. Gays and lesbians are not entitled to a religious ceremony, only the right to register their partnerships with the state. Other common exceptions include prohibitions on the joint custody of children (with the exception of Iceland) and the right to adopt children.

In the United States, the right of gay men and lesbians to marry has been thrust into the forefront of political debate because of the impending decision of the Hawaii Supreme Court (*Baehr v. Miike* [q.v.]) concerning the constitutionality of gay and lesbian marriage. Hawaii could be the first state to legalize gay and lesbian unions. In the United States, where marriage contracts are governed by state law and where reciprocity between the states is stipulated by the "Full Faith and Credit" clause of the U.S. Constitution, it is assumed that a full-fledged legal battle will erupt if gay men and lesbians attempt to assert their prerogatives in other states after marrying in Hawaii. The Defense of Marriage Act (q.v.) was signed into law in 1996 by President Bill Clinton in anticipation of the eventuality of gay and lesbian marriages in Hawaii.

MATTACHINE REVIEW. The *Mattachine Review* began publication in January 1955, two years after the initiation of *One*, published by One Inc. (q.v.), and a year prior to the first issue of *The Ladder*, a publication of the Daughters of Bilitis. Together, these three magazines were the primary sources of information for gay men and lesbians in the United States during the 1950s and 1960s. They operated under severe legal and financial constraints, existed under constant threat of censorship, and their circulation figures were so meager that they were produced on shoestring budgets.

A publication of the Mattachine Society (MS) (q.v.), the *Mattachine Review* contained short works of fiction, literary reviews, bibliographies, personal narratives, psychological and sociological studies of homosexuality, and articles on the gay liberation movement in Europe and North America (qq.v.). As a publication of the MS, it also provided a regular source of information about the activities of MS to its subscribers. Thus, it was a forerunner of such contemporary U.S. publications as *The Advocate* and *Gay Community News*.

The journal ceased publication in the mid-1960s, a few years after the dissolution of the national structure of the MS. At its height, its circulation was a few thousand, and it gradually lost readership in the late 1950s and early 1960s. Despite its limited readership, the *Mattachine Review* provided one of the first opportunities for gays and lesbians to develop a sense of national and international identity through the publication of information relevant to the emerging gay and lesbian subculture in North America and Europe.

MATTACHINE SOCIETY (MS). Founded in the autumn of 1950 in Los Angeles by Harry Hay (q.v.), Rudi Gernreich, Robert Hull, Charles Rowland, and subsequently Dale Jennings, Konrad Stevens, and James Gruber, the MS became the most prominent pre-Stonewall (q.v.) homosexual rights organization in the Americas.

Originally known to the founders as the Society of Fools, the name *Mattachine Society* was adopted in April 1951. The name was derived from Les sociétés mattachines, a secret medieval French society with counterparts in other countries. These all-male societies cultivated forms of social parody characteristic of the ancient Roman New Year celebration of Saturnalia. They satirized the pretenses of social custom through the performance of forbidden songs and rituals and, according to Hay, featured men dressed as women.

Motivated by a need for secrecy in an era intolerant of sexual as well as political deviance, the organizational structure of the MS was inspired by the Freemasons, an illegal eighteenth-century European brotherhood. As conceived by Harry Hay, the MS was to be composed of five "orders." At the base of the pyramid were the public

discussion groups or "guilds." Representatives of the guilds constituted the second order, while the third and fourth orders were envisioned to be composed of representatives of the second and third orders, respectively. At the top of this hierarchical structure was the
fifth order, the founders. In this way, Hay reasoned, the anonymity
of the membership, particularly that of the founders, could be protected. Not only were the founders homosexual, but three had also
been members of the Communist Party of the United States of
America.

A mission statement drafted in the spring of 1951 and ratified in
July set forth the goals of the organization. Unification, education,
and political action were the cornerstones of the "Missions and Purposes" of the MS. Calling for the creation of "an ethical homosexual culture," the founders argued that only through public education
and vigorous political action could homosexuals ever expect to lead
productive and fulfilling lives.

The organizational structure and militant political posture of the
early MS became the object of heated controversy among the membership in 1953 when a syndicated columnist for the *Los Angeles
Daily Mirror* identified Fred Snyder, an uncooperative witness before the House Un-American Activities Committee, as the lawyer of
the MS. The rank and file became increasingly uneasy at the prospect of the organization being affiliated with communism and with
the anonymity of the fifth order.

In response to these concerns, a democratic convention was called
to draft a constitution for the organization in the spring of 1953. A
conservative faction led by Hal Call, David Finn, and Marilyn Reiger succeeded in convincing the convention membership that the MS
had to dissociate itself from communism and direct political action.
The founders were accordingly forced to resign and the organization
charted a new, more accommodationist course.

One of the MS's most noteworthy accomplishments was the publication of the *Mattachine Review* (q.v.), a magazine devoted to the
literary, artistic, and political interests of the emerging gay subculture. At the height of its popularity MS had numerous chapters
throughout the country. Its membership, however, never exceeded
several thousand individuals. The MS dissolved as a national organization in March 1961. It was succeeded by its various local chapters,
which carried on its activities. Together with the Daughters of Bilitis
the Mattachine Society was the most significant gay rights organization in the United States until the mid-1960s when new gay and lesbian rights organizations appeared. Shortly after the Stonewall (q.v.)
riots on 28–29 June 1969, the political landscape of the movement

was transfigured, and MS chapters steadily declined in membership and influence.

MAYNE, XAVIER (1868–1942). Born Edward Irenaeus Prime Stevenson, he is remembered for his book on homosexuality, *The Intersexes: A History of Similisexualism As a Problem in Social Life.* First printed in 1908, it is the first such work by an American. The first edition consisted of 125 privately printed copies, published in Rome because of the difficulties in securing an Anglo-American printer. Mayne is also the author of *Imre: A Memorandum*, a short novel with a homosexual subplot.

Mayne published *The Intersexes* in order that the burgeoning literature on homosexuality, what he preferred to call "similisexualism," or the intersexes, be available to the English-speaking world. (Most of the literature on homosexuality at the turn of the century was in German, French, and Russian.) Most of its 641 pages consist of extensive summaries and abstracts from anthropological, biographical, criminological, historical, legal, literary, psychiatric, and religious sources.

Mayne's own ideas were largely influenced by the leading German psychiatrists and sexologists of the day such as Karl Heinrich Ulrichs and Magnus Hirschfeld (qq.v.). The book is dedicated to Richard von Krafft-Ebing whom Mayne credits for his inspiration and help in bringing the work to fruition. His own theory of the intersexes follows Ulrichs's idea of the "third sex" (q.v.).

Mayne argues that it has been a great error to have assumed that there are only two sexes. The male and female homosexual constitute intersexes, literally "between-men" and "between-women." They are physiologically males and females, but unlike heterosexuals they are naturally attracted to the same sex. As Mayne defined sex as the sexual passion, he concluded that there were at least four sexes, heterosexual and homosexual males and females.

At a time when the subject of homosexuality was rarely discussed in scientific terms, Xavier Mayne gave to the English-speaking world a wealth of information about a subject still cloaked in religious mythology and superstition.

MEDICAL MODEL OF HOMOSEXUALITY. Medical models of psychopathological conditions attempt to explain and treat abnormal or peculiar behaviors in the same fashion as medicine explains and treats physical ailments. Accordingly, homosexuality is explained in medical literature as a biological or psychological abnormality.

The medical model of homosexuality has been a topic of recurrent inquiry throughout the history of Western medicine. This vast and growing scientific literature now spans more than two centuries and remains characterized by a lack of consensus over fundamental issues. Debates have focused on whether the etiology of homosexuality is primarily biological or behavioral (including debates over the veracity of specific biological or behavioral models) and whether homosexuality is a mental illness. Further doubts have been cast on the intrinsic veracity of medical explanations of gay and lesbian sexuality.

The origins of modern medical research on homosexuality can be traced to 17th-century and 18th-century medical literature linking masturbation to various illnesses. Madness, consumption, impotence, and constipation, among other illnesses, were associated with excessive expenditures of semen. Even the propensity to engage in sexual relations with the same sex was attributed to masturbation.

Examples of such 18th-century literature include Hermann Boerhaave's *Institutiones medicae* (1728), John Brown's *Elements of Medicine* (1780), Samuel Tissot's *Onanism: or, a Treatise upon the Disorders of Masturbation* (1766), and Johann Valentine Müller's *Outline of Forensic Medicine* (1796). Tissot and Müller were perhaps the first to link same-sex love to masturbation. Tissot claimed that the "disorder" was even more apparent in women than in men. Anglo-American writers such as John Harvey Kellogg and William Acton were profoundly influenced by their European counterparts and perpetuated the notion of masturbatory insanity well into the 19th-century.

By the mid-19th century, linkages between masturbation and illness became increasingly suspect. Karl Heinrich Ulrichs (q.v.) ridiculed onanism as an explanation of same-sex eroticism, calling it the "product of a fantastic dream." Ulrichs countered with the "third sex" theory (q.v.), the proposition that anomalous embryological developments were responsible for same-sex eroticism. Although his third sex theory attracted few adherents, the idea that homosexuality developed in utero influenced many of the leading students of sexuality, such as Magnus Hirschfeld, Havelock Ellis (qq.v.), Richard von Krafft-Ebing, and Carl von Westphal.

Closely related to this idea were theories of congenital degeneracy, which became common by the turn of the century. Explanations for alcoholism, crime, poverty, and even theories of racial inferiority were supported by theories of hereditary degeneracy. Treatises linking homosexuality and congenital degeneracy were also common. Whereas Ulrichs claimed that homosexuality was no more than a natural biological variation, many others, including Krafft-Ebing, Westphal, and Ellis, explained at least some cases of sexual inversion or homosexuality as one manifestation of physiological degeneration.

Sigmund Freud remains noteworthy for proffering a behavioral model of sexual orientation and rejecting the association of homosexuality and congenital degeneracy. Freud criticized prior research on the grounds that it was dependent on subjects culled from insane asylums, leading to the inevitable conclusion that homosexuality was coincident with mental illness. Freud found no correlation between homosexuality and mental illness and disputed those who claimed that it resulted from physiological degeneration. Instead, Freud proposed that human beings were constitutionally bisexual and that homosexuality could be explained primarily in psychological terms, especially in light of early childhood development. Freud attached much importance to the Oedipus complex in explaining the development of gender roles and sexual orientation. Although Freud explicitly denied that homosexuality was pathological, he asserted that it constituted a developmental disturbance in the maturation of the child, thus perpetuating the notion that it was an abnormality.

Oedipal theories gradually came to dominate the discussion of homosexuality. Some writers, such as Otto Rank, Hans Sachs, and Sandor Ferenczi, refined and adapted Freud's theories. Others, such as Edmund Bergler, Charles Socarides, Sandor Rado, and Irving Bieber, challenged the validity of Freud's explanation of homosexuality, including his assurances that homosexuality was not an illness. Bergler, Socarides, and Bieber were particularly strident in their insistence that homosexuality was a psychopathology. Thus, although Freud can be credited with transforming the terms of the debate, he did not succeed in convincing other researchers that the oedipal basis of homosexuality was completely valid or that it was a benign personality maladjustment.

Although psychoanalytical paradigms dominated the discussion of homosexuality by mid-century, biological theories continued to attract attention. Early empirical research in biology focused on the endocrine system. Magnus Hirschfeld, among others, speculated that hormonal imbalances might be the source of a homosexual orientation. However, studies designed to detect differences in testosterone levels between homosexual and heterosexual men (including attempts to change the sexual orientation of homosexual men through testosterone supplements) failed to establish a correlation between testosterone and sexual orientation.

Beginning in the 1960s, a new approach to hormonal research emphasized the influence of perinatal hormone levels on sexual orientation. Reminiscent of Ulrichs's theory, this research suggests that the early stages of gestation are crucial for determining the sexual orientation of children. Based primarily on mammalian experiments, these studies concluded that, whether owing to maternal stress during pregnancy, drugs, immunity factors, or hormones, sexual inversions were the result of the neuro-organization of the fetus during the earliest phases of gestation.

Most recently, scientific research has focused on genetic explanations of homosexuality. The research of Simon LeVay and Dean Hammer, for example, has dominated the discussion concerning the etiology of homosexuality during the 1990s. Writing for *Scientific American*, LeVay and Hammer claim that their research into the genetic origins of sexual orientation was influenced by the studies conducted by Roger Gorski and Laura Allen, as well as those done by Richard Pillard and James Weinrich.

Gorski and Allen were the first to observe that a cell group (INAH3) in the preoptic region of the hypothalamus was larger in men than in women. This led LeVay to investigate the relationship between the INAH3 and sexual orientation. LeVay found that just as the INAH3 was larger in men than in women, so it was also larger in heterosexual men than in homosexual men, leading him to speculate that this region of the hypothalamus might be responsible for sexual orientation in males.

Pillard and Weinrich are credited with the first modern studies of homosexuality within families. Pillard and Weinrich observed much higher correlations between the sexual orientation of identical twins and fraternal twins than among mere brothers. This tendency was confirmed by Dean Hammer, among others, who also claimed that there was evidence that the genetic link between gay men and their gay male relatives was through the mother's line. This led Hammer to suggest that the genetic marker for male homosexuality might be located on the X chromosome, more specifically the Xq28 region. Exactly why the Xq28 region might influence sexual orientation remains speculative, but one of the possibilities mentioned by LeVay and Hammer is the possibility that "the Xq28 gene product bears directly on the development of sexually dimorphic brain regions such as INAH3." (Simon Levay and Dean H. Hamer. "Evidence for a Biological Influence in Male Homosexuals," *Scientific American*, May, 1994, p.49.)

Thus, as was the case at the dawn of the early homosexual rights movement, contemporary medical etiologies of homosexuality are once again focused on biology. The results of contemporary genetic research into homosexuality, however, have been as problematic as previous biological and psychological etiologies. There is no greater consensus today concerning the causes of homosexuality than there was 100 years ago. Biological and psychological models abound, but there is no generally accepted explanation of homosexuality in the medical community.

Similarly, there has never been a consensus concerning the intrinsic relevance of medicine to an understanding of homosexuality, and the advent of genetic research has done little to allay the suspicions of those who feel that homosexuality is far from a medical condition and is instead a cultural or ethical alternative to heterosexuality. This point of view also boasts an extensive history. Scholars of sexuality such as Vern Bullough, Michel Foucault, and Judith Butler; notable gay and lesbian leaders such as Karl Maria Kertbeny and Adolph Brand; Gay Liberation Front (qq.v.) activists; and contemporary leaders such as Urvashi Vaid have all questioned the veracity of the medical model of homosexuality. Thus, to a great extent, the scholarly community as well as the gay and lesbian liberation movement have been polarized over the scientific validity and political efficacy of the medical model of homosexuality. This polarization has irrevocably affected the goals and strategies of the movement.

METROPOLITAN COMMUNITY CHURCH. Founded in Los Angeles by the Reverend Troy Perry in 1968 to serve the needs of homosexual Christians. The organization grew rapidly: The first meeting took place in Troy Perry's house, but the initial response was so great that meetings were soon relocated to other venues to accommodate the large number of gays and lesbians who wanted to attend services. Within nine months of the initial meeting, the church had elected a board of directors, established an office, and put Perry on the payroll. Its rapid expansion continued with the creation of a wide range of support services, such as a legal and medical referral service, a hotline, and a youth group. The nationwide press coverage of the organization led to the formation of Metropolitan Community Church groups in cities around the United States, and, in 1970, the formation of the Universal Fellowship of Metropolitan Community Churches to coordinate their activities. In 1971, the church moved out of its temporary quarters into its first church building.

Beginning with the establishment of Metropolitan Community Churches in San Francisco, Chicago, San Diego, Miami, Dallas, Phoenix, and Honolulu, the Universal Fellowship of Metropolitan Community Churches spread rapidly around the United States and are now found in 45 of the 50 states. In 1973, London became the site of the first Metropolitan Community Church outside of the United States, only a year after an address by Troy Perry sponsored by the Committee for Homosexual Equality (q.v.). Shortly thereafter, churches were founded in Canada and in Australia (owing to the efforts of the Campaign against Moral Persecution [q.v.]). Universal

Fellowship of Metropolitan Community Churches can now also be found in Denmark, Indonesia, Mexico, New Zealand, and Nigeria. In 1998, the first African American conference of the Universal Fellowship of the Metropolitan Community Churches took place in the United States.

Aside from providing services for gay and lesbian Christians, the Metropolitan Community Church has participated in numerous political activities on behalf of the rights of gays and lesbians. The MCC is a cosponsor of the "Millennium March on Washington," scheduled for the year 2000.

MIDDLE EAST. The gay liberation movement does not exist in the Middle East, although covert organizations might exist. Very strong social and religious taboos against homosexuality are operative throughout the region, even though the region has a history of male homosexuality and contemporary reports of homosexuality abound. Most Middle Eastern states apply Islamic law, which views homosexuality as a sin and which proscribes the practice. Even in states where Islamic law is not the basis of the secular legal code, proscriptions are common. Laws against homosexuality exist in Iran, Jordan, Kuwait, Lebanon, Libya, Oman, Qatar, Saudi Arabia, United Arab Emirates, and Yemen. Notable exceptions include Egypt, Iraq, Israel, and Turkey.

Even where not legally proscribed, homosexuality is taboo. Thus, for example, in Egypt, where the practice of male homosexuality has persisted for centuries, the subject is not discussed in public, and networks of male homosexuals are rarely noted. The words of a recent visitor to Cairo sum up the situation succinctly: "In this, the most cosmopolitan city in the Arab world, there were no gay organizations or gay bars. It was unusual for someone to refer to himself as 'gay' or even 'homosexual,' and generally indicated the speaker had lived for many years in the West. There was no women's movement to speak of in Cairo, either." (Neil Miller. *Out in the World.* New York: Random House, 1992, p. 70.)

In Turkey, where there are also no legal proscriptions pertaining to homosexual intercourse, an international conference of gay and lesbian rights leaders was suppressed by the authorities, there are reports of police persecution of gays and lesbians, and one of the nation's leading gay rights leaders, Ibrahim Eren (q.v.), has been imprisoned on two occasions.

The situation is little better in Israel. Until 1988, male homosexual intercourse was punishable under Article 351 of the Israeli Penal Code, a legacy of the British occupation. Although it fell into disuse in the 1960s, it was not rescinded by the Knesset until 1988. Few social outlets exist for either gays or lesbians, however, and the first Israeli gay and lesbian rights organization, the Society for the Protection of Personal Rights, was not founded until 1975, ironically, in New York. Unlike other Middle Eastern countries, however, in Israel there are signs of progress. Gays and lesbians are accepted in the military service (q.v.) and, since 1992, have enjoyed statutory protection from discrimination in the job market.

MILITARY SERVICE. Together with the extension of civil rights (q.v.) to gays and lesbians, as well as marriage (q.v.) rights, the contemporary gay and lesbian movement has worked to achieve the rights of gays and lesbians to serve in the military.

Generally speaking, the countries where gays and lesbians have achieved the right to serve in the armed forces are those countries where gays and lesbians have achieved more comprehensive civil rights protections. Thus, for example, gays and lesbians serve in the armed forces of Australia, Canada, Denmark, France, the Netherlands, Norway, and Sweden, all of which have statutes prohibiting discrimination on the basis of sexual orientation. But gays and lesbians also serve in the armed forces of countries where they have yet to achieve full civil rights, such as Germany, Finland, Israel, Spain, and Switzerland.

In the United States, the first attempt to extend to gays and lesbians the right of military service was undertaken by Bill Clinton during the 1992 presidential campaign. After his election, President Clinton proposed that the military ban on the recruitment of homosexuals be ended. However, strong opposition to Clinton's proposal surfaced among the members of the Joint Chiefs of Staff, especially from the Chairman Colin Powell, and from members of the Senate Armed Services Committee and its Chair Senator Sam Nunn. When it appeared to Clinton that the Congress would not support his proposal, the president agreed to a compromise that has come to be known as the "Don't Ask, Don't Tell" (q.v.) policy. Gays and lesbians have challenged the constitutionality of this policy in the federal courts, but there has yet to be a definitive ruling from the Supreme Court on this issue.

MILK, HARVEY (1930–1978). The first openly gay man elected to the San Francisco Board of Supervisors, and reputedly the first openly gay man elected to public office in the United States. Milk's election to the San Francisco Board of Supervisors (San Francisco City Council) in 1977 was the culmination of his fourth campaign for public office. He ran unsuccessfully for supervisor in 1973 and in 1975. Shortly after his 1975 defeat, he lost a Democratic Party primary to Art Agnos for a seat in the California Assembly.

Milk was born in Woodmere, New York, and lived most of his life on the East Coast before migrating to San Francisco. He served in the U.S. Navy during the Korean War, and worked as a financial analyst on Wall Street, later as a producer on Broadway. His political concerns stemmed from his involvement in the antiwar movement during the Vietnam War and his interest in the Watergate scandal that resulted in the resignation of President Richard Nixon.

Milk ran his campaigns for supervisor out of a camera store that he owned with his companion and business partner Scott Smith in the Castro district of San Francisco. His election to the Board of Supervisors in 1977 was a reflection of the growing political influence of San Francisco's burgeoning gay and lesbian population. As early as 1961, San Francisco witnessed its first openly gay candidate for supervisor, José Sarria. The 1960s also witnessed the impact of increasingly militant gay and lesbian political organizations, such as the Society for Individual Rights and the Gay Liberation Front (qq.v.). Gays and lesbians became increasingly visible and politically active during the 1960s, especially after the 1969 Stonewall (q.v.) riots in New York City.

Harvey Milk's two greatest accomplishments during his brief 11 months as supervisor were the enactment of a gay and lesbian civil rights (q.v.) ordinance in San Francisco and the defeat of Proposition Six, better known as the Briggs Initiative. The civil rights ordinance Milk sponsored was enacted in 1978; it protected the rights of gays and lesbians in housing, public accommodations, and employment. The Briggs Initiative, a ballot initiative proposed by State Senator John Briggs, attempted to prohibit gays and lesbians from teaching in the California public school system. Under Milk's leadership the "No on Six" campaign was successful. Proposition Six was defeated by California voters in the November elections by a wide margin.

Shortly after the defeat of the Briggs Initiative, Harvey Milk and San Francisco Mayor George Moscone were assassinated by Supervisor Dan White. White had cast the only vote in opposition to the gay and lesbian civil rights bill and was demoralized by the increasingly liberal tenor of city hall politics in San Francisco. White resigned from the Board of Supervisors shortly after the enactment of the aforementioned legislation. Within a few days, however, he petitioned Mayor Moscone for reinstatement as supervisor. When it became apparent to White that Moscone was not going to reappoint him to the Board of Supervisors, he entered City Hall on 27 November and shot both the mayor and his archenemy Harvey Milk. Thus ended the mercurial political career of the first openly gay male elected official in the United States.

Named in honor of the slain civil rights leader, the Harvey Milk Gay Democratic Club remains active in Bay Area politics. In January 1998, *Harvey Milk,* an opera based on Milk's life and career, premiered in Houston, Texas.

MOSCOW UNION OF LESBIANS AND HOMOSEXUALS (MULH). *See* SEXUAL MINORITIES ASSOCIATION.

N

NATIONAL FEDERATION OF HOMOPHILE ORGANIZA-TIONS (NFHO). The National Federation of Homophile Organizations (NFHO) was the by-product of the 1970 York Social Needs Conference, cosponsored by the Yorkshire Council of Social Service and the Albany Trust (AT) (q.v.). The 1970 meeting at York University included representatives of most British homophile organizations and selected representatives from the clergy, social work, and education. Its purpose was to assess the continuing needs of gays and lesbians in the aftermath of the 1967 Sexual Offenses Act (q.v.). Although the 1967 statute had liberalized the criminal law in England and Wales pertaining to gay men, it remained highly punitive, and gays and lesbians remained objects of derision.

One of the decisions of the conference was to create a national organization of homophile groups to address issues of relevance to gays and lesbians in a centralized and coordinated fashion. The NFHO was created in 1971, and Antony Grey (q.v.) became its first chair.

The approach of the NFHO to counseling was in stark contrast to that of Icebreakers, an antipsychiatry group associated with the Gay Liberation Front (GLF) (q.v.). The GLF was suspicious of professional counselors because of psychiatry's historical association of homosexuality with mental illness. Icebreakers consisted of untrained gays and lesbians who sought to help isolated homosexuals adjust to life as a gay or lesbian, whereas the AT took a more conventional approach to counseling, and relied on professionals.

The influence of the GLF and its philosophy was at a high-water mark in the early 1970s, and these differences, along with the impatience of some constituent groups of the NFHO with its cumbersome constitutional structure, caused irreparable conflicts. Like its U.S. counterpart, the North American Congress of Homophile Organizations (q.v.), the NFHO disintegrated soon after its formation, in large part because of the growing influence of the GLF. When the Scottish Minorities Group and the Campaign for Homosexual Equality (qq.v.) left in 1973, the NFHO effectively came to an end.

NATIONAL GAY AND LESBIAN TASK FORCE (NGLTF). *See* NATIONAL GAY TASK FORCE.

NATIONAL GAY TASK FORCE (NGTF). The NGTF was founded in New York City, in 1973, by Martin Duberman, Barbara Gittings, and Frank Kameny (q.v.), among others; its first executive director was Dr. Bruce Voeller. The NGTF operated out of its Greenwich Village location until 1986 when it moved its national office to Washington, D.C., and changed its name to the National Gay and Lesbian Task Force (NGLTF). The NGLTF subsequently embraced the interests of bisexuals and transgendered people. In 1998 the NGLTF celebrated its 25th anniversary, making it the oldest U.S. gay, lesbian, bisexual, and transgendered rights organization in existence.

Like the Human Rights Campaign (HRC) (q.v.), the NGLTF has a broad agenda. It recruits and trains political activists, stages conferences, and publishes works of interest to lesbians, gays, bisexuals, and transgendered people. Its primary focus is the legislative process at the state and national level, where the NGLTF has worked to defeat legislation inimical to the interests of its members, such as the Defense of Marriage Act (q.v.), and to promote favorable legislation, such as the Employment Non-Discrimination Act (q.v.), the expansion of federal hate crimes legislation to include sexual minorities, and the Domestic Partnership Benefits and Obligations Act of 1997, which would make same-sex and opposite-sex partners of federal employees eligible for benefits heretofore reserved to married spouses. The NGLTF will serve as the coordinator of the Federation of Statewide Lesbian, Gay, Bisexual, and Transgendered groups, which is working to sponsor the 1999 "Equality Begins at Home" campaign to focus the attention of gay political activity on statehouses around the country.

The NGLTF has also worked with groups such as the Lambda Legal Defense and Education Fund on legal battles of concern to gays and lesbians, such as *Bowers v. Hardwick*, *Romer v. Evans*, and *Baehr v. Lewin* (qq.v). Finally, as a member of the Leadership Conference on Civil Rights, the NGLTF has worked to fight discrimination and to expand opportunities for racial minorities and women, thus broadening its agenda to embrace a full range of civil rights (q.v.) issues. Perhaps more than any other current gay and lesbian rights organization, the NGLTF has attempted to forge a broad coalition among a variety of marginalized groups, an objective first articulated in the United States by the Gay Liberation Front (q.v.). This represents the newest stage in the evolution of gay and lesbian rights organizing, and it remains to be seen whether (or to what extent) such broad coalitions can cooperate effectively in the civil rights arena.

NEDERLANDSCH WETENSCHAPPELIJK-HUMANITAIR KOMITEE / DUTCH SCIENTIFIC-HUMANITARIAN COMMITTEE (DSHC). Founded in 1911 by Jacob Anton Schorer, the DSHC emulated the principles of Magnus Hirschfeld's Wissenschaftlich-humanitäres Komitee (Scientific-Humanitarian Committee [SHC]) (qq.v.).

France's imposition of the Napoleonic Code in the Netherlands in 1811 had a profound effect on the regulation of sexual relations. Among other things, sodomy, which had theretofore been the object of severe criminal penalties, was decriminalized. Although criminal penalties prohibiting sexual relations between adults and minors were reintroduced in 1886, sexual relations between consenting adults, regardless of sexual orientation, remained beyond the purview of the law.

The emergence of a Christian political coalition at the turn of the century, however, eventually succeeded in imposing legislation intended to limit the spread of homosexuality. Led by Calvinists and Roman Catholics, the Dutch government enacted Article 248bis, in 1911, which changed the age of consent for homosexual relations (lesbians and gay men alike) from 16 to 21. Sixteen remained the age of consent for heterosexual relations. It was this act that provided the impetus for the formation of the DSHC.

From its founding in 1911 until 1940, the DSHC led the fight against Article 248bis and the reimposition of sodomy laws governing adults. Like the SHC, the DSHC attempted to influence the course of events by enlisting the support of influential citizens, jurists, medical doctors, scientists, and so forth, in the hope that a rational discourse on sexual orientation would result in enlightened legislation. Similar to the SHC's campaign against Paragraph 175 in Germany, the DSHC also relied in part on a petition drive to influence the course of parliamentary debate. Progress toward the repeal of 248bis, however, was negligible. Prosecutions steadily increased over the next three decades until the German invasion of the Netherlands in 1940 suspended the effort to repeal 248bis. The Nazis reinstituted criminal punishments for sex between adult men and dissolved the DSHC shortly thereafter.

The DSHC did not reemerge after the war, but its place was taken by the emergence of another homosexual rights group, the Cultuur-en-Ontspannings Centrum (Culture and Recreational Center) (q.v.) in 1946. One of the DSHC's objectives was realized when the government adopted the recommendations of the Speijer Report (q.v.) and equalized the age of consent for homosexuals and heterosexuals in 1971.

NEDERLANDSE VERENIGING TOT INTEGRATIE VAN HOMOSEKSUALITEIT COC/NETHERLANDS ASSOCIATION FOR THE INTEGRATION OF HOMOSEXUALITY COC. *See* CULTUUR-EN-ONTSPANNINGS CENTRUM (CULTURE AND RECREATIONAL CENTER).

NEW ZEALAND. *See* AUSTRALIA/NEW ZEALAND.

NEW ZEALAND HOMOSEXUAL LAW REFORM SOCIETY (NZHLRS). *See* DORIAN SOCIETY.

NKOLI, SIMON (1961–). Prominent South African gay rights leader, founder of the Gay and Lesbian Organization of the Witwatersrand (GLOW) (q.v.), the Gay Men's Health Forum, and member of the African National Congress (ANC).

Active in the antiapartheid struggle as a student leader in the Congress of South African Students, Nkoli brought his zeal for racial equality to the Gay Association of South Africa (GASA) (q.v.). Nkoli came out as a gay man in 1981. He joined GASA two years later and committed himself to integrating the predominantly white group and reorienting its apolitical focus.

Although he succeeded in attracting blacks to GASA, Nkoli's efforts were frustrated by racial tensions within the group. He formed the Saturday Group, an independent organization of black gays and lesbians in 1984. Although the Saturday Group was affiliated with GASA, his objective of integrating GASA and aligning it with other antiapartheid forces failed. Nkoli's arrest on 23 September 1984, after a rent boycott demonstration, caused the collapse of the Saturday Group.

His arrest also provoked a crisis within GASA. The reticence of GASA to support Nkoli during his detention and ultimate indictment for murder contributed to the disintegration of the organization in 1986. The International Lesbian and Gay Association (q.v.) voted to expel the group for its failure to support the antiapartheid movement and Simon Nkoli's cause, and GASA ceased to exist as a national organization a short time later.

Nkoli founded GLOW shortly after his acquittal on murder

charges in 1986. Unlike previous gay and lesbian rights organizations in South Africa, GLOW's purpose was predominantly political. It was interracial, and it took a forthright position in opposition to apartheid. Although it also promoted social functions and served as a social support system for its members, GLOW succeeded in wedding the struggle for gay and lesbian rights with the struggle for racial justice. A longtime member of the ANC, Nkoli deserves much of the credit for the ANC's support of gay and lesbian rights and the incorporation of gay and lesbian civil rights (q.v.) in the 1996 Constitution of South Africa.

NORTH AMERICA. As was the case with Europe (q.v.), early on the United States produced authors such as Earl Lind and Xavier Mayne (qq.v.) whose works protested the social and political plight of homosexuals. There was even an attempt to found a gay rights organization in the United States modeled on the Bund für Menschenrechte (League for Human Rights) (q.v.), an early German homosexual rights group. But, unlike its German namesake, the Society for Human Rights (q.v.) was shortlived and attracted little or no attention. Thus, whereas the homosexual rights movement began in Europe during the 1860s with the protests of such individuals as Karl Heinrich Ulrichs and Karl Maria Kertbeny (qq.v.) and the 1897 foundation of the Wissenschaftlich-humanitäres Komitee (Scientific-Humanitarian Committee) (q.v.), the American movement did not begin in earnest until the emergence of organizations such as the Veterans Benevolent Association and the Mattachine Society (MS) (qq.v.) after World War II.

Between the foundation of the MS in 1951 and Stonewall (q.v.) in 1969 organizations such as the MS and early Canadian organizations—such as the Association for Social Knowledge (ASK) (q.v.)—fought to establish groups where gays and lesbians could socialize, develop friendships, and exchange information. Although these organizations also engaged in a limited range of political activities, such as opposition to sodomy statutes (q.v.) in the United States and Canada, they were not overtly political in comparison with contemporary gay and lesbian rights organizations.

Stonewall changed the character of the gay rights movement. The revolutionary zeal of the Gay Liberation Front (q.v.) transformed gay and lesbian organizations into a political movement of millions of individuals. Shortly after Stonewall, U.S. organizations such as the Gay Activist Alliance (q.v.) began to press not only for rescinding sodomy statutes but also for civil rights (q.v.) ordinances protecting the rights of gays and lesbians in housing, employment, and public accommodations. Today, in the United States, groups such as the National Gay and Lesbian Task Force and the Human Rights Campaign Fund (qq.v.) continue the work begun 30 years ago on behalf of the civil rights of gays and lesbians. In Canada, similar initiatives have been undertaken by such organizations as the Coalition for Gay Rights in Ontario (q.v.).

The process of enacting human rights protections for lesbians and gays has proceeded much more quickly in Canada than in the United States. Whereas in the United States only 10 states and 150 cities and counties offer degrees of civil rights protection to gays and lesbians, most Canadian provinces have such statutes, and gays and lesbians enjoy federal guarantees that do not exist in the United States. Furthermore, Canadian gays and lesbians may enlist openly for military service (q.v.), something that has yet to be achieved south of the border.

Thus, in the Americas, Canada is the only nation abreast of the most progressive European nations. Europe remains far ahead of the Americas, however, in the extension of marriage (q.v.) rights to gays and lesbians. In no jurisdiction in the Americas can gays or lesbians be legally married. *See also Baehr v. Lewin*; Canadian Charter of Rights and Freedoms.

NORTH AMERICAN CONFERENCE OF HOMOPHILE ORGA-NIZATIONS (NACHO). In February 1966 members of 15 U.S. homosexual rights organizations (the National Planning Conference of Homophile Organizations) met in Kansas City, Kansas. Their agenda was to create a unified national organization to lead the homosexual rights movement. A subsequent meeting in San Francisco in August resulted in the creation of the North American Conference of Homophile Organizations. NACHO was a loose federation of homophile organizations, not the single unified group envisioned by those who originally met in Kansas City. Nevertheless, it did succeed in accomplishing many common objectives.

There were three regional affiliates of NACHO. The most active was the Eastern Regional Conference of Homophile Organizations (ERCHO) (q.v.); there were also western and midwestern regional conferences. Through these regional conferences NACHO was able to seed homosexual rights organizations in locations where none had previously existed, such as in Syracuse, New York, and Cincinnati, Ohio. NACHO also produced two legal studies on the status of homosexuals in the United States: *The Challenge and Progress of Homosexual Law Reform* in 1968, and *Homosexuals and Employment* in 1970. It coordinated the first simultaneous demonstrations in U.S. cities protesting the treatment of gays and lesbians by the federal government and the military and established a legal fund to finance attacks on various aspects of discrimination. Finally, at its 1968 national conference, NACHO crystallized its strident opposition to psychiatry's categorization of homosexuality as a mental illness by adopting "Gay Is Good" as a movement slogan. Like ERCHO, NACHO can be seen as a bridge between pre-Stonewall (q.v.) and post-Stonewall gay rights activism. NACHO became a forum for those who were interested in direct action as well as legal challenges to discrimination. But, like ERCHO, NACHO did not survive the challenges posed by the Gay Liberation Front (GLF) (q.v.). Not only did the GLF advocate increasingly confrontational tactics, but it also advocated a common front against a wide variety of oppressions. This caused a split in NACHO between those who felt that NACHO should remain a single-issue group and supporters of the GLF who advocated building alliances with other groups. The 1970 NACHO convention was riven with disputes and a struggle for power between the more mainstream members and those in the Radical Caucus. Although plans were made for a convention in 1971, the 1970 convention was its last. NACHO had disintegrated and with it the hopes for a national organization to defend the interests of gays and lesbians.

O

ONE INC. One Inc. was created in the autumn of 1952 in Los Angeles by activists associated with the Mattachine Society (MS) (q.v.) and the Knights of the Clock.

The founders' first objective was the publication of a magazine catering to the interests of gays and lesbians. Martin Bloc and Dale Jennings were its first editors. The first edition appeared in January 1953, and the magazine remained in print until 1968. *One Magazine: The Homosexual Viewpoint* competed for subscribers with the *Mattachine Review* (q.v.) and the *Ladder*, publications of the MS and the Daughters of Bilitis (DOB). At its height in the mid-1960s its circulation surpassed that of either of its two main competitors.

One Magazine was conceived in the midst of an internecine struggle between the founders of MS, led by Harry Hay (q.v.), and a more conservative faction headed by Hal Call and Marilyn Reiger. The founders of the MS viewed homosexuals as a legitimate minority group and advocated the creation of a homosexual culture as an alternative to heterosexuality. Call and Reiger believed that homosexuals and heterosexuals differed only in their sexual preference and could best advance their interests through assimilation.

At the May 1953 MS convention, the founders of the organization were ousted. Hay's communist affiliations and his militant homosexual rights agenda proved to be out of step with the rank and file of the MS. Call and Reiger charted a much more conservative course for the MS, using legal, psychiatric, and social work professionals to educate the public and to speak on behalf of homosexuals.

Because most of the board of directors of *One Magazine* were either cofounders of the MS or sympathetic with its original goals, *One Magazine* often found itself in opposition to the MS. *One Magazine* was also publicly opposed to the DOB's ideology whose assimilationist objectives paralleled those of the MS. *One Magazine* consistently advocated civil rights (q.v.) policies as the answer to the discrimination faced by gays and lesbians. Nevertheless, members of the MS, DOB, and One Inc. attended each others' annual conventions and collaborated on a number of issues.

Less than two years after its first edition, the October 1954 issue of *One Magazine* was impounded by the Los Angeles postmaster on the grounds that it constituted an obscene publication. The ensuing litigation initiated by One Inc. resulted in a 1958 U.S. Supreme Court decision sustaining One's contention that the impoundment constituted a violation of the freedom of the press. This decision remains one of the most important legal victories for the homosexual rights movement in the United States, because it eliminated an important impediment to the publication of information crucial to its survival.

The demise of *One Magazine* was precipitated in 1965 by a dispute between the editor, Don Slater, and the business manager, Dorr Legg, over the future direction of the organization. With the board of directors evenly divided, Slater appropriated the library, business records, and miscellany of the corporation for himself and his followers. The ensuing civil suits left the organization's assets evenly divided between the contending parties. For a brief time two *One Magazine*s were published. Eventually, Slater renamed his publication *Tangents* and founded an alternative organization, the Homosexual Information Center.

One Magazine ceased publication in 1968. It was briefly revived in 1972 but did not survive. However, chapters of One Inc., including the highly successful and now formally independent One of Long Beach, still serve gays and lesbians around the country.

Other successful projects of One Inc. include the annual Midwinter Institutes, which have served as an important forum for the exchange of information; the Institute of Homophile Studies, a forerunner of contemporary gay and lesbian studies programs; and the Institute for the Study of Human Resources, a tax-exempt research foundation. In 1981 the Institute of Homophile Studies and the Institute for the Study of Human Resources were authorized by the California State Board of Education to confer M.A. and Ph.D. degrees in the field of homophile studies. The many and varied activities of One Inc. continue in the 1990s.

ORDER OF CHAERONEA. A secret British society of homosexual rights activists dating from the mid-1890s. The Order of Chaeronea took its name from the battle between the Macedonians and the Athenians on the plains of Chaeronea in 338 B.C. Here, so it is told, the Sacred Band of Thebes (Band of Lovers) fought to the death against Philip of Macedon for the liberty of Athens. Hence, the organization's adopted name symbolized the struggle for homosexual rights.

Born in the oppressive environment of Victorian England, the Order of Chaeronea's secrecy was the result of antihomosexual legislation such as the Labouchère Amendment (q.v.) and the notorious trials of Oscar Wilde (q.v.). In such an environment a support and advocacy group such as this one would have become the object of police surveillance, making the confidentiality of its membership a necessity.

The society's chief significance lies in the connection of its members with other organizations that played a role in fighting for the rights of gays and lesbians in Britain. Although little is known about its internal proceedings, the identities of some of its members are now known. For example, the two principal figures in the Order of Chaeronea, Laurence Housman and Charles Cecil Ives (qq.v.) were active in the British Society for the Study of Sex Psychology (q.v.), an organization that did much to promote the cause of homosexual rights. Thus, the Order of Chaeronea indirectly contributed to the cause of gay and lesbian rights through fostering interconnections between its members and other better-established institutions.

OSVOBOZHDENIE (LIBERATION). *See* SEXUAL MINORITIES ASSOCIATION.

P

PARAGRAPH 175. Enacted shortly after the consolidation of the modern German state in 1871, Paragraph 175 of the German legal code criminalized sodomy between men. The repeal of Paragraph 175 was the primary objective of the early homosexual rights movement in Germany (1864–1935), an objective that was reiterated by homosexual rights activists after World War II in both the Federal

Republic of Germany (FRG) and the German Democratic Republic (GDR).

Paragraph 175 derived from Prussia's Paragraph 143 and Paragraph 152 of the North German Federation. Prussia had a long history of criminalizing sexual relations between men. Paragraph 143 imposed criminal penalties of up to four years' imprisonment for homosexual acts between men.

Prussian expansionism in the wake of its success in the Austro-Prussian War led to the formation of the Prussian-dominated North German Federation in 1866. Despite the efforts of such individuals as Karl Heinrich Ulrichs, Karl Maria Kertbeny (qq.v.), and Carl von Westphal and the opposition of the prestigious Royal Prussian Deputation for Public Health, Paragraph 143 was imposed on other members of the federation and subsequently became the basis for Paragraph 152 of the North German Federation.

With the consolidation of modern Germany in 1871, Paragraph 175 supplanted 143 and 152. Paragraph 175, which remained on the statute books for roughly a century, penalized sexual relationships between men with imprisonment. A 1911 attempt to extend 175's provisions to lesbians failed.

Opposition to 175 was led by two prominent homosexual rights groups, the Wissenschaftlich-humanitäres Komitee (Scientific Humanitarian Committee [SHC]) and the Gemeinschaft der Eigenen (Community of the Special [COS]); their respective leaders Magnus Hirschfeld and Adolf Brand (qq.v.); and several coalitions, including the Aktionsausschuss (Action Committee) (q.v.), and the Kartell für Reform des Sexualstrafrechts (Coalition for the Reform of the Sexual Crimes Code). From its inception in 1897 until its demise in 1933, the SHC and Magnus Hirschfeld led the fight to repeal Paragraph 175 in the Reichstag.

Although repeal seemed imminent in 1928, the ensuing economic depression overshadowed all other business, and the Reichstag tabled further consideration of 175. With the rise of the Nazi Party to power after the 1932 elections, homosexual rights advocates lost all influence over the course of events. In 1935, 175 was supplemented by 175a, which broadened the definition of sexual offenses. Paragraph 175 referred only to oral and anal intercourse between men (and bestiality). Paragraph 175a included acts of sexual foreplay, importuning others to commit such acts, and public indecency. Penalties ranged from three months' to 10 years' imprisonment. Although the extension of criminal penalties for sodomy to lesbians was debated within the Nazi Party at this time, the Nazis continued to restrict sodomy prosecutions to male homosexuals. Punishment for bestiality was relegated to 175b.

Paragraphs 175 and 175a were used by the Nazis to incarcerate thousands of homosexual men in concentration camps. They were forced to wear the insignia of a pink triangle (q.v.) to distinguish them from other inmates. Estimates of the total number of pink triangles vary widely; most estimates put the total between 5,000 and 15,000. Thousands more homosexuals served sentences in civilian prisons.

After Germany's defeat in 1945, a new generation of homosexual rights activists called for the deletion of Paragraphs 175 and 175a from the statutes of the GDR and the FRG. But it was not until 1968 that the campaign to repeal Germany's sodomy statutes (q.v.) began to yield results. The GDR decriminalized private sexual relations between adults in 1968; the FRG followed suit in 1969.

Most recently, the reunification of the FRG and the GDR spawned negotiations to eliminate the last vestige of Paragraph 175, the unequal age of consent laws (q.v.) in East and West Germany. Whereas the GDR equalized the age of consent for homosexual and heterosexual sexual relations at 16, the FRG retained the provisions of Paragraph 175, in which the age of consent for homosexual relations was 18, though the corresponding heterosexual age of consent was 16. The reunification of East and West Germany, in 1989 led to renewed demands for the repeal of the unequal age of consent in the FRG and, in 1991, the FRG consented to the provisions of the GDR statute. Thus, the long history of Paragraph 175 came to an end. Ironically, the age of consent law governing the reunified Germany includes lesbians for the first time in the history of the German nation state. *See also* Sodomy Statutes.

PARENTS AND FRIENDS OF LESBIANS AND GAYS (PFLAG). Founded in 1981 in the United States, PFLAG serves as both a social support network and a political advocacy group for gays, lesbians, bisexuals, and their families and friends. It now claims affiliates in more than 380 communities across the United States as well as in 11 other countries.

Among its most recent political initiatives were its efforts on behalf of the anti-Amendment 2 campaign in Colorado, its efforts to defeat the passage of the Defense of Marriage Act (DOMA) (q.v.), and Project Open Mind.

Although its efforts to prevent the enactment of Amendment 2 to the Colorado Constitution were unsuccessful, PFLAG's opposition to Amendment 2 was eventually upheld by the U.S. Supreme Court in *Romer v. Evans* (q.v.). Thus, the effort to nullify existing as well as prospective gay and lesbian civil rights (q.v.) protections in Colorado, was defeated by a coalition of gay and lesbian organizations.

PFLAG played a prominent role in this strategic battle. PFLAG's opposition to the DOMA, in 1996, however, failed to prevent the enactment of the first federal statute defining marriage (q.v.). The DOMA's passage restricts the legal definition of marriage to heterosexual couples. PFLAG is hoping that the DOMA, like Colorado Amendment 2, will be overturned in the federal courts.

Project Open Mind was initiated by PFLAG in Atlanta, Georgia, Tulsa, Oklahoma, and Houston, Texas, in 1995. The purpose of the project was to sponsor ads to counteract the effects of hate speech directed against gays and lesbians and to act as a spearhead for PFLAG's outreach programs in these communities. The initial success of Project Open Mind led PFLAG to extend its efforts in 1996 to Minneapolis, Minnesota, St. Louis, Missouri, and Seattle, Washington. Many social organizations, businesses, and local politicians have endorsed the project and contributed funds in support of PFLAG activities.

PERRY, REV. TROY (1940–   ). *See* METROPOLITAN COMMUNITY CHURCH.

PINK TRIANGLES. Insignia worn by homosexual men interned in German concentration camps during the Nazi regime.

Homosexual intercourse between men had been forbidden by the German criminal code since the adoption of Paragraph 175 (q.v.) in 1871. The rise of the Nazi Party, however, posed an even greater threat to the security and well-being of gay men than did the statutory penalties contained in Paragraph 175.

As early as 1928, the Nazi Party proclaimed its opposition to homosexuality in response to a questionnaire mailed to party headquarters by Adolf Brand (q.v.). The movement to rescind Paragraph 175 was at its peak, and Brand was canvassing the major political parties in preparation for the final stages of parliamentary debate. Overtly hostile to the idea, the Nazi Party declared its support of Paragraph 175, associating homosexuality with degeneracy, frailty, and a lack of patriotism.

Five years later, on 6 May 1933, a group of Nazi youth ransacked the building that housed Magnus Hirschfeld's Wissenschaftlich-humanitäres Komitee (Scientific Humanitarian Committee), the Institut für Sexualwissenschaft (Institute for Sexual Science), and the World League for Sexual Reform (qq.v.). Hirschfeld was a well-known sexologist and a leader of the German homosexual emancipation movement. The building was viewed as a den of iniquity by the Nazi Party, and its contents were burned in a public square three days later.

In June 1934 Ernst Röhm, chief of the Sturmabteilung (SA), was arrested at the Hotel Hanselbauer together with other high-ranking officers of the SA. Often referred to as the "Blood Purge" or the "Night of the Long Knives," the arrest and subsequent execution of Röhm and his colleagues is often attributed to his overt homosexuality and the threat he posed to Hitler's leadership of the Nazi Party.

Finally, in 1935, a revision of Paragraph 175 extended the range of sexual behavior deemed criminal. Paragraph 175a criminalized such acts as kissing, importuning, and possessing homoerotic literature. The number of arrests for violations of Paragraph 175a far exceeded the number of men prosecuted under 175. Furthermore, by 1936, prison sentences for violations of Paragraphs 175 and 175a were most often followed by incarceration in concentration camps.

Identifiable by the triangular pink cloth they were forced to wear on their lapels, homosexual men were often the most vilified prisoners in the camps. In addition to the thousands of "pink triangles" incarcerated because of violations of 175 and 175a, men suspected of homosexuality in the armed services, the police, the SS, and so forth, were also interned in concentration camps. After the outbreak of war, homosexual men in the occupied territories were also confined in the camps.

Estimates of the number of deaths vary widely. Most of the records were destroyed by the Schutzstaffel (SS) as the Allied armies advanced toward Germany in 1945. Aside from the inestimable numbers of gay men and lesbians who died at the hands of the SS for reasons other than their sexual orientation, the number of pink triangles who died in the work camps and gas chambers of Nazi Germany is most often put between 5,000 and 15,000.

Unlike other survivors of the Holocaust, who were financially compensated for their sufferings by the Federal Republic of Germany after World War II, pink triangles were excluded because they had been interned in the camps legally. The commemoration of the pink triangles has been one of the objectives of gay and lesbian rights leaders in Germany since the end of the war.

PRECIADO, PEDRO (1956–). The acknowledged leader of the Grupo de Orgullo Homosexual de Liberación (Group Pride for Homosexual Liberation [GPHL]) (q.v.) in Guadalajara, Mexico, from its founding in 1982.

The GPHL was founded shortly after the July 1982 national elections. Pedro Preciado and Lupita Garcia de Alba ran on the ticket of the Partido Revolucionario de los Trabajadores (PRT) as, respectively, openly gay and lesbian candidates for the National Chamber of Deputies. Preciado became interested in the gay and lesbian rights movement because of reports of the movement's emergence in Mexico City a few years earlier. Preciado and others organized a committee of gays and lesbians to promote the candidacy of Rosario Ibarra, PRT's candidate for the presidency. Preciado, Garcia de Alba, and two gay and lesbian candidates from Mexico City, were all defeated along with Ibarra in the 1982 elections. The GPHL was founded in response to the recriminations between gays and lesbians and the PRT following the electoral defeat.

Many gays and lesbians were offended by the association of the movement with the socialist politics of the PRT, and the PRT was criticized by some of its heterosexual supporters for its alliance with gays and lesbians. Thus, the Committee of Lesbians and Homosexuals in Support of Rosario Ibarra evolved into the GPHL and all ties with the PRT were suspended. Under Preciado's leadership, the GPHL became an independent gay and lesbian rights organization, the first such group in Guadalajara.

The candidacies of an openly gay man and a lesbian in Guadalajara created an immediate backlash. All gay bars were closed, and the police began a campaign of harassment. In response, Preciado organized a media campaign and street demonstrations. By 1983 city officials and the police relented, and bars began to reopen. It was at this time that Preciado decided to open a gay bar to help underwrite the activities of the GPHL, AIDS education in particular. Named Boops, the bar was on the ground floor of the house that served as the GPHL headquarters. Preciado and his lover lived in rooms adjacent to the GPHL's offices on the second floor for five years.

In 1988, a new mayor was elected to office. Once again, the GPHL found itself under attack. Gay bars, including Boops, were closed, and harassment of gays and lesbians resumed. Although Preciado was able to negotiate the reopening of some bars, Boops remained closed, and the environment for gays and lesbians in Guadalajara deteriorated. The loss of revenue from the bar also forced the GPHL to find new accommodations, and Preciado was forced to move. A major setback for the GPHL was the cancellation of the annual meeting of the International Lesbian and Gay Association (ILGA) (q.v.) scheduled for Guadalajara in 1991. The meeting had been arranged by Preciado, but local officials responded to criticism by the church and influential families and rescinded their agreement to allow the ILGA meeting to take place in Guadalajara. The meeting was forced to move at the last minute to Acapulco.

The GPHL's future is uncertain. In 1994, after years of struggle, Preciado and his lover, Jorge, opened another bar, which they hoped would generate sufficient profits to help finance GPHL activities.

Preciado is still the principal figure in the organization, though he has admitted to becoming weary of his leadership role.

R

RADICAL FAERIES. *See* HAY, HENRY (HARRY) JR.

RIKSFÖRBUNDET FÖR SEXUELLT LIKABERÄTTIGANDE/ NATIONAL ALLIANCE FOR SEXUAL EQUAL RIGHTS (NASER). Although there are a number of Swedish gay and lesbian organizations such as Homosexuella Socialister and EKHO, the NASER is the national gay and lesbian organization, with roughly two dozen chapters. The NASER also supports a youth group.

The NASER was instrumental in lobbying the Swedish Parliament to establish a commission in 1978 to make recommendations regarding the elimination of discrimination against gays and lesbians. Its recommendations were presented in 1984. Although the commission did not recommend the legalization of gay or lesbian marriage (q.v.) or the right of gay and lesbian couples to adopt children, it did recommend banning discrimination against homosexuals, granting political asylum to gays and lesbians, and subsidizing gay and lesbian organizations.

Based on the commission's recommendations, the Swedish Parliament enacted civil rights (q.v.) provisions in 1987. Similar to the groundbreaking 1981 civil rights legislation in Norway, the Swedish Parliament enacted laws prohibiting "hate speech" and the refusal to provide goods or services to gays and lesbians in the private sector.

Also based on the commission's recommendations, gay and lesbian couples were granted limited partnership rights in 1987. Because these rights stopped far short of the rights granted to married heterosexual couples, however, the NASER worked for the adoption of a partnership law similar to the Danish Registered Partnership Act (q.v.), a goal that was recently realized.

Prior to 1987, the Swedish government equalized the age of consent laws (q.v.) for heterosexuals and homosexuals (1978), declassified homosexuality as a disease (1979), and accepted gays and lesbians into the armed services (1979). It now funds gay and lesbian organizations such as the NASER.

Together with those of Norway and Denmark, Sweden's laws are among the most progressive in the world pertaining to the rights of lesbians and gays. In 1995, the three Scandinavian countries agreed to mutually recognize the rights of domestic partnerships formed in the respective countries.

ROBINSON, SVEND (1952–   ). "Liberation, pride, exhilaration, freedom all of these emotions and more I felt on the evening of February 29, 1988, when I spoke on Canadian national television to tell the nation that I am a member of Parliament who is a proud gay man." (Svend J. Robinson. "Coming Out as an MP in Canada," in *The Third Pink Book*, edited by Aart Hendricks, Rob Tielman, Evert van der Veen. Buffalo, New York: Prometheus Books, 181).

With those words, Svend Robinson became the first Member of Parliament in Canada to openly declare his homosexuality and one of only a very few openly gay politicians worldwide. Others include Representative Barney Frank in the United States and the British Member of Parliament Chris Smith (who in 1998 was appointed Secretary of State for Culture, Media, and Sport), but they are rare exceptions to the rule.

A member of the New Democratic Party, Robinson was first elected to represent the Burnaby-Kingsway district, British Columbia, in 1979. He is significant not only because he has forged a successful parliamentary career but because of his advocacy of gay and lesbian rights in Canada. As early as 1980, in the parliamentary debates over the Charter of Rights, Robinson unsuccessfully attempted to amend Section 15 of the proposed charter to include protections for the civil rights (q.v.) of gays and lesbians. He has also been a vocal supporter of other civil rights initiatives such as opening up the Canadian armed forces to the enlistment of gays and lesbians and the inclusion of gays and lesbians in the Canadian Human Rights Act, both of which represent milestones for gays and lesbians in Canada, and the world. *See also* Canadian Charter of Rights and Freedoms.

RÖMER, L. S. A. M. VON (1873–1965). Lucien Sophie Albert Marie von Römer, Arnold Aletrino, and Jacob Israël de Haan were among the first to speak in defense of homosexual love in the Netherlands. Aletrino was a physician and friend of Jacob de Haan, a poet and novelist. In 1901, Aletrino defended homosexuality as a sexual preference at the Fifth Congress for Criminal Anthropology and in a Dutch psychiatric journal, *Actes du Cinquième Congrès International d'Anthropologie Criminelle*. De Haan's 1904 homoerotic autobiographical novel, *Pijpelijntjes*, created a public scandal because of its subject material and because of its dedication to Aletrino, a married man.

Of the three, von Römer was the most significant. Von Römer was a physician who was acquainted with Magnus Hirschfeld (q.v.), the German sexologist and founder of the Wissenschaftlich-humanitäres Komitee (Scientific Humanitarian Committee [SHC]), (q.v.). Both von Römer and Hirschfeld knew the work of Karl Heinrich Ulrichs (q.v.), the pioneering homosexual rights advocate and author of the third sex theory (q.v.). Ulrichs had contended as early as the 1860s that homosexuals were biological anomalies, a third sex, and that homosexuality was tantamount to left-handedness. Like Hirschfeld, von Römer subscribed in general terms to the idea that homosexuality was a biological phenomenon. He collaborated with Hirschfeld and wrote for the *Jahrbuch für sexuelle Zwischenstufen* (Yearbook for Sexual Intermediates), the SHC's journal.

Before an audience of Christian socialists, the Reinlevenbeweging (Pure Life Movement), von Römer spoke openly of homosexual love which he argued was on a par with heterosexual love. This angered many, and von Römer's thesis was rebutted by Louis Heijermans in *De Nieuwe Tijd* (The New Age), a party organ of the Sociaaldemocratische Arbeiders Partij (Social Democratic Workers Party). This, in turn, provoked an exchange between von Römer and Heijermans in the pages of the magazine, where he again set forth his view that homosexuality was a natural instinct.

Von Römer's exchange with Heijermans in the pages of *De Nieuwe Tidj* took place at a time when the Dutch Parliament was debating the introduction of new laws restricting sexual expression. The parliamentary debates were characterized by a high degree of hostility to homosexuality, with little sympathy for the ideas of those such as von Römer. After numerous attempts to criminalize homosexual relations, Article 248bis was eventually passed in 1911. Introduced by the minister of justice, Edmond Regout, Article 248bis raised the age of consent for homosexual intercourse to 21, while leaving the corresponding age for heterosexual intercourse at 16. In response to this act of parliament, the Nederlandsch Wetenschappelijk-Humanitair Komitee (Dutch Scientific-Humanitarian Committee) was founded by Jacob Anton Schorer (qq.v.), a jurist and opponent of the growing animosity toward homosexuality in the Netherlands.

***ROMER V. EVANS* (1996).** In this historic decision, the U.S. Supreme Court ruled in a six-to-three decision that states may not prohibit the enactment of civil rights (q.v.) legislation protecting the rights of gays, lesbians, and bisexuals.

The increased militancy of gays and lesbians following the Stonewall (q.v.) riots in the United States took many forms. One was the movement to enact civil rights legislation to protect gays and lesbians from discrimination in employment, housing, and public accommodations. In 1974, a bill (HR 14752) was introduced in the House of Representatives to extend the civil rights protections of the 1964 Civil Rights Act to gays and lesbians, the first such piece of legislation in U.S. history. Neither this bill nor any subsequent piece of federal civil rights legislation has been enacted into law.

However, gay and lesbian activists have succeeded in enacting civil rights legislation at the state and local levels. Between 1972 and 1996, major metropolitan areas and counties, as well as smaller cities and towns, enacted laws providing degrees of civil rights protection for gays and lesbians. In addition, 10 states have enacted statewide legislation. Executive orders in 18 states and numerous municipal and county proclamations also provide degrees of protection to lesbian and gay citizens. This progress has not been without its setbacks. Many civil rights statutes have been overturned in referenda sponsored by such groups as the 1977 Save Our Children campaign in Dade County, Florida. Most recently, religious conservatives have countered the growing impetus to extend civil rights protections to gays and lesbians with a new legal strategy. In states such as Oregon and Colorado, groups such as Colorado for Family Values have promoted referenda and initiatives designed not only to repeal existing county, municipal, and state protections but also to prohibit the future enactment of similar legislation.

It was just such an initiative that occasioned the *Romer v. Evans* Supreme Court decision. Colorado Amendment 2, enacted by Colorado voters in 1992, provided for the repeal of existing civil rights protections in cities such as Denver and Boulder and forbade the enactment of similar legislation by the State of Colorado or any of its agencies, subdivisions, municipalities, and so forth. The passage of Colorado Amendment 2 was hailed by religious conservatives as the answer to the growing political influence of the gay and lesbian rights movement.

In overturning the initiative, the Supreme Court sustained a 1994 Colorado Supreme Court decision by declaring that Amendment 2 violated the constitutional rights of gays and lesbians to the equal protection of the laws. The broader impact of *Romer v. Evans* on the future of civil rights litigation for gays and lesbians, and its implications for the 1986 *Bowers v. Hardwick*, (q.v.) decision is uncertain.

S

SAMTÖKIN 78. Iceland's national gay and lesbian rights organization since 1978, Samtökin 78 is recognized by the government and receives government appropriations to help finance its activities. Samtökin 78 has advocated the elimination of all legal distinctions between homosexuals and heterosexuals and has attempted to counteract homophobic representations of gays and lesbians in Icelandic media.

Iceland's penal code does not criminalize gay or lesbian sexual relations. Thus, Samtökin 78 has focused its energies on other inequities in Icelandic law, such as the unequal age of consent for heterosexuals and homosexuals and the lack of domestic partnership legislation.

Until 1992, age of consent laws (q.v.) differed for heterosexuals and homosexuals; the age of consent for heterosexuals was 16, as it was for sexual relations between women; for gay men it was 18. In 1992, one of Samtökin 78's objectives was fulfilled when the Icelandic Parliament, the Altinget, legislated the equalization of the age of consent for all citizens regardless of sexual orientation. The age of consent in Iceland is now 14.

More recently, in 1996, the Altinget enacted legislation providing for registered partnerships between same-sex couples. The legislation was inspired by the Danish Registered Partnership Act (q.v.). Like the Danish law, Iceland's statute confers on gay and lesbian couples the same rights and responsibilities as married heterosexual couples, with the exception of adoption and insemination rights. Unlike the Danish law, however, Iceland's statute provides for joint custody of children, making it the most progressive domestic partnership act in the world.

Samtökin 78 is currently lobbying for the enactment of an antidiscrimination law similar to the trend-setting 1981 Norwegian antidiscrimination legislation.

SCHORER, JACOB ANTON (1866–1957). Jurist and founder of the Nederlandsch-Wetenschappelijk Humanitair Komitee (Dutch Scientific-Humanitarian Committee [DSHC]) (q.v.) in 1911.

Together with other outspoken supporters of the rights of homosexuals in the Netherlands, such as L. S. A. M. von Römer (q.v.), Jacob Schorer fought against the enactment of legislation that was intended to discriminate against homosexuals.

At the turn of the century, politics in the Netherlands was increasingly dominated by a coalition of Christian parties, whose agenda included the enactment of morals legislation. Adult homosexual relations had been legal since 1811 and, although the Dutch penal code of 1886 introduced criminal penalties for consensual sex with minors, the age of consent for homosexual and heterosexual intercourse alike was established at 16. But the attitude toward homosexuality in Parliament began to change during the first decade of the twentieth century. Even though prominent doctors, such as von Römer, and liberal jurists, such as Schorer, spoke against attempts to criminalize homosexuality, a bill increasing the age of consent for homosexual intercourse to 21 was finally enacted in 1911.

Fearing that this might only be the opening act in a campaign to recriminalize adult homosexuality, Schorer founded the DSHC in 1911. From its founding until its eventual closure in 1940, Schorer was the mainstay of this small but resilient group. Schorer modeled the DSHC on the Wissenschaftlich-humanitäres Komitee (Scientific-Humanitarian Committee) (q.v.) in Berlin, accumulated a library on homosexuality, wrote in defense of the dignity of homosexual love, and led the effort to repeal Article 248bis, which established differential ages of consent for homosexual and heterosexual intercourse.

After almost 40 years of work, however, 248bis was still on the statute books when the Germans invaded the Netherlands in 1940 and closed the DSHC. Schorer's worst fears came true when the Nazis recriminalized adult homosexuality in the Netherlands. He and other members of the DSHC went into hiding until the cessation of hostilities. Although the DSHC was not reconstituted after the war, Schorer's homosexual rights campaign was assumed by the formation of a new group, the Cultuur-en-Ontspannings Centrum (Culture and Recreational Center) (q.v.). In 1971, Schorer's objective was realized when the government, acting on the recommendations of the Speijer Report (q.v.), rescinded Article 248bis.

SCHWULENVERBAND DER DDR (GAY FEDERATION OF THE GDR). A federation of more than 30 gay and lesbian groups in the former German Democratic Republic (GDR), founded by Edward Stapel in 1990 in Leipzig. Many of these groups were affiliated with Protestant churches, whereas others were affiliated with Communist youth organizations or were independent.

The first organized homosexual groups in the GDR originated in 1982 after a conference on homosexuality sponsored by the Evangelical Academy Berlin-Brandenburg. Working groups immediately sprang up around the country in small cities and large metropolitan areas. Although heavily infiltrated by the state security police, these groups provided the basis for the emerging gay and lesbian movement in East Germany.

In addition to church-sponsored homosexual groups, the GDR organized a series of conferences on homosexuality, beginning with a 1985 conference in Leipzig. The three conferences effected a change in the official attitude toward homosexuality. Open discussions of homosexuality were undertaken by the mass media, and gay and lesbian groups affiliated with communist youth organizations were now sanctioned. A television program (*Visite*) devoted to health issues, for example, produced the first documentary on homosexuality, in

1987, and the first documentary film on homosexuality, *Die Ander Liebe* (The Other Love), appeared in 1988. The official party line urged tolerance and the integration of homosexuals into society. This dramatic change was reflected in a government-sanctioned publication by Reiner Werner, *Homosexualität. Herausforderung an Wissen und Toleranz* (Homosexuality. Challenge to Knowledge and Tolerence), which called for the creation of support services for gays and lesbians and domestic partnership legislation, among other things. Thus, on the eve of its merger with the Federal Republic of Germany, the GDR for the first time opened the door to gay and lesbian organizations and the first nationwide federation of gay and lesbian groups.

The Schwulenverband der DDR demanded reparations for the pink triangles (q.v.), gay men who suffered imprisonment and death in German concentration camps under the Nazis. The new federation also demanded recognition of the rights of gay and lesbian couples, similar to the provisions of the Danish Registered Partnership Act (q.v.), as well as the right to adopt children and other antidiscrimination legislation.

The reunification of Germany ended discussions between the Schwulenverband and representatives of the GDR concerning these reform proposals.

SCOTTISH HOMOSEXUAL RIGHTS GROUP. *See* SCOTTISH MINORITIES GROUP.

SCOTTISH MINORITIES GROUP (SMG). The Scottish Minorities Group (SMG) was founded in 1969 by Ian Dunn, among others, to take up the fight to repeal two criminal statutes pertaining to gay men. Although the Act of 25 Henry VIII, c.6, and the Labouchère Amendment to the Criminal Law Amendment Act of 1885 had been superseded by the 1967 Sexual Offenses Act (qq.v.), the 1967 statute excluded Scotland and Northern Ireland. Thus, in effect, homosexual relations between men remained a crime in Scotland at a time when private sexual relations between adult men had been decriminalized in England and Wales. The principal objective of the SMG was the extension of the Sexual Offenses Act to Scotland. A small organization, the SMG nevertheless engaged in a wide variety of activities, including sponsoring social activities for its members. In March 1973 it staged a teach-in on homosexuality, and in 1974 it hosted the first International Gay Rights Congress, both in Edinburgh. Along with most other gay and lesbian rights groups in Britain, the SMG was affiliated for a brief time with the National Federation of Homophile Organizations (q.v.). The SMG withdrew in 1973. In 1975 it collaborated with the Campaign for Homosexual Equality (q.v.) and the Union for Sexual Freedom in Ireland in promoting a draft bill proposing a liberalization of the provisions of the 1967 Sexual Offenses Act and the extension of the revised statute to Scotland and Northern Ireland. In 1980, 13 years after the enactment of the Sexual Offenses Act, the provisions of the 1967 statute were finally extended to Scotland. The SMG has continued its campaign on behalf of gays and lesbians since 1978 under the banner of the Scottish Homosexual Rights Group and is currently known as OUTRIGHT Scotland. Ian Dunn died unexpectedly in 1998.

SEXUAALINEN TASAVERTAISUUS R.Y./SEXUAL EQUAL RIGHTS (SER). Sexuaalinen Tasavertaisuus R.Y. (Sexual Equal Rights [SER]) is the Finnish national gay and lesbian rights organization. Since 1971 SER has been active in the attempt to repeal Finland's censorship law, a law that makes it illegal to promote, endorse, or encourage homosexuality.

In 1971 Finland decriminalized homosexual relations. The final version of the statute, however, also contained a ban on incitement of homosexual acts, a provision that was introduced to appease critics of the statute, such as the Lutheran Church. Thus, since 1971, Chapter 20 of the Finnish Penal Code has subjected those found guilty of violating this censorship law to fines or to imprisonment (six months maximum).

In 1979 SER and several employees of Finnish radio and television stations filed a complaint with the United Nations Human Rights Committee alleging that their rights to free speech had been abridged by the censorship law between 1975 and 1979. All the cases in question involved informational programs about gays and lesbians broadcast over radio or television. After three years of deliberation, the UN Human Rights Committee found in favor of the Finnish government, citing the legitimate authority of sovereign nations to regulate public morality.

In 1991, the Finnish Parliament began discussions on a revision of the Constitution of Finland and the Finnish Penal Code. From the outset, SER has lobbied the Parliament to eliminate all vestiges of discrimination against lesbians and gays. The revised Finnish Constitution now includes a statement specifically prohibiting discrimination based on sexual orientation, and the revised Finnish Penal Code also contains provisions prohibiting discrimination on the basis of sexual orientation in the provision of public or private goods and services. In light of these changes, the fate of the censorship law remains uncertain.

Most recently, SER launched a campaign to enact legislation

granting the right of marriage (q.v.) to gay and lesbian couples. On 28 May 1996, a bill was submitted to Parliament that would give gay and lesbian couples rights similar to those accorded to married heterosexual couples. Its provisions are based on the Danish Registered Partnership Act (q.v.). The bill would make it possible for gays and lesbians to enter into legally binding domestic partnerships with the rights and privileges of married heterosexual couples, with the exception of the right of adoption. The prospects for adoption of the legislation are uncertain.

SEXUAL LAW REFORM SOCIETY. *See* HOMOSEXUAL LAW REFORM SOCIETY.

SEXUAL MINORITIES ASSOCIATION. Renamed the Union of Lesbians and Homosexuals shortly after its founding in 1989 in Moscow, this Russian organization was perhaps the first overt gay and lesbian rights organization to appear in the USSR. It was preceded by the Leningrad Gay Laboratory, but this organization was clandestine and disintegrated shortly after the arrest of its founder, Alexander Zaremba, in 1986. Shortly after the founding of the Sexual Minorities Association, it began to publish its own newspaper, *Tema*.

One of its declared purposes was the repeal of Article 121.1 (q.v.) of the Russian legal code (which criminalized male homosexual relations) together with amnesty for those currently serving prison terms. Other objectives included dispelling myths about homosexuality and AIDS through the Soviet mass media and providing social outlets for gays and lesbians.

Within a year of its founding, the Union of Lesbians and Homosexuals was rife with internal disagreements and, by 1991, had ceased to exist. Out of its ashes, however, appeared a new organization that took up the struggle for gay and lesbian rights, the Moscow Union of Lesbians and Homosexuals (MULH). Formed in 1990, the new organization's first cochairs were Roman Kalinin (q.v.) and Yevgenia Debryanskaya. MULH was affiliated with the Libertarian Party, which endorsed the repeal of Article 121.1. Kalinin also assumed the responsibility for editing and publishing *Tema*. In 1990, *Tema's* offices were robbed of its distribution lists and other publication materials. Despite this assault that some have attributed to the Soviet KGB, *Tema* reopened and continued to publish until 1993.

But organizational difficulties once again emerged. By 1991 the MULH had dissolved and been replaced by Osvobozhdenie (Liberation), again under the leadership of Kalinin and Debryanskaya.

Despite the obvious organizational instability of the first gay and lesbian groups in the Soviet Union, one of the primary objectives of the original Sexual Minorities Association was fulfilled when Armenia, Estonia, Latvia, Moldova, and the Ukraine nullified their antihomosexual statutes after the dissolution of the Soviet Union. Russian President Boris Yeltsin followed shortly thereafter, annulling Article 121.1 by presidential decree. The annulment of Article 121.1 in May 1993 decriminalized adult male homosexuality in Russia; those aspects of the statute pertaining to sexual relations with adolescent boys and to the use of force remain in effect.

The first gay and lesbian associations in Russia have been joined by many others in Moscow, St. Petersburg, and other Russian cities, as well as in some of the former Soviet republics such as Belarus, Estonia, Latvia, and the Ukraine. The Rossiyskaya assotsiatsiya lesbiyanok, geev i biseksualov "Treugolnik" (Russian Lesbian, Gay, and Bisexual Association "Triangle") was formed in 1993 to attempt to coordinate the activities of 27 separate groups. And although *Tema* has ceased publication, it has been replaced by a number of other gay and lesbian publications, and the subject of homosexuality is now discussed much more openly in the Russian mass media than it was at the beginning of the decade.

SEXUAL OFFENSES ACT (1967). In Britain, the Sexual Offenses Act superseded the Act of 25 Henry VIII, c.6, and the Labouchère Amendment to the Criminal Law Amendment Act of 1885 (qq.v.). The former had criminalized anal sex, while the Labouchère Amendment broadened the criminal definition of homosexual relations to include all forms of homosexual behavior, not only anal penetration. The Labouchère Amendment made even consensual homosexual relations between adult males in private a crime. Hundreds of years of legal persecution were partially undone with the enactment of the Sexual Offenses Act in 1967.

The initiative for reforming Britain's harsh legal penalties was the Homosexual Law Reform Society (HLRS) (q.v.), an organization that was created after the Report of the Committee on Homosexual Offenses and Prostitution (q.v.) in 1957. Many unsuccessful attempts to repeal the provisions of existing legislation were undertaken by the HLRS and its supporters in Parliament between 1958 and 1967. Finally, in 1967, a bill introduced by Leo Abse in the House of Commons and Lord Arran in the House of Lords succeeded in gaining a majority in Parliament. It was given Royal Assent and became law on July 27, 1967.

Although, in effect, the Sexual Offenses Act repealed existing criminal penalties against adult male homosexuality, its language remained highly restrictive. Its applicability extended only to England

and Wales; Scotland and Northern Ireland were unaffected by the new law. The age of consent was raised from 20 to 21, and the punishment for engaging in homosexual relations with an underaged male was increased from two to five years. In addition, the statute contained a provision to punish those who conspired to corrupt public morals, a provision that was used effectively against the gay press. Also, for purposes of the statute, privacy referred not merely to non-public venues, but also to situations where not more than two individuals were present. Finally, due to intensive pressure from prominent former officers and the National Union of Seamen, the armed services and the merchant navy were entirely excluded from the provisions of the new bill.

Thus, the Sexual Offenses Act was at best a mixed blessing for those who had campaigned to decriminalize homosexual relations between men. Enforcement of the provisions of the new statute was vigorous, and public attitudes toward gays and lesbians remained hostile and punitive.

Subsequent attempts to liberalize the Sexual Offenses Act have come to naught, although the provisions of the 1967 statute were extended to Scotland in 1980 and to Northern Ireland in 1982.

SOCIETY FOR HUMAN RIGHTS (SHR). The first homosexual rights organization in the United States, the Society for Human Rights (SHR) was chartered as a nonprofit organization on 10 December 1924 by the state of Illinois. The founder of the group was Henry Gerber (q.v.), with six others. Gerber is listed on the charter as secretary of the organization.

The name of the organization was derived from a German homosexual emancipation group, the Bund für Menschenrechte (League for Human Rights) (q.v.). Seeking to emulate the progress of the homosexual emancipation movement in Germany during the first quarter of the 20th century, Gerber decided that the plight of homosexuals in the United States could only be addressed through an organization devoted to the reform of public opinion and the law. The group's focus was to have been reform of the laws of the state of Illinois.

However, the organization was shortlived. Only two issues of the society's newsletter, *Friendship and Freedom* (named after the German publication *Freundschaft und Freiheit*), were published before the officers of the organization were arrested in Chicago on trumped up morals charges. The date of the arrest remains uncertain, but it occurred either in December 1924 or early 1925. Although the charges were dismissed in court, Gerber lost his job as a postal employee, and the organization effectively came to an end before it could begin to organize.

SOCIETY FOR INDIVIDUAL RIGHTS (SIR). The Society for Individual Rights (SIR) originated in San Francisco in the autumn of 1964. Created as an alternative to existing gay and lesbian rights organizations in the Bay Area by William Beardemphl, Mark Forrester, Jim Foster, and Bill Plath, the SIR's purpose was to broaden the gay and lesbian rights constituency.

The Mattachine Society (MS) (q.v.) and the Daughters of Bilitis (DOB) were composed of small bands of stalwarts who were never able to transform their groups into mass-action organizations. The national structure of the MS dissolved in 1961, leaving only a few chapters in larger cities to carry on the fight for gay and lesbian rights. Although the San Francisco chapter was one of the first and most active chapters of the MS, it too was in decline.

By the early 1960s San Francisco had developed the beginnings of a gay subculture. Gay bars began to multiply, gay literature became more available, homoerotic films were screened in select theaters, and so forth. With the increasing size and visibility of the gay subculture came increasingly frequent confrontations with the city and the police. As early as 1957, the obscenity trial of Lawrence Ferlinghetti for the distribution of Allen Ginsberg's poem "Howl" began to galvanize the city's gay and lesbian population. Several years later, the city and the police department engaged in a systematic attack on gays and lesbians. Many gay bars lost their licenses, gay men were arrested for a variety of public indecency offenses, and homoerotic films and literature were confiscated.

Evidence of the growing influence of the city's gay and lesbian population was the candidacy of the first gay man for city supervisor (city council) in 1961. Although José Sarria's campaign was not successful, the mere existence of an openly gay candidate for city supervisor was an indication of the increasing politization of San Francisco's gay and lesbian population.

Two new homosexual rights organizations, the League for Civil Education (LCE) and the SIR, emerged to fill the gap left by the politically ineffective MS and DOB chapters. Although the LCE's membership was even smaller than that of the MS and DOB, it did publish a highly successful newspaper, the *LCE News*, for several years. Of the two, the SIR was far more effective in attracting members. The SIR claimed a membership of 1,000 in 1967.

The key to the SIR's relative success was its organizational priorities. Eschewing the staid and accommodationist posture of the MS and DOB, the SIR was unapologetic about the gay and lesbian lifestyle and actively cultivated social outlets for gays and lesbians. Dances, buffets, bowling, art exhibitions, a thrift shop, anything that its members had the motivation to organize, were used by the SIR to create a sense of community and to generate income for the organization. With this income, in 1966 it purchased a building in downtown San Francisco that became a community center for the city's gay and lesbian population.

The SIR was also politically active. Its "Candidates Nights," held at the community center before each regularly scheduled election, provided a forum to air issues of concern to gay and lesbian residents. It also created a political action committee to help finance the campaigns of supportive candidates; engaged in voter registration drives; and published *Vector*, a monthly newsmagazine. Its most prominent role was an alliance with the Tavern Guild, an organization of gay bars formed to defend their establishments from intimidation by the police. The SIR, together with the Tavern Guild, the LCE, and the Council on Religion and the Homosexual (q.v.), was successful in putting an end to police harassment of gay establishments. By 1968 the incidents of intimidation had decreased markedly.

The SIR played a significant role in transforming the nature of the gay and lesbian community in San Francisco during the 1960s. Its active support of cultural activities widened the base of support for political initiatives. But the SIR was also soon seen to be too reformist in the context of the more militant civil rights (q.v.) and antiwar movements. Leo Laurence, editor of *Vector* in 1969, attempted to no avail to radicalize the SIR and left the group to form the Committee for Homosexual Freedom, an organization more in tune with the politics of the Gay Liberation Front (q.v.). The SIR persisted in its more traditional political agenda and was soon overwhelmed in significance by New Left organizations.

SODOMY STATUTES. Although sodomy statutes vary considerably from one jurisdiction to the next, the objective of all such statutes has been the prohibition of specific sexual acts, most commonly oral and anal sex. Penalties have typically been severe, ranging from incarceration in prison to the death penalty. Although sodomy statutes do not typically criminalize sexual orientation, per se, they have been enforced disproportionately against gay men. Many sodomy statutes have also been enforced against lesbians. Because authorities have routinely used sodomy statutes to repress homosexual relations, their elimination has been at the forefront of the gay and lesbian rights movement since its inception in the 1860s.

The first secular legal code prohibiting sodomy in the West was the Roman *Codex Justinianus* in the 6th century A.D. Together with compilations of Christian canon law, such as Gratian's 11th century *Concordia discordantium canonum*, the *Codex* became the basis for early modern legislation criminalizing sodomy in Europe (q.v.). In rapid succession, most European jurisdictions enacted sodomy laws so that, by the 18th and 19th centuries, such statutes had become commonplace. As a general rule, only France (subsequent to 1789) and other territories governed by the Code Napoléon escaped the influence of sodomy statutes in Europe.

The most notorious early modern European sodomy laws were the Act of 25 Henry VIII, c.6, and the Labouchère Amendment (qq.v.), British statutes; Article 995 of the Code of Laws of the Russian Empire, its successors Article 154a and Article 121.1 (q.v.) of the USSR code of laws; and Paragraph 175 (q.v.) of the German legal code. All are of particular significance because of their wide jurisdictional influence and because they became the principal targets of the homosexual rights movement in Europe.

The Act of 25 Henry VIII, c.6, and the Labouchère Amendment, for example, were impediments to the freedom of sexual expression not only in Great Britain but also in many territories that were, at one time or another, part of the British empire. Australia, Canada, Hong Kong, Ireland, Israel, New Zealand, and the United States all based their sodomy statutes, in part, on British law. Likewise, Article 995 had a pervasive influence throughout the Russian Empire after its enactment in 1845. Although the enforcement of Article 995 was suspended in 1917, similar statutes (Article 154a [between 1934 and 1960] and Article 121.1 [between 1960 and 1993]) extended the prohibition against sodomy throughout the Soviet Union. Paragraph 175 was especially notorious because of its association with the Nazi Party's incarceration of homosexuals (the pink triangles [q.v.]) in concentration camps during the Third Reich.

Because sodomy statutes are inimical to the welfare of gays and lesbians, their repeal has been at the forefront of the gay and lesbian rights movement. The first advocates of homosexual rights, Karl Heinrich Ulrichs and Karl Maria Kertbeny (qq.v.), spoke against the adoption of Paragraph 175 prior to its enactment in 1871, and the repeal of Paragraph 175 was a principal objective of the first homosexual rights organization in the world, the German Wissenschaftlich-humanitäres Komitee (The Scientific-Humanitarian Committee) (q.v.). In Britain, a long tradition of protest literature on the subject of sodomy laws also existed. Sir Richard Burton, Edward Carpenter, John Addington Symonds, and Havelock Ellis (qq.v.) all protested the illogic of British sodomy laws. The British Society for the Study of Sex Psychology (q.v.) was also an important early 20th-century professional organization to advocate the repeal of sodomy statutes. Similarly, a tradition of protest existed in Czarist Russia, involving such people as the anarchists Alexander Berkman and Emma Goldman, poets such as Mikhail Kuzmin, and the jurist Vladimir Nabokov. Two political parties, the Anarchists and the Constitutional Democrats (Cadets), were remarkable for their support of homosexual rights prior to the 1917 revolution.

Despite years of protest, it was not until the late 1960s that the sodomy laws in Great Britain, Germany, and the Soviet Union were effectively challenged. In Britain, the repeal of the Act of 25 Henry VIII, c.6, and the Labouchère Amendment occurred as a result of the enactment of the 1967 Sexual Offenses Act (q.v.), which embodied the reforms suggested by the Committee on Homosexual Offenses and Prostitution and advocated by the Homosexual Law Reform Society (qq.v.).

The repeal of Paragraph 175 remained a goal of gay and lesbian rights groups in both East and West Germany after the defeat of the Nazis in 1945. East Germany decriminalized sexual relations between adult homosexuals in 1968. West Germany followed in 1969. *See also* Schwulenverband der DDR.

Efforts to repeal Article 154a of the USSR code of laws were effectively repressed by the Stalinist regime, and it was not until the formation of the Sexual Minorities Association (q.v.) in 1989 that the gay and lesbian rights movement in Russia began to publicly campaign for the elimination of Article 121.1. But the political liberalization that followed the decline in the power of the Communist Party in Russia, as well as the disintegration of the Soviet Union, created the opportunity to reform Soviet law. In 1993, Article 121.1 was repealed by President Boris Yeltsin.

In North America, the drive to repeal sodomy statutes has also been a key feature of the gay and lesbian rights movement. Sodomy statutes in both Canada and the United States were derived from British law. Thus, for example, Canada enacted in 1859 its own version of Britain's Act of 25 Henry VIII, c.6, and, in 1892, a gross indecency statute modeled on the Labouchère Amendment. Both were opposed by early Canadian gay and lesbian rights groups such as the Association for Social Knowledge (q.v.).

Sodomy statutes also have a long history in the United States, where the regulation of sexual practices has traditionally been the province of the states. All but two of the original 13 colonies had sodomy statutes. Modeled on the British "buggery" statute, the Act of 25 Henry VIII, c.6, most defined sodomy as anal sex and proscribed the practice without regard to the gender of the parties involved. By the end of the 19th century, state statutes commonly prohibited oral as well as anal sex, and many states extended the prohibition even to married couples. On the eve of the Stonewall (q.v.) riots, every state in the union except Illinois had laws prohibiting anal and/or oral sex between consenting adults in private. The prescribed penalties were harsh, often involving long prison terms, including life imprisonment. The Mattachine Society (q.v.) and the Daughters of Bilitis were the first gay and lesbian rights organizations in the United States to call for the repeal of sodomy laws.

Criticisms of sodomy statutes in American legal circles led to reform movements in Canada and the United States. The enactment of the 1967 Sexual Offenses Act in Britain had a great impact on the debate in Canada. The Canadian Criminal Code Reform (q.v.) of 1969 followed the British example by decriminalizing homosexual relations between adults 21 years of age or older in private. In the United States, the American Law Institute also made recommendations to abolish the enforcement of sodomy statutes between adults. Between 1966 and 1986, sodomy statutes in 25 states were rescinded. In 1986, however, in the *Bowers v. Hardwick* (q.v.) decision, the U.S. Supreme Court reaffirmed the constitutionality of states proscribing sexual relations between homosexual adults. Today, almost 40 percent of U.S. states still retain sodomy statutes in their legal codes.

Other sodomy statutes, also the remnants of British colonialism, have been rescinded recently in Australia, Hong Kong, and New Zealand, owing in large part to the groundwork laid by such gay and lesbian rights organizations as the Campaign Against Moral Persecution, the Ten Percent Club, and the Dorian Society (qq.v.). Despite the accomplishments over the last 30 years, the elimination of sodomy statutes remains a priority of gay and lesbian organizations, because sodomy is still a criminal offense in 86 countries.

SOMOS (WE ARE). Somos emerged in São Paulo in 1977 at roughly the same time that the Lampião (q.v.) collective began publishing the first national gay and lesbian newspaper in Brazil from Rio de Janeiro.

Originating as a discussion group, Somos functioned as a semisecret organization for two years before its public debut. The occasion was a debate between leftist students and faculty and representatives of Somos before the Social Sciences Faculty of the University of São Paulo in February 1979. During a frank exchange of opinions, Marxist students and faculty asserted that gay rights were secondary to the primacy of the class struggle, and gays and lesbians countered with ironic instances of discrimination at the hands of those professing a commitment to social justice.

The immediate consequence of the confrontation between the handful of activists affiliated with Somos and the Left at the University of São Paulo was a tenfold increase in the membership of Somos. Somos organized social affairs, public debates, and protests; facilitated international contacts with other gay groups; and participated in the short-lived Committee for the Defense of Homosexual Rights, a coalition of three São Paulo gay rights groups.

Members of Somos also participated with eight other organizations in the 1980 Brazilian Congress of Organized Homosexual Groups, the first such meeting of its kind in Brazil. This meeting proved to be a turning point for Somos. Trotskyists proposed that gay rights groups align themselves with organizations of the Left, such as the Workers' Party, in order to inculcate a proletarian consciousness. Although a motion to this effect was rejected, Somos was soon taken over by Trotskyists, and the group splintered. Within two years, Somos was subsumed by the Workers' Party, and, by 1982, it no longer functioned as an independent group. In the 1982 elections, the Workers' Party put forward a plank on gay rights and nominated candidates who spoke openly on behalf of gay rights, but the membership of Somos dwindled in proportion to the decline in its effectiveness as a gay rights organization.

Since the emergence of Somos, gay and lesbian organizations such as the Gay Group of Bahia, Nós Também, and Adé Dudu have become a more familiar feature of the Brazilian political landscape. Although their influence does not equal that of organizations in North America, their educational and political campaigns, such as the effort to eliminate the designation of homosexuality as a mental illness, are indications of a growing sense of political commitment and strength, and a new nationwide association of gay and lesbian groups appears to be in the offing.

SPEIJER REPORT (1969). Named after Dr. N. Speijer, professor at the State University of Leyden. In 1968, the Dutch government commissioned a report on the probable effects of reducing the age of consent for homosexuals. Since 1911, the age of consent for homosexuals had been 21, even though the corresponding age for heterosexuals was 16. Because of Dr. Speijer's credentials in social psychiatry, he was appointed to chair the committee of five eminent psychiatrists and neurologists (the inspector for public moral welfare was a sixth member).

The committee report emphasized the congenital etiology of homosexuality. Most homosexuals, it reported, were biologically predisposed to their sexual orientation or were otherwise influenced by early childhood experiences. Thus, the fear that young adults might be seduced into homosexuality was greatly exaggerated. Furthermore, the committee concluded that homosexual teenagers have as great a need as their heterosexual counterparts for sexual outlets and the criminalization of homosexuality below the age of 21 was irrational. Accordingly, the Speijer committee recommended the repeal of the existing age of consent for homosexuals and the adoption of the same age of consent for homosexuals as for heterosexuals.

In 1971, the Dutch government repealed 248bis, the statute that fixed the age of consent for homosexuals at 21. Sixteen, the existing standard for heterosexuals, was made the new age of consent for homosexuals, thus culminating a 60-year initiative begun by the Nederlandsch Wetenschappelijk-Humanitair Komitee (Dutch Scientific-Humanitarian Committee) (q.v.).

An English translation of the Speijer committee report, distributed by the Albany Trust (AT) (q.v.), was used by the AT's enemies in the British Parliament to discredit its work, which led to the demise of the AT in 1980.

STEVENSON, EDWARD IRENAEUS PRIME. *See* MAYNE, XAVIER.

STONEWALL. Perhaps more than any other term, Stonewall has come to symbolize the spirit of the contemporary gay and lesbian liberation movement.

A popular gay bar, the Stonewall Inn operated at 53 Christopher Street in the heart of Greenwich Village. Because New York State and New York City had laws forbidding importuning others of the same sex, cross-dressing, same-sex dancing, and so forth, it was only police corruption that enabled gay bars to remain open. Thus, like most other gay bars in New York City during the 1960s, the Stonewall Inn was run by a Mafia family. And like other gay bars it was subject to periodic police raids and closures in order to preserve the reputation of the police department as well as elected public officials.

The Stonewall Inn catered to a diverse crowd; most of the clientele was nonwhite, and included transvestites and transsexuals, underage gay men, lesbians, prostitutes, and drug dealers. On 27 June 1969 the New York City police raided the Stonewall Inn shortly before midnight. What began as a routine event ended up in a violent confrontation between the patrons of the bar, onlookers, and the police, which carried over into further demonstrations the following evening and into the next week.

This was certainly not the first protest against police harassment of gays and lesbians or gay bars. But in the highly volatile political environment of the late 1960s, the protests received an enormous amount of press coverage and created an opportunity for younger gays and lesbians to challenge the leadership of existing homosexual rights organizations. Neither the New York Mattachine Society nor the New York chapter of the Daughters of Bilitis was prepared for the outrage felt by many younger gays and lesbians. Where the established organizations originally called for calm, the militants called for more aggressive leadership, direct action, and confrontational techniques. Within the space of a few weeks, a new organization, the Gay Liberation Front (GLF) (q.v.), came into being. The GLF transformed the gay and lesbian political movement from a predominantly legalistic and traditional one into a more assertive, open, and confrontational movement for human rights.

The events of 27–29 June in New York City are celebrated each year across the United States and around the world with marches commemorating the birth of the contemporary gay and lesbian liberation movement.

STONEWALL GROUP. In 1990, representatives of the Stonewall Group and the International Lesbian and Gay Association (ILGA) (q.v.) met with Andre-Guy Kirchberger to press the European Community (EC) to amend its Social Charter to prohibit discrimination against lesbians and gay men. Kirchberger was a ranking official in the cabinet of Vasso Papandreou, the EC's social affairs commissioner.

Although the meeting produced no concrete results, Kirchberger did request the Stonewall Group to produce a report on the plight of lesbians and gays in the EC. The report, entitled *Harmonization within the European Community: The Reality for Lesbians and Gay Men*, was presented to the European Commission of the EC later that year. The report documented impediments to the achievement of several objectives of the EC posed by differences in the laws of the member states. The objective of harmonizing the laws of EC members, the freedom of movement across the borders of EC states, and a barrier-free EC market were all undermined by the widely varying legal statuses of gays and lesbians in the member states.

Although the commission refused to act on the report's proposals to end discrimination, it was instrumental in paving the way for a subsequent meeting between the social affairs commissioner of the EC and representatives of gay and lesbian groups throughout the EC. The meeting that occurred in December 1990 resulted in several concessions. The social affairs commissioner appointed an official to be responsible for gay and lesbian concerns and to act as liaison between the commission and gays and lesbians. The commissioner also authorized a study of the ramifications of the Single European Market for gays and lesbians and recommended that the commission's forthcoming Code of Practice prohibit harassment in the workplace on the basis of sexual orientation. The Code of Practice does not have the force of law, but its recommendation that sexual orientation be a protected category was a first for the EC.

STUDENT HOMOPHILE LEAGUE (SHL). The first organization of gays and lesbians on a university campus in the United States, the Student Homophile League (SHL) was founded at Columbia University in October 1966 and received university recognition in April 1967. One of its first political acts was the disruption, in 1968, of a panel discussion on the etiology of homosexuality at Columbia. This attack on psychiatry's preoccupation with homosexuality as a pathology preceded the antipsychiatry movement sponsored by the Front Homosexuel d'Action Révolutionnaire (Revolutionary Homosexual Action Front) (q.v.) in Paris and the 1970 disruption of the American Psychiatric Association's annual meeting in San Francisco by gay and lesbian militants. Thus, the SHL's act of resistance to the power of mainstream psychiatry over the lives of gays and lesbians may have been the first step toward the eventual delisting of homosexuality as a mental illness by such professional associations as the American Psychiatric Association and the World Health Organization.

The founding of the SHL at Columbia spawned SHL chapters at New York University and other East Coast Universities such as Cornell. It presaged, as well, the rapid development of gay and lesbian organizations on college campuses throughout North America after Stonewall (q.v.).

SYDNEY GAY LIBERATION (SGL). Founded in 1972, its origins can be traced to a radical clique within the Campaign against Moral Persecution (CAMP) (q.v.). As opposed to the more conservative objectives of its parent organization, it functioned initially as a Gay Liberation Front (GLF) (q.v.) faction of CAMP, focusing on consciousness raising, critiques of straight society, and overt displays of gay pride. Finding CAMP to be inhospitable to their objectives, the SGL was founded to afford its members the opportunity to pursue alternative courses of action.

Like its GLF counterparts in the United States and Britain, SGL stressed the revolutionary implications of homosexuality. From their perspective, the goal of gay liberation should not be toleration by the dominant heterosexist/patriarchal society but the overthrow of institutions that privileged male heterosexual values. Leading theoreticians included Martha Shelley and Dennis Altman. Altman's book, *Homosexual: Oppression and Liberation* was one of the first contemporary gay liberation critiques of gay and lesbian oppression. Altman participated in many of the activities sponsored by the SGL and influenced its course of development.

Like other GLF organizations, the SGL was also critical of hierarchal organizational structures, preferring instead a more open and participatory decisionmaking structure. In practice this meant that everyone was expected to participate in one of the many subgroups of the SGL. In addition, members were expected to take care of the day-to-day business of the group and to participate in the general business meetings where the objectives of SGL were decided. This emphasis on participatory democracy plagued the group from the outset and proved to be one of the reasons for its undoing.

Despite the ideological differences between the SGL and CAMP, they cooperated on many projects. They often participated in open forums on homosexuality, protest demonstrations, and gay pride rallies. The SGL also participated with other Sydney GLF groups in a wide variety of political activities such as "kiss-ins" and "zaps" of psychiatric presentations of homosexuality as a pathology.

In the end, however, like other GLF groups, the SGL finally succumbed to the diverse interests that characterized its membership, including its inability to appeal to the interests of lesbians as well as its organizational problems. Shortly after the 1973 Gay Pride Week in Sydney, SGL dissolved into a number of semiautonomous groups, renaming itself the Gay Liberation Front. The organization eventually disintegrated in 1974.

Despite the failure of SGL's major objective, the revolutionary transformation of Australian society, organizations such as the SGL, Melbourne Gay Liberation, and CAMP initiated the contemporary gay liberation movement in Australia and thus set in motion reform movements which have liberalized Australian attitudes towards gays and lesbians.

SYMONDS, JOHN ADDINGTON (1840–1893). Historian, poet, and sexologist, John Addington Symonds was one of the first British writers to protest the inhumane treatment of homosexuals. Like Edward Carpenter and Havelock Ellis (qq.v.), with whom he corresponded regularly, Symonds was influenced by the poetry of Walt Whitman (q.v.). Symonds was also acquainted with Karl Heinrich Ulrichs (q.v.), the German writer and homosexual activist who initiated the early homosexual rights movement. Symonds visited Ulrichs in Aquila, Italy, shortly before Ulrichs's death and was responsible for stimulating an interest in Ulrichs's work in the English-speaking world.

John Addington Symonds was a prolific writer. He is remembered for his seven-volume *Histories of the Renaissance*, *Studies of the Greek Poets*, and the English translation of *The Life of Benvenuto Cellini*. His works on sexology include *A Problem in Greek Ethics*, and *A Problem in Modern Ethics*. His last work, *Walt Whitman*, was published on 19 April 1893, the day of his death in Rome.

In *A Problem of Greek Ethics*, Symonds was concerned with documenting the integral nature of male-male love in ancient Greek society, its veneration of masculinity, and its nobility. By understanding the cultural relativity of sexual customs, Symonds hoped to dispel prevailing opinion about homosexuality, attitudes perpetuated by Christian churches, the medical profession, and the law. In his study of ancient Greek society, Symonds concluded that pederasty was a deeply ingrained social custom, so ingrained that it became a quasi-religious institution. He further argued that Greek male-male love did not resemble the image of effeminacy—or degeneracy—portrayed by modern medical authorities on the subject. Quite the contrary. Far from being considered a symptom of degeneracy, male-male love was a badge of masculinity, a venerated emotion. Consequently, unlike in modern Europe (q.v.), in ancient Greece there had been no attempt to legislate against its practice.

Symonds continued his attacks on modern opinion in his *A Problem in Modern Ethics*. In this treatise, he critically reviewed the extant medical opinion on the subject of homosexuality and found that it was little more than irrational bigotry dressed up in scientific language. Comparing Walt Whitman's celebration of male camaraderie in the Calamus section of *Leaves of Grass* with the works of Plato, he again found little in common with their idealization of the love between men and the picture of the pathological invert painted by modern science. *A Problem in Modern Ethics* concluded with a condemnation of 19th-century British law, such as the Labouchère Amendment (q.v.), and an appeal for legislative reform. The models for such legal reform were the Code Napoléon (1804) and the Italian penal code (1889), because they had decriminalized male homosexual relations with no apparent negative side effects.

Despite Symonds's outspoken defense of male homosexuality in his writings, he remained very reserved in his personal life, disclosing his sexual preference to only a close circle of friends and family. On the advice of his father, in 1864 he married Catherine North, with whom he subsequently had four daughters. *A Problem in Greek Ethics* and *A Problem in Modern Ethics* were both privately printed in limited numbers and circulated to friends and associates. His collaboration with Havelock Ellis in the writing of *Sexual Inversion* was suppressed by his family after his death, as were all his publications on the subject of homosexuality. It was only some years after his death that his defense of homosexual love became general knowledge. The reticence of his family in disclosing his sexual preference is evident in the fact that his memoirs were not published until 1976.

SZIVARVANY (RAINBOW). A prominent Hungarian gay and lesbian rights organization, Rainbow played a key role in lobbying the Hungarian Parliament to adopt legislation legalizing same-sex marriages (q.v.).

In March 1995 the Constitutional Court of Hungary ruled that the failure of the government to recognize common-law marriages between individuals of the same sex violated the Constitution of Hungary. In its decision, the court ordered the government to rectify the inequity within one year.

Together with other gay and lesbian rights organizations, Rainbow organized gays and lesbians to support the decision of the court through the pages of *MASOK*, Hungary's gay magazine, as well as radio and television programs. Parliament voted gay and lesbian couples the rights of married heterosexual couples on 21 May 1996. Following the precedent set by the Danish Registered Partnership Act (q.v.), the only exception to the equality between heterosexual and homosexual partnerships, or common-law marriages, was that gays and lesbians were to be prohibited from adopting children.

Hungary's policy on same-sex marriages makes it the first Eastern European country to legalize same-sex unions. Currently, in addition to Denmark and Hungary, Norway, the Netherlands, Sweden, Greenland, and Iceland have domestic partnership laws. Similar legislation is now under consideration in Finland, Spain, Portugal, and in the state of Hawaii.

Regardless of the recent action, much remains to be done to improve the lives of gays and lesbians in Hungary. Official and unofficial attitudes toward gays and lesbians remain intolerant, making the enactment of antidiscrimination legislation of paramount importance.

T

TEN PERCENT CLUB. At the time of the reunification of Hong Kong and the People's Republic of China, in 1997, the Ten Percent Club was the first and foremost homosexual organization in the city devoted to legal reform.

Laws pertaining to homosexuality in Hong Kong were derived from British law. Male homosexuality was proscribed, but, as in Britain, no laws proscribed sexual relations between women. Mirroring the penalties of the 1861 Offenses against the Person Act, the maximum penalty for consensual homosexual relations between adult men was life imprisonment. The changes in Britain brought about by the 1967 Sexual Offenses Act (q.v.) did not affect the laws of the Crown Colony of Hong Kong.

The Ten Percent Club is a small, unofficial organization that serves primarily as a social outlet for gay men in Hong Kong's repressive environment. Official government recognition is required for an organization to function publicly, but the organizers of the Ten Percent Club were never able to garner enough signatures to petition the government for recognition. Nevertheless, organizers did conduct negotiations with members of the Hong Kong Legislative Council concerning the possibility of reforming Hong Kong's sodomy statute (q.v.), and reform was realized in 1990 when the Legislative Council rescinded the statute.

There is no visible gay or lesbian movement in the People's Republic of China. Although the criminal code does not explicitly mention homosexuality, homosexual behavior is punished as "hooliganism." Lengthy prison sentences are not uncommon, and the official position of the government toward gays and lesbians is that it is a Western affliction that must be eradicated.

Given the reunification of Hong Kong with the People's Republic of China, the obstacles facing the only known Chinese homosexual rights organization are great, and the fate of Hong Kong's fledgling gay and lesbian subculture is highly problematic owing to the long history of repression of homosexuality in the People's Republic of China.

TERRIS, WYKEHAM. *See* HAIRE, NORMAN.

THIRD SEX THEORY. Over a 15-year period (1864–1879) Karl Heinrich Ulrichs (q.v.) published 12 treatises on the nature of love between men. Known in English as *The Riddle of "Man-Manly" Love*, the 12 booklets include anthropological, historical, and legal studies of love between men and love between women. The core of Ulrichs's attempt to explain this riddle of nature was his third sex theory.

Ulrichs maintained that the human embryo originates as neither male nor female. Rather, it is hermaphroditic until the third or fourth month of gestation when, under normal circumstances, natural processes shape the embryo into a boy or girl. The fully developed child retains vestigial features of the opposite sex. On occasion, however, the result is the birth of a true hermaphrodite, an individual with the sexual organs of both the male and the female.

Ulrichs also maintained that just as the embryo originates as hermaphroditic, the embryo contains a dormant hermaphroditic "germ" of sexual attraction. As the normal embryo evolves from its primitive hermaphroditic state into that of a distinct physical sex, it also acquires a sexual attraction harmonious with its physical constitution, the sexual attraction of a man for a woman or of a woman for a man. Just as, on occasion, nature produces physical hermaphrodites, nature also produces psychic-sexual hermaphrodites, individuals whose sexual attraction is not in harmony with their physical constitution. The result is love between men or love between women.

Consequently, Ulrichs claimed that there was a third sex corresponding to that of man and woman. *Urnings* and *Urningins* (male and female homosexuals) were neither men nor women in the strict sense, because, although Urnings and Urningins were fully developed males and females, they lacked the corresponding sexual attraction to the opposite sex.

Ulrichs's third sex theory had a great impact on the subsequent development of modern conceptions of sexual orientation. Richard von Krafft-Ebing, the prominent Viennese sexologist; Havelock Ellis and Edward Carpenter (cofounders of the British Society for the Study of Sex Psychology [BSSP]); John Addington Symonds; and Magnus Hirschfeld (the founder of the Institute for Sexual Science [ISS] and the World League for Sexual Reform [WLSR]) (qq.v.) were all indebted to Ulrichs. Although none adhered to the strict details of his third sex theory, all, in their own distinctive fashion, borrowed ideas and terminology from Ulrichs.

The influence of the third sex theory was not limited to the specialized field of sexology. Literary works such as Radclyffe Hall's *The Well of Loneliness*, Edward Stevenson's *The Intersexes*, and Marcel Proust's *A la recherche du temps perdu* (Remembrance of Things Past) bear the unmistakable influence of the third sex theory and helped propel Ulrichs's ideas into popular culture.

The third sex theory has also had a lasting impact on the politics of the homosexual rights movement. Magnus Hirschfeld, founder of the first homosexual rights organization, embraced the idea that homosexuality was an inborn condition over which the individual had no control. Throughout the entire campaign to repeal Paragraph 175 (q.v.) of the German legal code, the Wissenschaftlich-humanitäres Komitee (Scientific-Humanitarian Committee) (q.v.) argued that it was irrational to imprison individuals because of a biological condition tantamount to left-handedness. Havelock Ellis used similar logic in his efforts to reform British law. Arguments not entirely dissimilar to the third sex theory are still in fashion today.

Ulrichs hoped that his research would liberate Urnings and Urningins from centuries of misunderstanding by demonstrating that abnormal sexual preferences were the result of biological causes, not individual moral debauchery. He further argued that the condition was an explicable biological variation induced in the gestation of the embryo, not the result of physiological degeneration. Indeed, Ulrichs's vision was responsible for changing the climate of opinion concerning the issue of moral responsibility. Most sexologists came to accept the idea that inversion was primarily innate. Ulrichs was less successful on the issue of degeneracy. Most research continued to link inverted sexual desire and congenital degeneracy for years to come. *See also* Medical Model of Homosexuality.

U

ULRICHS, KARL HEINRICH (1825–1895). Lawyer, author, and political activist, Karl Heinrich Ulrichs is remembered as the forefather of the modern homosexual rights movement.

A citizen of the kingdom of Hanover, Ulrichs protested the annexation of Hanover by Prussia in 1866. He was concerned about Prussian expansionism, in part because of Prussia's traditional Judeo-Christian taboos regarding sodomy and his fear that Prussia would reinstate criminal prohibitions against homosexuality in Hanover (they had, in effect, been rescinded by the introduction of the Code Napoléon by the French during their occupation of Hanover). He was incarcerated for one year for his resistance to the Prussian takeover of Hanover in 1866.

As a lawyer, Ulrichs was familiar with the Code Napoléon, the French legal code that had left its imprint on those German principalities formerly under French control. The Napoleonic Code, among other things, decriminalized same-sex love. Ulrichs argued that there was absolutely no evidence that the decriminalization of sodomy in France or elsewhere had any adverse consequences on the health or morals of the people. He thus embarked on a crusade to extend the decriminalization of same-sex love to all of Germany, even to those areas dominated by Prussia.

Ulrichs's principal contribution was the publication of 12 books on same-sex love between the years 1864 and 1879. The first five were published under a pseudonym, Numa Numantius; the balance were published under his own name. In addition to Ulrichs's own ideas, the collection of essays incorporates excerpts from historical, anthropological, medical, moral, and legal studies by a wide variety of authors. Essays appealing for legal justice and equity are prominently featured throughout the collection. Now collectively referred to as *The Riddle of "Man-Manly" Love*, Ulrichs's studies had an enormous impact on the subsequent development of the early homosexual rights movement.

In his studies, Ulrichs advanced the idea that same-sex love was a congenital condition and that *Urnings* and *Urningins* (terms he used to refer to male and female homosexuals), were "psychical hermaphrodites," a "third sex," individuals whose sexual desires did not correspond to their sexual organs. Although his third sex theory (q.v.) found few adherents, the idea that Urnings/Urningins developed in utero influenced some of the most prominent sex researchers of the day, including Carl von Westphal, Richard von Krafft-Ebing, Havelock Ellis, and Magnus Hirschfeld (qq.v.). Thus, Ulrichs was also instrumental in the development of the medical model of homosexuality (q.v.).

Ulrichs was also a political activist. He attempted to advance the interests of homosexuals at two German legal congresses. In 1865 at Graz and in 1867 in Munich he argued to no avail that the prohibitions against homosexuality in the Prussian law code were irrational and that same-sex love was not a vice. His campaign to forestall the recriminalization of homosexual sodomy ultimately came to naught owing to the consolidation of the modern German state in 1871 and the subsequent enactment of a harsh homosexual sodomy statute (q.v.), Paragraph 175 of the German imperial legal code (q.v.). Nevertheless, his initial efforts are remembered as the first public remarks in defense of homosexual rights.

Ulrichs is also remembered as the author of *Auf Bienchens Flügeln* (On the Wings of a Bee), a collection of homoerotic poems; *Kritische Pfeile* (Critical Arrows), a polemic addressed to political authorities in Berlin and Vienna; *Matrosengeschichten* (Sailor Stories); and *Alaudae* (Larks), a literary journal. He memorialized the death of Prince Ludwig II of Bavaria with a small collection of poems in 1886.

Karl Heinrich Ulrichs died in Aquila, a small town in northern Italy, where he lived the last years of his life in self-imposed exile. Before his death, he was visited by John Addington Symonds (q.v.), who carried his ideas to England. Two years after his death the first homosexual rights organization was established in Berlin by Magnus Hirschfeld, who was animated in large part by Ulrichs's works.

UNION OF LESBIANS AND HOMOSEXUALS. *See* SEXUAL MINORITIES ASSOCIATION.

UNION FOR SEXUAL FREEDOM IN IRELAND (USFI). Founded in the mid-1970s, the Union for Sexual Freedom in Ireland engaged primarily in providing support services and social outlets for gays and lesbians in Northern Ireland. Its political objective was the extension of the 1967 Sexual Offenses Act (q.v.) to Northern Ireland. Like Scotland, Northern Ireland had been excluded from the provisions of the 1967 Sexual Offenses Act, which decriminalized private homosexual relations between adult males. Gays in Northern Ireland were still governed by the provisions of the Act of 25 Henry VIII, Ch. 6, and the Labouchère Amendment to the Criminal Law Amendment Act (qq.v.). Both provided for severe punishments for men convicted of a wide range of homosexual activities. The USFI joined with the Campaign for Homosexual Equality (CHE) and the Scottish Minorities Group (SMG) (qq.v.) in drafting legislation that proposed both the liberalization of the 1967 Sexual Offenses Act and its extension to Northern Ireland. Fifteen years of work finally paid off in 1982 when the provisions of the 1967 Sexual Offenses Act were finally extended to Northern Ireland. The provisions of the statute, however, have yet to be liberalized.

V

VETERANS BENEVOLENT ASSOCIATION (VBA). The VBA emerged in the United States after World War II to serve the needs of gay and lesbian service personnel. It was the first U.S. homosexual rights organization since the short-lived Society for Human Rights (q.v.) in the mid-1920s, and even preceded the Mattachine Society (q.v.) as the first mass-membership homosexual rights organization in the United States. Thus the VBA, together with the Cultuur-en-Ontspannings Centrum (Culture and Recreational Center) (q.v.) in the Netherlands, were the first homosexual rights organizations to emerge after World War II.

The VBA originated in New York City in 1945 and served as a social and legal support network for its roughly 100 members until 1954.

W

WERTHER, RALPH. *See* LIND, EARL.

WHITMAN, WALT (1819–1892). American poet whose *Leaves of Grass* had a profound impact on the ideas of three British proponents of homosexual emancipation. In the "Calamus" section of the 1860 edition of *Leaves of Grass*, Whitman celebrated loving relationships between men and idealistically foretold a day when these attachments would transform not only friendships but political and social relationships as well.

Whitman's poems were read with great enthusiasm in England by John Addington Symonds and Edward Carpenter (qq.v.). Symonds's first encounter with *Leaves of Grass*, in 1865, inspired a lifelong correspondence with the American poet. Symonds was interested in Whitman's ideas on love between men and in his reaction to Symonds's own work on the subject. A recurrent theme in Symonds's letters to Whitman was his persistent question concerning the intent and meaning of the "Calamus" section of *Leaves of Grass*. Symonds saw in Whitman's poetry not only a defense of comradely love but also a justification of sexual relations between men, and he hoped to enlist Whitman's support for the idea of homosexual emancipation. This proved to be a source of great frustration for Symonds as well as increasing irritation for Whitman, who refused either to explicate the meaning of his poetry or endorse the idea of homosexual emancipation. Whitman went to his grave without satisfying Symonds on either score.

Whitman also had a great impact on Edward Carpenter who became acquainted with his poetry in 1869. Like Symonds, Carpenter was inspired to initiate a correspondence with Whitman because of Whitman's avowal of love between men and his idealistic social and political philosophy, values that also animated Carpenter. Carpenter visited with Whitman on two occasions in the United States, in 1877 and again in 1884. In 1883, Carpenter published "Towards Democracy," a poem indebted to Walt Whitman's ideas.

Whitman was also responsible in an indirect way for the professional relationships between Symonds, Carpenter, and Havelock Ellis (q.v.), the prominent British sex researcher and author. Ellis was also influenced by Whitman's poetry. An essay on Whitman in Ellis's book, *The New Spirit*, inspired Symonds to strike up a relationship with Ellis, which culminated in their joint authorship of *Sexual Inversion*. Similarly, Edward Carpenter's long professional association with Ellis and his wife, Edith, was due in part to their mutual admiration for the poetry of Walt Whitman.

As cofounders of the British Society for the Study of Sex Psychology, and through their involvement in the World League for Sexual Reform (qq.v.), Havelock Ellis and Edward Carpenter carried Walt Whitman's ideas to an international audience. Thus, although Whitman never spoke openly in defense of homosexual emancipation, his ideas were formative in the works of John Addington Symonds, Edward Carpenter, and Havelock Ellis and in the formation of national and international societies dedicated to sex reform.

WILDE, OSCAR (1854–1900). Internationally renowned Irish playwright, social critic, and proponent of homosexual love, Oscar Wilde's persecution by British authorities for his relationship with Lord Alfred Douglas became a worldwide symbol of discrimination against homosexuals.

In 1892 when Wilde became romantically involved with Lord Alfred Douglas, he was the most prominent playwright in London, known as much for his outspoken criticism of British customs and politics as for a succession of well-received plays. Married to Constance Holland and the father of two children, Wilde struck up a relationship with the son of John Douglas, the marquess of Queensberry. The elder Douglas took great exception to Wilde's courtship of his son and accused Wilde of being a pederast. This accusation precipitated a civil suit for defamation of character against Lord Alfred's father, which proved to be Wilde's undoing. Wilde not only lost the civil suit, but the evidence submitted to the court by John Douglas in defense of his accusation was subsequently used by prosecutors in a criminal proceeding against Wilde. The basis for the prosecution was Britain's Labouchère Amendment (q.v.). Although the first trial resulted in a hung jury, Wilde was subsequently convicted in a second trial and sentenced to two years "hard labour." Wilde died in exile in Paris several years after his release from prison.

Oscar Wilde's imprisonment became a rallying cry for those who sought to reform British law pertaining to homosexual offenses, such as John Addington Symonds, Edward Carpenter, and Havelock Ellis (qq.v.), as well as others such as Magnus Hirschfeld (q.v.) who were engaged in the struggle for homosexual emancipation abroad.

WISSENSCHAFTLICH-HUMANITÄRES KOMITEE / SCIENTIFIC-HUMANITARIAN COMMITTEE (SHC). The SHC was founded on 15 May 1897 by Magnus Hirschfeld (q.v.), Max Spohr, Erich Oberg, and others in Berlin. It was the principal homosexual rights organization in Germany between 1897 and 1933, and Magnus Hirschfeld was its acknowledged leader. Max Spohr, a publisher, republished the collected works of Karl Heinrich Ulrichs (q.v.) shortly after Ulrichs's death. Erich Oberg was a well-placed civil servant.

The SHC had a national and international following, with chapters in Munich, Leipzig, and Frankfurt and in Amsterdam, London, and Vienna. World War I interrupted its work and hindered its growing international influence. During the Weimar period, the SHC reasserted its role as the leading homosexual rights organization in Germany and throughout the world.

Magnus Hirschfeld was much influenced by Karl Heinrich Ulrichs. Like Ulrichs, Hirschfeld felt that homosexuals were an intermediate gender, neither masculine nor feminine. Also like Ulrichs, Hirschfeld argued that a scientific understanding of homosexuality was necessary if homosexuals were to be liberated from ancient fears and misunderstandings. Accordingly, the motto of the SHC was "per scientiam ad justitiam" ("justice through science").

The main goals of the SHC over its 35-year history were to educate the public about homosexuality, to enlist homosexuals in their own liberation struggle, and to effect the repeal of Paragraph 175 (q.v.) of the German penal code, which was adopted in 1871. Ulrichs and Karl Maria Kertbeny (q.v.) had struggled to prevent its adoption, to no avail. The SHC saw the repeal of Germany's harsh antihomosexual sodomy statute (q.v.) as its paramount objective.

The SHC lobbied extensively against Paragraph 175 with Roman Catholic priests, the criminal courts, police officials, mayors, newspapers, and so forth. In 1901 it produced a pamphlet "Was soll das Volk vom dritten Geschlecht wissen?" ("What Should the People Know about the Third Sex?"), which went through several revisions before the onset of World War I. Its total circulation was approximately 50,000.

The SHC also published the results of an unscientific survey of students and workers in Berlin. Of the 6,611 individuals surveyed, the SHC claimed that roughly 2.2 percent of them reported that they were homosexual. This constituted an unexpectedly high percentage, and the SHC hoped that this research might help underscore the fact that the homosexual population of Germany was much larger than had previously been believed. The results of the research became widely known in part because of the 1903 prosecution of Magnus Hirschfeld on the grounds of publishing "indecent" material. Hirschfeld defended his research in court, and the proceedings received wide coverage in the German press. Hirschfeld was found innocent but was fined 200 marks for the mere mention of perversions to the youths included in the survey.

The core of the SHC's parliamentary strategy was a petition drive aimed at influencing deliberations in the Reichstag. The petition was circulated for the first time in 1897. Its objective was to garner signatures of prominent individuals in the sciences and arts who subscribed to the principle of decriminalizing consensual adult male homosexuality. The SHC claimed that over 6,000 signatures were ultimately secured, including those of the prominent sexologists

Richard von Krafft-Ebing and Sigmund Freud, August Bebel (the Social Democratic Party leader), and other notables such as Martin Buber, Albert Einstein, Karl Jaspers, and Thomas Mann.

Although parliamentary consideration of the petition began in 1898, the first and only major debate on Paragraph 175 during Kaiser Wilhelm's reign did not take place until 1905. Beyond a narrow circle of supporters, it mustered little support.

The support for the SHC waned in the years prior to World War I as a result of testimony given by Hirschfeld in the trial of Count Kuno von Moltke, a close personal associate of the kaiser and mayor of Berlin. The count, along with other advisors to the kaiser, had been exposed as a homosexual in the pages of a prominent socialist newspaper, *Die Zukunft*. Hirschfeld's expert testimony regarding the count's sexual orientation was widely regarded to be a betrayal of confidentiality and led to a decline in financial support for the SHC. World War I effectively brought the work of the SHC to a halt.

The adoption of the Weimar Constitution in 1919 produced a renewed emphasis on the petition drive. Together with the Gemeinschaft der Eigenen (Community of the Special) and the Deutscher Freundschaftsverband (German Friendship Association), the SHC formed the Aktionsausschuss (Action Committee) (qq.v.), in 1920, to further the effort to repeal Paragraph 175. The SHC also joined with six other groups in the Kartell für Reform des Sexualstrafrechts (Coalition for Reform of the Sexual Crimes Code) in 1925. The coalition published a progressive draft penal code in 1927. Reichstag deliberations on 175 resumed in 1928–29. In 1929, the Reichstag Committee for Penal Code Reform voted by a narrow margin to legalize homosexual acts between consenting adults. The bill was tabled by the Reichstag, however, and Paragraph 175 was never again debated before the demise of the Weimar Republic in 1933.

Among its other accomplishments, the SHC published the *Jahrbuch für sexuelle Zwischenstufen* (Yearbook for Sexual Intermediates) between 1899 and 1923. Edited by Hirschfeld, this was a scholarly journal devoted to anthropological, historical, legal, and medical studies of homosexuality. The yearbook also served to inform members of the SHC's activities. Beyond the yearbook, the SHC helped produce *Anders als die Andern* (Different from the Others), the first motion picture devoted to the subject of homosexuality. Hirschfeld was instrumental in the film's production and played one of its lead roles.

The SHC did not survive the rise of the Nazi Party and the demise of the Weimar Republic. The SHC was housed in the same building as the Institut für Sexualwissenschaft (Institute for Sexual Science) and the World League for Sexual Reform (qq.v.), and its activities were brought to an ultimate halt when the building was ransacked by Nazi youth on 6 May 1933. The contents of the building were removed and never recovered. Most of the possessions were burned on 10 May 1933 as part of a nationwide mass book burning devoted to purging the nation of un-German publications.

WOLFENDEN REPORT. *See* COMMITTEE ON HOMOSEXUAL OFFENSES AND PROSTITUTION, REPORT OF.

WORLD LEAGUE FOR SEXUAL REFORM (WLSR). The First Congress for Sexual Reform was convened by Magnus Hirschfeld (q.v.) on 15 September 1921 at the Institut für Sexualwissenschaft (Institute for Sexual Science) (q.v.) in Berlin. The creation of the WLSR was one of the principal accomplishments of the congress. Magnus Hirschfeld, Havelock Ellis (q.v.), and August Forel were named its first copresidents at the 1928 meeting in Copenhagen, where the WLSR was formally established. Three further conferences of the WLSR were held; in London in 1929, Vienna in 1930, and Brno in 1932. At the height of its influence the WLSR, together with its affiliated organizations, claimed a membership of 130,000.

Similar to the British Society for the Study of Sex Psychology (q.v.), the announced purposes of the WLSR were to reform laws that discriminated against women and homosexuals and to promote contraception and abortion rights. WLSR worked to achieve sexual freedom and the right of consenting adults to engage in sexual activities free from the fear of criminal prosecution.

The WLSR was racked by internal political disputes concerning the issue of the league's responsibility for combating fascism. Some, most notably Wilhelm Reich, argued that the purpose of the organization (sexual reform based on scientific knowledge) was being undermined by the policies of the Nazi Party. Others felt that the WLSR should remain committed to the advancement of science and should not engage in politics. Citing deep and irreconcilable differences over the politics of the WLSR, its co-presidents Norman Haire (q.v.) (England) and J. H. Leunbach (Denmark) disbanded the organization in 1935.

WU, GARY (1969–   ). Since his arrest and imprisonment in the People's Republic of China (PRC) in 1995, Gary Wu has emerged as one of the leading advocates of gay and lesbian rights in the PRC. His arrest and imprisonment for organizing a lesbian social event at the Fourth Annual Conference on Women in Beijing caused Wu to seek asylum (q.v.) in the West. Now living in exile, Wu has devoted most of his energy to publicizing the plight of gays and lesbians in the PRC and to the promotion of the International Chinese Comrades Organization, an organization cofounded by Wu to provide information about gay life to gays and lesbians in the PRC. He has also been involved in the promotion of the Overseas Chinese Gay and Lesbian Center and a film festival featuring Chinese gay and lesbian cinema.

A professional reporter, Wu is the author of *Black Souls Under a Red Sun*, a book documenting gay and lesbian life in the PRC. The book, which is banned in the PRC, contains interviews with Chinese gays and lesbians and discusses the oppressive social and political climate for homosexuals. Although homosexuality is not proscribed by law, it is officially condemned by the Communist Party, and familial pressures stifle gays and lesbians from coming out. Reminiscent of recent psychological practices in the West, are Wu's recorded incidents of the use of shock therapy in attempts to change the sexual orientation of gays and lesbians. The difficulties facing the fledgling gay and lesbian movement in the PRC are many and varied, but Wu hopes that his promotional activities in Western Europe and the United States will contribute to the eventual success of the movement.

Based on Wu's impressions of his country, the takeover of Hong Kong by the PRC in 1997 looms like a dark cloud over the aspirations of those involved in organizations such as the Ten Percent Club (q.v.), who have campaigned for the legal and social rights of gays and lesbians in Hong Kong.

Bibliography

Introduction

Scholarly literature on homosexuality and the gay liberation movement is primarily a 20th-century phenomenon, although references to homosexuality can be found in Eastern as well as Western languages that antedate the modern period. Since the end of World War II, the volume of publications on the subject has grown exponentially. I have attempted to present a bibliography that reflects the enormity of recent scholarship on the phenomenon of love between men as well as the gay liberation movement. Most of the sources are in English, but many important sources that reflect the history of gay politics in other countries remain untranslated, and I have included as many as space will permit.

In keeping with my periodization of the gay liberation movement, I have included bibliographical entries corresponding to the early homosexual rights movement, the modern homosexual rights movement, and the contemporary homosexual rights movement. Many original classics (such as the works of early movement leaders) are included. In addition, there are numerous entries reflecting the ancient history of same-sex love throughout the world, long before the gay liberation movement erupted in the 19th century.

Because our understanding of "homosexuality" has been constructed from publications in fields as diverse as anthropology, law, literature, psychology, religion, social and political theory, and sociology, I have included selected references from each of these fields. Similar concerns associated with the diversity of social practices related to male homosexuality motivated me to include bibliographical entries reflecting gay culture, including the cross-cultural nature of gayness and gay politics. Finally, I have included a section in the bibliography on contemporary issues.

Organization of the Bibliography

1. Bibliographies
2. Periodicals/Journals

1. Bibliographies

Bell, Alan P., and Martin S. Weinberg, eds. *Homosexuality: An Annotated Bibliography*. New York: Oxford University Press, 1972.

Bullough, Vern, and W. Dorr Legg et al., eds. *An Annotated Bibliography of Homosexuality* (2 vols.). New York: Garland, 1976.

Courouve, C. *Bibliographie des Homosexualités*. Paris, 1978.

Crawford, William. *Homosexuality in Canada: A Bibliography*. Toronto: Canadian Gay Archives, 1984.

Dall'Orto, G. *Leggere Omosessuale: Bibliografia*. Turin, 1984.

Dynes, Wayne R. "A Bibliography of Bibliographies of Homosexuality."*Cabirion and Gay Books Bulletin* (10) (1984): 16–22.

Foster, Stephen Wayne. "Bibliography of Homosexuality among Latin-American Indians." *Cabirion and Gay Books Bulletin* 12 (1985): 17–19.

Fout, John. *A Select Bibliography on the History of Sexuality*. Annandale-on-Hudson, N.Y.: Committee on Lesbian and Gay History, Bard College, 1989.

Garza, Luis Alberto de la. *Preliminary Chicano and Latino Lesbian and Gay Bibliography*. Berkeley, Calif.: Archivos Rodrigo Reyes, 1994.

Gittings, B. B. *A Gay Bibliography*. Philadelphia: Task Force on Gay Liberation, American Library Association, 1974.

Herzer, Manfred. *Bibliographie zur Homosexualität*. Berlin: Verlag Rosa Winkel, 1982.

Kertbeny, Karl Maria. *Kertbeny: Bibliographie der Werke, publiziert von K. M. Kertbeny, 1846–1874*. Berlin: Druckerei des Berliner Tageblatt, 1873.

Parker, W. *Homosexuality: A Selective Bibliography of over Three Thousand Items*. Metuchen, N.J.: Scarecrow Press, 1971.

Porter, Jack Nunan. *Sexual Politics in the Third Reich: The Persecution of Homosexuals During the Holocaust: A Bibliography and Introductory Essay*. Montreal: Concordia University, 1991.

Retief, Glen. *The Policing of Subjugated Sexualities: A Bibliography*. Cape Town: Institute of Criminology, University of Cape Town, 1992.

Ridinger, Robert B. Marks. *The Homosexual and Society: An Annotated Bibliography*. New York: Greenwood Press, 1990.

———. *The Gay and Lesbian Movement: References and Resources*. Boston: G. K. Hall, 1996.

Smith, Aaron Stratton. *A Cross-Cultural Bibliography on Homosexuality*. [s.l., s.n., 1992].

Steakley, James. *The Writings of Dr. Magnus Hirschfeld: A Bibliography*. Toronto, 1985.

Task Force on Lesbian and Gay Issues, Council on Social Work Education. *An Annotated Bibliography of Lesbian and Gay Readings*. New York: The Council, 1983.

Verstraete, Beert C. *Homosexuality in Ancient Greek and Roman Civilizations: A Critical Bibliography with Supplement*. Toronto: Canadian Gay Archives, 1982.

2. Periodicals/Journals

The Advocate. Los Angeles: LPI, September 1967– .

Australasian Gay and Lesbian Law Journal. Annandale, N.S.W.: The Federation Press, 1993– .

Erickson Educational Foundation Newsletter. Baton Rouge, La.: Erickson Educational Foundation, 1968– .
Gay Community News. Boston: G.C.N., 1973–1992, 1994– .
Gay Sunshine. San Francisco: Gay Sunshine Press, (nos. #1–47) 1970–82.
Journal of Gay, Lesbian, and Bisexual Identity. New York: Human Sciences Press, 1996– .
Journal of Homosexuality. New York: Haworth Press, 1974– .
The Mattachine Review (12 vols.). New York: Arno Press, 1975.
The Ladder (16 vols.). San Francisco: Daughters of Bilitis, 1956–1972.
One Magazine: The Homosexual Viewpoint. Los Angeles: One Inc., 1953–68.

3. Archives/Libraries

Archives Gaies du Québec. 4067 St-Laurent, Suite 202, Montreal, Québec, Canada.
Black Gay Archives. Box 30004, Philadelphia, Pennsylvania.
Blanche Baker Memorial Library and Archives (One Inc.). 3340 Country Club Drive, Los Angeles, California.
Canadian Gay Archives. P.O. Box 639, Station A, Toronto, Ontario, Canada.
Gough, Cal, and Ellen Greenblatt, eds. *Gay and Lesbian Library Service.* Jefferson, North Carolina: McFarland, 1990.
Henry Gerber/Pearl M. Hart Library and Archives. 3352 N. Paulina Street, Chicago, Illinois.
International Gay and Lesbian Archives. P.O. Box 38100, Los Angeles, California.
Metropolitan Community Church Library. 1919 Decatur, Houston, Texas.
National Museum and Archive of Lesbian and Gay History. Lesbian and Gay Community Services Center, 208 W. Thirteenth Street, New York, New York.
New York Public Library. Division of Humanities, Social Sciences, and Special Collections, New York, New York.

4. Almanacs/Encyclopedias/Dictionaries/Indices

The Alyson Almanac: A Treasury of Information for the Gay and Lesbian Community. Boston: Alyson, 1989.
Copely, Ursla Enters. *Directory of Homosexual Organizations and Publications: A Field Guide to the Homosexual Movement in the*

United States and Canada with Topical Index. Hollywood, Calif.: Homosexual Information Center, 1985.

Dynes, Wayne R. *Homolexis: A Historical and Cultural Lexicon of Homosexuality.* New York: Scholarship Committee, Gay Academic Union, 1985.

————. *Homosexuality: A Research Guide.* New York: Garland, 1987.

Dynes, Wayne R., ed. *Encyclopedia of Homosexuality* (2 vols.). New York: Garland, 1990.

Fitch, J. Harrison, and the editors of *Out* Magazine. *Out's Gay and Lesbian Guide to the WEB.* Emeryville, Calif: Lycos Press, 1997.

Greenberg, Alan. *Gay/Lesbian Periodicals Index.* Charlotte, N.C.: Integrity Indexing, 1992.

Malinowski, H. Robert. *International Directory of Gay and Lesbian Periodicals.* Phoenix: Oryx Press, 1987.

Murray, R. *Images in the Dark: An Encyclopedia of Gay and Lesbian Film and Video.* Philadelphia: TLA Publications, 1994.

National Museum and Archive of Lesbian and Gay History. *The Gay Almanac.* New York: Berkeley Books, 1996.

Ridinger, Robert B. Marks. *An Index to The Advocate, The National Gay Newsmagazine, 1967–1982.* Los Angeles: Liberation Publications, 1987.

Walker, Bill. *San Francisco Bay Area Gay and Lesbian Serials: A Guide to the Microfilm Collection.* Berkeley: University of California, 1991.

5. Biographies/Correspondence/Memoirs

Alexander, Jeb. *Jeb and Dash: A Diary of a Gay Life, 1918–1945.* Edited by Ina Russell. Boston: Faber and Faber, 1993.

Aronson, Theo. *Prince Eddy and the Homosexual Underworld.* London: J. Murray, 1994.

Bauman, Robert. *The Gentleman from Maryland: The Conscience of a Gay Conservative.* New York: Arbor House, 1986.

Beith, Gilbert, ed. *Edward Carpenter: In Appreciation.* London: G. Allen and Unwin, 1931.

Brodie, Fawn M. *The Devil Drives: A Life of Sir Richard Burton.* New York: W. W. Norton, 1967.

Burton, Peter. *Parallel Lives.* London: GMP; Boston: Alyson Publications, 1985.

Carpenter, Edward. *My Days and Dreams: Being Autobiographical Notes.* London: G. Allen and Unwin, 1916.

Crisp, Quentin. *The Naked Civil Servant.* New York: New American Library, 1978.

Duberman, Martin B. *Cures: A Gay Man's Odyssey*. New York: Dutton, 1991.

————. *Midlife Queer: Autobiography of a Decade: 1971–1981*. New York: Scribner, 1996.

Faas, Ekbert. *Young Robert Duncan: Portrait of the Poet as Homosexual in Society*. Santa Barbara, Calif.: Black Sparrow Press, 1983.

Freeman, Simon, and Barrie Penrose. *Conspiracy of Silence: The Secret Life of Anthony Blunt*. London: Grafton, 1986.

Grosskurth, Phyllis. *John Addington Symonds, a Biography*. London: Longmans, 1964.

Grosskurth, Phyllis, ed. *The Memoirs of John Addington Symonds*. London: Hutchinson, 1984.

Guérin, Daniel. *Proudhon, oui ou non*. Paris: Gallimard, 1978.

————. *Autobiographie de Jeunesse*. Paris: Pierre Belfond, 1972.

————, ed. *Charles Fourier: Vers la liberté en amour*. Paris, 1975.

Gunderson, Steve, and Rob Morris with Bruce Bawer. *House and Home*. New York: Dutton, 1996.

Hall Carpenter Archives. Gay Men's Oral History Group. *Walking After Midnight: Gay Men's Life Stories*. London, New York: Routledge, 1989.

Hernandez, Tony. *A mi manera—: la vida de un homosexual*. Mexico D.F.: Costa-Amic Editores, 1988.

Hodges, Andrew. *Alan Turing*. New York: Simon and Schuster, 1984.

Holroyd, Michael. *Lytton Strachey: The New Biography*. New York: Farrar, Straus, and Giroux, 1995.

Hooven, F. Valentine. *Tom of Finland: His Life and Times*. New York: St. Martin's Press, 1993.

Hyde, H. Montgomery. *Lord Alfred Douglas: A Biography*. London: Methuen, 1984.

Isherwood, Christopher. *Christopher and His Kind, 1929–1939*. New York: Farrar, Straus, and Giroux, 1976.

Kennedy, Hubert. *Ulrichs: The Life and Works of Karl Heinrich Ulrichs: Pioneer of the Modern Gay Movement*. Boston: Alyson Publications, 1988.

Liebman, Marvin. *Coming Out Conservative: An Autobiography*. San Francisco: Chronicle Books, 1992.

Lind, Earl, a.k.a. Ralph Werther. *Autobiography of an Androgyne*. New York: Arno Press, 1975 (c. 1918).

Martin, Robert K., and George Piggford, eds. *Queer Forester*. Chicago: University of Chicago Press, 1997.

Meier, Karl. *Heinrich Hössli: On the 100th Year of His Death*. Trans. Michael Lombardi. Los Angeles: Urania Manuscripts, 1982.

Mixner, David. *Stranger among Friends*. New York: Bantam Books, 1996.

Persichetti, Nicoló. *In Memory of Karl Heinrich Ulrichs*. Trans. Michael Lombardi. Los Angeles: Urania Manuscripts, 1982.

Peters, Robert L., and Herbert M. Schueller, eds. *The Letters of John Addington Symonds* (3 vols.). Detroit: Wayne State University Press, 1967–1969.

Pollard, Patrick. *Andre Gide: Homosexual Moralist*. New Haven, Conn.: Yale University Press, 1991.

Porter, Kevin, and Jeffrey Weeks, eds. *Between the Acts: Lives of Homosexual Men, 1885–1967*. New York: Routledge, 1991.

Rowbotham, Sheila, and Jeffrey Weeks. *Socialism and the New Life: The Personal and Sexual Politics of Edward Carpenter and Havelock Ellis*. London: Pluto Press, 1977.

Shilts, Randy. *The Mayor of Castro Street: The Life and Times of Harvey Milk*. New York: St. Martin's Press, 1982.

Siciliano, Enzo. *Pasolini: A Biography*. Trans. John Shepley. New York: Random House, 1982.

Spencer, Colin. *Which of Us Two? The Story of a Love Affair*. London; New York: Viking, 1990.

Sucipto. *Jalan Sempurna*. Jakarta: Apresiasi Gay Jakarta, 1992.

Symonds, John Addington. *Walt Whitman: A Study*. New York: B. Blom, 1967.

Timmons, Stuart. *The Trouble with Harry Hay: Founder of the Modern Gay Movement*. Boston: Alyson Publications, 1990.

Tsuzuki, Chushichi. *Edward Carpenter, 1844–1929*. New York: Cambridge University Press, 1980.

Ulrichs, Karl Heinrich. *Letters to His Publisher and Other Correspondence*. Trans. Michael Lombardi. Los Angeles: Urania Manuscripts, 1985.

Vacha, Keith. *Quiet Fire: Memoirs of Older Gay Men*. Edited by Cassie Damewood. Trumansburg, N.Y.: Crossing Press, 1985.

White, Edmund. *Genet: A Biography*. New York: Alfred A. Knopf, 1993.

Wojnarowicz, David. *Close to the Knives: A Memoir of Disintegration*. New York: Vintage Books, 1991.

Wolfenden, Sir John. *Turning Points: The Memoirs of Lord Wolfenden*. London: Bodley Head, 1976.

Wolff, Charlotte. *Magnus Hirschfeld: A Portrait of a Pioneer in Sexology*. London: Quartet, 1986.

6. Literature/Film and Video

Aldrich, Robert. *The Seduction of the Mediterranean: Writing, Art, and Homosexual Fantasy*. New York: Routledge, 1993.

Almendros, Néstor and Orlando Jiménez-Leal, eds. *Conducta Impropia*. Madrid: Editorial Playor, 1984.

Bad Object Choices, ed. *How Do I Look: Queer Film and Video*. Seattle: Bay Press, 1991.

Bergman, David. *Gaiety Transfigured: Gay Self-Representation in American Literature*. Madison: University of Wisconsin Press, 1991.

Bergmann, Emile L., and Paul Julian Smith, eds. *¿Entiendes? Queer Readings, Hispanic Writings*. Durham, N.C.: Duke University Press, 1995.

Bersani, Leo. *Homos/Leo Bersani*. Cambridge, Mass.: Harvard University Press, 1995.

Binding, Paul. *Lorca: The Gay Imagination*. London: GMP, 1985.

Burroughs, William. *Queer*. New York: Viking Press, 1985.

Butters, Ronald R., John M. Clum, and Michael Moon, eds. *Displacing Homophobia: Gay Male Perspectives in Literature and Culture*. Durham, N.C.: Duke University Press, 1989.

Clark, J. Michael. *Liberation and Disillusionment: The Development of Gay Male Criticism and Popular Fiction a Decade after Stonewall*. Las Colinas, Tex.: Liberal Press, 1987.

———. *Pink Triangles and Gay Images: (Re)claiming Communal and Personal History in Retrospective Gay Fiction*. Arlington, Tex.: Liberal Arts Press, 1987.

Cocteau, Jean. *The White Paper*. New York: Macauley, 1958.

Craft, Christopher. *Another Kind of Love: Male Homosexual Desire in English Discourse, 1850–1920*. Berkeley: University of California Press, 1994.

Crew, Louie, ed. *The Gay Academic*. Palm Springs, Calif.: ETC Publications, 1978.

Cuseo, Allan A. *Homosexual Characters in YA Novels: A Literary Analysis, 1969–1982*. Metuchen, N.J.: Scarecrow Press, 1992.

Curtis, Wayne, ed. *Revelations: A Collection of Gay Male Coming Out Stories*. Boston: Alyson Publications; London: Distributed in the U.K. by GMP Publishers, 1988.

De Jongh, Nicholas. *Not in Front of the Audience: Homosexuality on Stage*. London; New York: Routledge, 1992.

Delavenay, Emile. *D. H. Lawrence and Edward Carpenter: A Study in Edwardian Transition*. London: Taplinger, 1971.

Dollimore, Jonathan. *Sexual Dissidence: Augustine to Wilde, Freud to Foucault*. Oxford: Clarendon Press, 1991.

Dyer, Richard. "Less and More than Women and Men: Lesbian and Gay Cinema in Weimar Germany." *New German Critique* 40 (1987): 5–60.

———. *Now You See It: Studies on Lesbian and Gay Film*. London; New York: Routledge, 1990.

Fichte, Hubert. *The Gay Critic*. Trans. Kevin Gavin. Ann Arbor: University of Michigan Press, 1996.

Fone, Byrne R. S. *A Road to Stonewall: Male Homosexuality and Homophobia in England and America Literature, 1750–1969*. New York: Twayne Publishers, 1994.

Fone, Byrne R. S., ed. *Hidden Heritage: History and the Gay Imagination, An Anthology*. New York: Avocation, 1980.

Foster, David William. *Gay and Lesbian Themes in Latin American Writing*. Austin: University of Texas Press, 1991.

Foster, David William, ed. *Latin American Writers on Gay and Lesbian Themes: A Bio-Critical Sourcebook*. Westport, Conn.: Greenwood Press, 1994.

Galloway, David, and Christian Sabisch, eds. *Calamus: Male Homosexuality in Twentieth-Century Literature—An International Anthology*. New York: Quill, 1982.

Genet, Jean. *Querelle*. Trans. Anselem Hollo. New York: Grove Press, 1974.

———. *Prisoner of Love*. Trans. Barbara Bray. Hanover, N.H.: University Press of New England, 1992.

Gever, Martha, John Greyson, and Pratibha Parmar, eds. *Queer Looks: Perspectives on Lesbian and Gay Film and Video*. New York: Routledge, 1993.

Gide, André. *Corydon*. Trans. Richard Howard. New York: Farrar, Straus, and Giroux, 1983.

Goldberg, Jonathan. *Sodometries: Renaissance Texts: Modern Sexualities*. Stanford, Calif.: Stanford University Press, 1992.

Hadleigh, Boze. *The Lavender Screen: The Gay and Lesbian Films: Their Stars, Makers, Characters, and Critics*. Secaucus, N.J.: Carol Pub. Group, 1992.

Karlinsky, Simon. "Russia's Gay Literature and History (11th to 20th Centuries)." *Gay Sunshine* 29–30 (1976): 1–7.

———. "Death and Resurrection of Mikhail Kuzmin." *Slavic Review* 38 (1979): 92.

Kirkup, James. *A Poet Could Not Be But Gay: Some Legends of My Lost Youth*. London; Chester Springs, Penn.: Peter Owen, 1991.

Kopelson, Kevin. *Love's Litany: The Writing of Modern Homoerotics*. Stanford, Calif. : Stanford University Press, 1994.

Koponen, Wilfred R. *Embracing a Gay Identity: Gay Novels as Guides*. Westport, Conn.: Bergin & Garvey, 1993.

Krouse, Matthew, ed. *The Invisible Ghetto: Lesbian and Gay Writing from South Africa*. East Haven, Conn.: Inbook, 1993.

Kuzmin, Mikhail. *Wings: Prose and Poetry*. Trans./ed. Neil Granoien and Michael Green. Ann Arbor, Mich.: Ardis, 1972.

Leyland, Winston, ed. *Now the Volcano: An Anthology of Latin Ameri-*

can Gay Literature. Trans. Erskine Lane, Franklin D. Blanton, and Simon Karlinsky. San Francisco: Gay Sunshine Press, 1979.

Lilly, Mark, ed. *Lesbian and Gay Writing: An Anthology of Critical Essays*. London: Macmillan, 1990.

Lucey, Michael. *Gide's Bent: Sexuality, Politics, Writing*. New York: Oxford University Press, 1995.

Mackay, John Henry. *The Hustler: The Story of a Nameless Love from Friedrich Street*. Trans. Hubert Kennedy. Boston: Alyson Publications, 1985.

Mailer, Norman. *The Homosexual Villain*. Los Angeles: One, 1955.

Marks, Elaine, and George Stambolain, eds. *Homosexualities and French Literature: Cultural Contexts/Critical Texts*. Ithaca, N.Y.: Cornell University Press, 1979.

Martin, Robert K. *The Homosexual Tradition in American Poetry*. Austin: University of Texas Press, 1979.

Meve, Jorn. *Homosexuelle Nazis: Ein Stereotyp in Politik und Literatur des Exils*. Hamburg: MannerschwarmSkript, 1990.

Mishima, Yukio. *Confessions of a Mask*. Trans. Meredith Weatherby. New York: New Directions, 1968.

Morrow, Bruce, and Charles H. Rowell, eds. *Shade: An Anthology of Fiction by Gay Men of African Descent*. New York: Avon, 1996.

Murphy, Timothy F., and Suzanne Poirier, eds. *Writing AIDS: Gay Literature, Language, and Analysis*. New York: Columbia University Press, 1993.

Nelson, Emmanuel S., ed. *Critical Essays: Gay and Lesbian Writers of Color*. Binghamton, N.Y.: Harrington Park Press, 1993.

Proust, Marcel. *Sodome et Gomorrhe*. Trans. C. K. Scott Moncrieff and Terrance Kilmartin. New York: Modern Library, 1993.

Reade, Brian, ed. *Sexual Heretics: Male Homosexuality in English Literature from 1850 to 1900*. London: Routledge and Kegan Paul, 1970.

Rivers, J. E. *Proust and the Art of Love: The Aesthetics of Sexuality in the Life, Times, and Art of Marcel Proust*. New York: Columbia University Press, 1980.

Robinson, Christopher. *Scandal in the Ink: Male and Female Homosexuality in Twentieth-Century French Literature*. London; New York: Cassell, 1995.

Russo, Vito. *The Celluloid Closet*. New York: Harper and Row, 1981.

Sartre, Jean-Paul. *St. Genet: Comedien et Martyr. St. Genet: Actor and Martyr*. Trans. Bernard Frechtman. New York: Pantheon Books, 1983.

Saslow, James M. *Ganymede in the Renaissance: Homosexuality in Art and Society*. New Haven, Conn.: Yale University Press, 1986.

Schmidgall, Gary. *The Stranger Wilde: Interpreting Oscar.* New York: Dutton, 1994.

Sedgwick, Eve Kosofsky. *Between Men: English Literature and Male Homosocial Desire.* New York: Columbia University Press, 1986.

Sergent, Bernard. *L'homosexualité dans la mythologie grecque.* Paris: Payot, 1984.

Shively, Charley, ed. *Calamus Lovers: Walt Whitman's Working-Class Camerados.* San Francisco: Gay Sunshine Press, 1987.

Sinfield, Alan. *The Wilde Century: Effeminacy, Oscar Wilde, and the Queer Moment.* London: Cassell, 1994.

Stehling, Thomas. *Medieval Latin Poems of Male Love and Friendship.* New York: Garland, 1984.

Straayer, Chris. *Deviant Eyes, Deviant Bodies: Sexual Re-Orientations in Film and Video.* New York: Columbia University Press, 1996.

Yingling, Thomas E. *Hart Crane and the Homosexual Text: New Thresholds, New Anatomies.* Chicago: University of Chicago Press, 1990.

7. Social and Political Theory

Abelove, Henry, Michele Aina Barale, and David Halperin, eds. *The Lesbian and Gay Studies Reader.* New York: Routledge, 1993.

Adam Barry D. *The Survivial of Domination: Inferiorization and Everyday Life.* New York: Elsevier/Greenwood, 1978.

———. "Sexual Outlaws." *Canadian Journal of Political and Social Theory* 4(2) (1980): 75.

———. "Where Gay People Come From." *Christopher Street* 64 (1982): 50.

———. "Structural Foundations of the Gay World." *Comparative Studies in Society and History* 27(4) (1985): 658–70.

———. "The Construction of a Sociological 'Homosexual' in Canadian Textbooks." *Canadian Review of Sociology and Anthropology* 23(3) (1986): 399.

Altman, Dennis. *Homosexual Oppression and Liberation.* New York: Outerbridge & Dienstfrey, 1971.

———. "The State, Repression, and Sexuality." *Gay Left* 6 (summer 1978): 4.

Altman, Dennis, et. al. *Homosexuality, Which Homosexuality: International Conference on Gay and Lesbian Studies.* Amsterdam: Uitgeverij An Dekker/Schorer; London: GMP, 1989.

Beemyn, Brett, and Mickey Eliason, eds. *Queer Studies: A Lesbian, Gay, Bisexual, and Transgender Anthology.* New York: New York University Press, 1996.

Blasius, Mark. *Gay and Lesbian Politics: Sexuality and the Emergence of a New Ethic*. Philadelphia: Temple University Press, 1994.

Bristow, Joseph, and Angelia R. Wilson, eds. *Activating Theory: Lesbian, Gay, Bisexual Politics*. London: Lawrence and Wishart, 1993.

Bronski, Michael. *Culture Clash: The Making of a Gay Sensibility*. Boston: South End Press, 1984.

Butler, Judith. *Gender Trouble: Feminism and the Subversion of Identity*. New York: Routledge, 1990.

———. "Sexual Inversions." In *Discourses of Sexuality: From Aristotle to AIDS*, edited by Donna C. Stanton, 344–61. Ann Arbor: University of Michigan Press, 1992.

———. *Bodies That Matter: On the Discursive Limits of "Sex"*. New York and London: Routledge, 1993.

Cohen, Ed. *Talk on the Wilde Side: Towards a Genealogy of a Discourse on Male Sexualities*. New York: Routledge, 1993.

Cohen, Jean. "Strategy or Identity." *Social Research* 52(4) (1985): 663.

Cohen, Steven F., and James Gallagher. "Gay Movements and Legal Change: Some Aspects of the Dynamics of a Social Problem." *Social Problems* 32 (1984): 72–81.

Dannecker, Martin. *Homosexuelle und die Homosexualität*. (Theories of Homosexuality). Trans. David Fernbach. London: Gay Men's Press, 1981.

De Cecco, John P., and John P. Elia, eds. *If You Seduce a Straight Person, Can You Make Them Gay? Issues in Biological Essentialism versus Social Constructionism in Gay and Lesbian Identities*. Binghamton, N.Y.: Harrington Park Press, 1993.

de Lauretis, Teresa, ed. *Queer Theory: Lesbian and Gay Sexualities*. Bloomington: Indiana University Press, 1991.

Dorenkamp, Monica, and Richard Henke, eds. *Negotiating Lesbian and Gay Subjects*. New York: Routledge, 1995.

Dynes, Wayne. "Privacy, Sexual Orientation, and the Self-Sovereignty of the Individual: Continental Theories, 1762–1908." *Gay Books Bulletin* 6 (1981): 20–23.

Edelman, Lee. *Homographesis: Essays in Gay Literary and Cultural Theory*. New York: Routledge, 1994.

Edwards, Tim. *Erotics and Politics: Gay Male Sexuality, Masculinity, and Feminism*. New York: Routledge, 1994.

Epstein, Julia, and Kristina Straub, eds. *Body Guards: The Culture and Politics of Gender Ambiguity*. London: Routledge, 1991.

Epstein, Steven. "Gay Politics, Ethnic Identity: The Limits of Social Constructionism." *Socialist Review* 93/94 (1987): 9–56.

Escoffier, Jeffrey. "Sexual Revolution and the Politics of Gay Identity." *Socialist Review* 81/82 (1985): 119–54.

Féray, Jean-Claude. "Une histoire critique du mot homosexualité." *Arcadie*. 325 (1981): 11–21; 326 (1981): 115–24; 327 (1981): 171–81; 328 (1981): 246–58.

Fernbach, David. *The Spiral Path: A Gay Contribution to Human Survival*. London: Gay Men's Press; Boston: Alyson, 1981.

Foucault, Michel. *The History of Sexuality: Introduction*. Vol. 1 of *The History of Sexuality*. Trans. Robert Hurley. New York: Pantheon Books, 1978.

———. "Sexual Choice, Sexual Act." *Salmagundi* 58–59 (1982–83): 10.

———. *The Use of Pleasure*. Vol. 2 of *The History of Sexuality*. Trans. Robert Hurley. New York: Pantheon Books, 1985.

———. *The Care of the Self*. Vol. 3 of *The History of Sexuality*. Trans. Robert Hurley. New York: Pantheon Books, 1986.

Freud, Sigmund. *Three Essays on the Theory of Sexuality*. Trans. James Strachey. New York: Basic Books, 1962.

Fuss, Diana. *Essentially Speaking: Feminism, Nature and Difference*. New York: Routledge, 1989.

Fuss, Diana, ed. *Inside/Out: Lesbian Theories, Gay Theories*. New York: Routledge, 1991.

Greenberg, David F. *The Construction of Homosexuality*. Chicago: University of Chicago Press, 1988.

Halperin, David, John J. Winkler, and Froma I. Zeitlin, eds. *Before Sexuality: The Construction of Erotic Experience in the Ancient Greek World*. Princeton, N.J.: Princeton University Press, 1988.

Hart, John, and Diane Richardson, eds. *The Theory and Practice of Homosexuality*. London: Routledge and Kegan Paul, 1981.

Henke, Richard, and Monica Dorenkamp, eds. *Negotiating Lesbian and Gay Subjects*. New York: Routledge, 1995.

Kaplan, Morris. *Sexual Justice: Democratic Citizenship and the Politics of Desire*. New York: Routledge, 1997.

McIntosh, Mary. "The Homosexual Role." *Social Problems* 16 (1968): 182–92.

Mieli, Mario. *Elementi di critica omosessuale*. (Homosexuality and Liberation: Elements of a gay critique). Trans. David Fernbach. London: Gay Men's Press, 1980.

Morton, Donald, ed. *The Material Queer: A LesBiGay Cultural Studies Reader*. Boulder, Colo.: Westview Press, 1996.

Murray, Stephen O. *Social Theory, Homosexual Realities*. New York: Gai Saber, 1984.

Padug, Robert. "Sexual Matters: On Conceptualizing Sexuality in History." *Radical History Review* (20) (spring–summer, 1979): 11–18.

Raffo, Susan, ed. *Queerly Classed*. Boston: South End Press, 1997.

Ringer, R. J., ed. *Queer Words, Queer Images: Communication and the*

Construction of Homosexuality. New York; New York University Press, 1994.

Sedgwick, Eve Kosofsky. *Epistemology of the Closet*. Berkeley and Los Angeles: University of California Press, 1990.

Seidman, Steven, ed. *Queer Theory/Sociology*. Cambridge, Mass.: Blackwell, 1996.

Stein, Edward, ed. *Forms of Desire: Sexual Orientation and the Social Constructionist Controversy*. New York: Routledge, 1992.

Tierney, William G. *Academic Outlaws: Queer Theory and Cultural Studies in the Academy*. Thousand Oaks, Calif.: Sage Publications, 1997.

Warner, Michael, ed. *Fear of a Queer Planet: Queer Politics and Social Theory*. Minneapolis: University of Minnesota Press, 1993.

Weeks, Jeffrey. *Sexuality and Its Discontents: Meanings, Myths, and Modern Sexualities*. London; Boston: Routledge and Kegan Paul, 1985.

———. *Against Nature: Essays on History, Sexuality, and Identity*. London: Rivers Oram, 1991.

———. *Invented Moralities: Sexual Moralities in an Age of Uncertainty*. New York: Columbia University Press, 1996.

Weinberg, Thomas S. *Gay Men, Gay Selves: The Social Construction of Homosexual Identities*. New York: Irvington, 1983.

Wilson, Angelia R., ed. *A Simple Matter of Justice? Theorizing Lesbian and Gay Politics*. London: Cassell, 1997.

8. Sociology/Anthropology/Social Work

Arboleda, Manuel. "Representaciones artisticos de actividades homoeroticos en la ceramica Moche." *Boletín de Lima* 16 (1981): 98–107.

Beach, Frank A., and Clellan S. Ford. *Patterns of Sexual Behavior*. New York: Harper, 1951.

Bell, Alan P., and Martin S. Weinberg. *Homosexualities: A Study of Diversity among Men and Women*. New York: Simon and Schuster, 1978.

Bell, David, and Gill Valentine. *Mapping Desire: Geographies of Sexualities*. London; New York: Routledge, 1995.

Blackwood, Evelyn, ed. *Anthropology and Homosexual Behavior*. New York: Haworth Press, 1985.

Blumenfeld, Warren J., ed. *Homophobia: How We All Pay the Price*. Boston: Beacon Press, 1992.

Blumenfeld, Warren J., and Diane Raymond. *Looking at Gay and Lesbian Life*. Boston: Beacon Press, 1993.

Callender, Charles, and Lee Kochems. "The North American Berdache." *Current Anthropology* 24(4) (1983): 443.

Carpenter, Edward. *The Intermediate Sex: A Study of Some Transi-
tional Types of Men.* London: Allen & Unwin, 1908.

————. *Intermediate Types among Primitive Folk.* New York: Arno,
Press 1975.

Carrier, Joseph Michel. " Cultural Factors Affecting Urban Mexican
Male Homosexual Behavior." *Archives of Sexual Behavior* 5(2)
(1976):

Carrier, Joseph Michel. *De Los Otros: Intimacy and Homosexuality
Among Mexican Men.* New York: Columbia University Press, 1995.

Churchill, Wainright. *Homosexual Behavior among Males: A Cross-
Cultural and Cross-Species Investigation.* New York: Hawthorn
Books, 1967.

Comstock, Gary David. *Violence Against Lesbians and Gay Men.* New
York: Columbia University Press, 1991.

Cory, Donald Webster, and John P. LeRoy. *The Homosexual and His
Society: A View from Within.* New York: Citadel Press, 1963.

Das, Man Singh, and Joseph Harry, eds. *Homosexuality in International Perspective.* New York: Advent, 1980.

De, Shobha, and Khushwant Singh, eds. *Uncertain Liaisons: Sex,
Strife, and Togetherness in Urban India.* New Delhi: Viking Pen-
guin, 1993.

De Cecco, John, ed. *Gay Relationships.* New York: Haworth Press,
1988.

————. *Homophobia: An Overview.* New York: Haworth Press, 1984.

Delph, Edward William. *The Silent Community: Public Homosexual
Encounters.* Beverly Hills, Calif.: Sage Publications, 1978.

Devall, William B., and Joseph Harry. *The Social Organization of Gay
Males.* New York: Praeger, 1978.

Devi, Shakuntala. *The World of Homosexuals.* New Delhi: Vikas Publishing House, 1977.

Donaldson, Stephen, and Wayne R. Dynes, eds. *Ethnographic Studies
of Homosexuality.* New York: Garland Publishing, 1992.

Downing, Christine. *Myths and Mysteries of Same-Sex Love.* New
York: Continuum, 1989.

Drake, Jonathan. " 'Le Vice' in Turkey." *International Journal of
Greek Love* 1 (1966): 13–27.

Endleman, Robert. "Homosexuality in Tribal Societies." *Transcultural
Psychiatric Research Review* 23 (1986): 187–218.

Enriquez, José Ramón. *El Homosexual ante la Sociedad Enferma.* Barcelona, Spain: Tusquets, 1978.

Evans-Pritchard, E. E. "Sexual Inversion among the Azande." *American Anthropologist* 72(6) (1970): 1430.

Gagnon, John H., and Simon, William. *Sexual Conduct: The Social Sources of Human Sexuality*. Chicago: Aldine, 1973.

Goldberg, Jonathan. "Sodomy in the New World: Anthropologies Old and New." *Social Text* 9 (1991).

Harry, Joseph. *Gay Children Grown Up: Gender Culture and Gender Deviance*. New York: Praeger, 1982.

————. *Gay Couples*. New York: Praeger, 1984.

Hauser, Richard. *The Homosexual Society*. London: Bodley Head, 1962.

Herdt, Gilbert. "Representations of Homosexuality: An Essay on Cultural Ontology and Historical Comparison, Parts I and II." *Journal of the History of Sexuality* 1(3–4) (1991).

————. *Guardians of the Flutes: Idioms of Masculinity*. With a new preface by the author. Chicago: University of Chicago Press, 1994.

Herdt, Gilbert, ed. *Ritualized Homosexuality in Melanesia*. Berkeley: University of California Press, 1984.

————. *Third Sex, Third Gender: Beyond Sexual Dimorphism in Culture and History*. New York: Zone Books, 1994.

Herdt, Gilbert, and Robert Stoller. "Theories of Origins of Male Homosexuality: A Cross-Cultural Look." In *Observing the Erotic Imagination*, edited by Robert Stoller. New Haven, Conn.: Yale University Press, 1985: 104–134.

Hidalgo, Hilda, Travis L. Peterson, and Natalie Jane Woodman, eds. *Lesbian and Gay Issues: A Resource Manual for Social Workers*. Silver Spring, Md.: National Association of Social Workers, 1985.

Hoffman, Martin. *The Gay World; Male Homosexuality and the Social Creation of Evil*. New York: Basic Books, 1968.

Humphreys, Laud. *Tearoom Trade: Impersonal Sex in Public Places*. Chicago: Aldine, 1970.

————. *Out of the Closets: The Sociology of Homosexual Liberation*. Englewood Cliffs, N.J.: Prentice-Hall, 1972.

Knauft, Bruce M. "Homosexuality in Melanesia." *Journal of Psychoanalytic Anthropology* 10 (1987): 155–91.

Lautmann, Rüdiger, ed. *Seminar: Gesellschaft und Homosexualität*. Frankfurt: Suhrkamp, 1977.

Levine, Martin P., ed. *Gay Men: The Sociology of Male Homosexuality*. New York: Harper & Row, 1979.

Levy, Robert. "The Community Function of Tahitian Male Transvestism." *Anthropological Quarterly* 44(1) (1971): 12.

Mathy, Robin M., and Frederick L. Whitam. *Male Homosexuality in Four Societies: Brazil, Guatemala, the Philippines and the United States*. New York: Praeger, 1985.

————. *Sexual Stigma: An Interactionist Account*. London; Boston: Routledge & Kegan Paul, 1975.

Plummer, Kenneth, ed. *The Making of the Modern Homosexual.* Totowa, N.J.: Barnes and Noble, 1981.

————. *Modern Homosexualities: Fragments of Lesbian and Gay Experiences.* London; New York: Routledge, 1992.

Rofes, Eric E. *"I Thought People Like That Killed Themselves": Lesbians, Gay Men, and Suicide.* San Francisco: Grey Fox Press, 1983.

Roscoe, Will. *The Zuni Man-Woman.* Albuquerque: University of New Mexico Press, 1992.

Ross, Michael W., ed. *Homosexuality and Social Sex Roles.* New York: Haworth Press, 1983.

Ruan, Fang Fu. *Sex in China: Studies in Sexology in Chinese Culture.* New York; London: Plenum Press, 1991.

Ruan, F. F., and Y. M. Tsai. "Male Homosexuality in Contemporary Mainland China," *Archives of Sexual Behavior* 17 (1988): 189–199.

Schmitt, Arno, and Jehoeda Sofer, eds. *Sexuality and Eroticism among Males in Moslem Societies.* New York: Haworth Press, 1991.

Schneebaum, Tobias. *Where the Spirits Dwell: An Odyssey in the New Guinea Jungle.* New York: Grove Press, 1988.

Shepherd, Gill. "Rank, Gender, and Homosexuality: Mombasa As a Key to Understanding Sexual Options." In *The Cultural Construction of Sexuality* edited by Pat Caplan. London: Tavistock, 1987: 240–270.

Southgate, Minoo S. "Men, Women, and Boys: Love and Sex in the Works of Sa'di." *Iranian Studies* 17 (1984): 413–52.

Sweet, Roxanna Thayer. *Political and Social Action in Homophile Organizations.* New York: Arno Press, 1975.

Taylor, Clark. "El Ambiente: Male Homosexual Social Life in Mexico City." Ph.D. diss. University of California, Berkeley, 1978.

Thorstad, David. "A Pueblo Journal: Homosexuality among the Zapotecs." *Christopher Street* 160 (March 1988).

Troiden, Richard. *Gay and Lesbian Identity: A Sociological Analysis.* Dix Hills, N.Y.: General Hall, 1988.

Veispak, Teet, ed. *Sexual Minorities and Society: The Changing Attitudes Towards Homosexuality in Twentieth-Century Europe.* Tallinn, Estonia: Eesti TA Ajaloo Instituut, 1991.

Weinberg, George. *Society and the Healthy Homosexual.* Garden City, N.Y.: Doubleday/Anchor Press, 1973.

West, Donald James. *Homosexuality.* Chicago: Aldine Pub, 1968.

West, Donald James, and Buz de Villiers. *Male Prostitution.* New York: Haworth Press, 1993.

Westwood, Gordon. *A Minority: A Report on the Life of the Male Homosexual in Great Britain.* London: 1960.

Williams, Walter. "Sex and Shamanism: The Making of a Hawaiian Mahu." *Advocate,* 2 April 1985.

————. "Persistence and Change in the Berdache Tradition among Contemporary Dakota Indians." *Journal of Homosexuality* 11(3–4) (1986): 191.

————. *The Spirit and the Flesh: Sexual Diversity in American Indian Culture*. Boston: Beacon Press, 1986.

Winkler, John J. *The Constraints of Desire: The Anthropology of Sex and Gender in Ancient Greece*. New York: Routledge, 1990.

9. Psychology

Abelove, Henry. "Freud, Male Homosexuality, and the Americans." *Dissent* 33 (1986):59–69.

American Psychological Association Task Force on the Status of Lesbian and Gay Male Psychologists. *Removing the Stigma: Final Report/Task Force on the Status of Lesbian and Gay Male Psychologists*. Washington, D.C.: American Psychological Association, 1979.

Bayer, Ronald. *Homosexuality and American Psychiatry: The Politics of Diagnosis*. New York: Basic Books, 1981.

Bell, Alan P., Sue Kiefer Hammersmith, and Martin S. Weinberg. *Sexual Preference, Its Development in Men and Women*. Bloomington: Indiana University Press, 1981.

Biery, Roger E. *Understanding Homosexuality-The Pride and the Prejudice*. Austin, Tex.: Edward-William Publishing, 1990.

Browning, Frank. *A Queer Geography: Journeys toward a Sexual Self*. New York: Crown, 1996.

D'Augelli, Anthony R., and Charlotte J. Patterson, eds. *Lesbian, Gay, and Bisexual Identities over the Lifespan: Psychological Perspectives*. New York: Oxford University Press, 1995.

Ellis, Havelock. *Studies in the Psychology of Sex*. New York: Random House, 1936.

Friedman, Richard C. *Male Homosexuality: A Contemporary Psychoanalytical Perspective*. New Haven, Conn.: Yale University Press, 1988.

Garnets, Linda D., and Douglas C. Kimmel, eds. *Psychological Perspectives on Lesbian and Gay Male Experiences*. New York: Columbia University Press, 1993.

Geuter, Ulfried. *Homosexualität in der deutschen Jugendbewegung: Jungenfreundschaft und Sexualität im Diskurs von 4 Jugendbewegung, Psychoanalyse und Jugendpsychologie am Beginn des 20. Jahrhunderts*. Frankfurt: Suhrkamp, 1994.

Hall. Marny. *The Lavender Couch: A Consumer's Guide to Psychotherapy for Lesbians and Gay Men*. Boston: Alyson, 1985.

Henley, Nancy, and Fred Pincus. "Interrelationship of Sexist, Racist, and Antihomosexual Attitudes." *Psychological Reports* 42 (1978): 83.

Herek, Gregory M. "The Social Psychology of Homophobia: Toward a Practical Theory." *New York University Review of Law and Social Change* 14 (1986).

———. *Stigma and Sexual Orientation: Understanding Prejudice Against Lesbians, Gay Men, and Bisexuals.* Thousand Oaks, Calif.: Sage Publications, 1998.

Hunter, Ski, Coleen Shannon, Jo Knox, and James I. Martin. *Lesbian, Gay, and Bisexual Youths and Adults: Knowledge for Human Services Practice.* Thousand Oaks, Calif.: Sage Publications, 1998.

Kimmel, Douglas C., and Linda D. Garnets, eds. *Psychological Perspectives on Lesbian and Gay Male Experiences.* New York: Columbia University Press, 1993.

Kinsey, Alfred C., Wardell B. Pomeroy, and Clyde E. Martin. *Sexual Behavior in the Human Male.* Philadelphia: W. B. Saunders, 1948.

Lewes, Kenneth. *The Psychoanalytical Theory of Male Homosexuality.* New York: Simon and Schuster, 1988.

Marmor, Judd, ed. *Sexual Inversion: The Multiple Roots of Homosexuality.* New York: Basic, 1965.

———. *Homosexual Behavior: A Modern Reappraisal.* New York: Basic, 1980.

Masters, William H., and Virginia E. Johnson. *Homosexuality in Perspective.* Boston: Little, Brown, 1979.

McWhirter, David, June Machover Reinisch, and Stephanie A. Sanders, eds. *Homosexuality/Heterosexuality: Concepts of Sexual Orientation.* New York: Oxford University Press, 1990.

Neilsen, Joseph H. "Heterosexism: Redefining Homophobia for the 1990s." *Journal of Gay and Lesbian Psychotherapy* 1(3) (1990): 21.

Ross, Michael W. *The Married Homosexual Man: A Psychological Study.* London; Boston: Routledge and Kegan Paul, 1983.

———. *Psychopathology and Psychotherapy in Homosexuality.* New York: Haworth Press, 1988.

Ruitenbeek, Hendrik Marinus, ed. *Homosexuality: A Changing Picture.* London: Souvenir Press, 1973.

10. Medical Model of Homosexuality

Allen, Clifford, and Charles Berg. *The Problem of Homosexuality.* New York: Citadel Press, 1958.

Bullough, Bonnie, and Vern Bullough. *Sin, Sickness and Sanity: A History of Sexual Attitudes.* New York: Garland, 1977.

Bullough, Vern. "The Physician and Research into Human Sexual Behavior in Nineteenth-Century Germany." *Bulletin of the History of Medicine* 63 (1989): 248.

Bullough, Vern, and Martha Voght. "Homosexuality and Its Confusion with the 'Secret Sin' in Pre-Freudian America."*Journal of the History of Medicine* 28 (1973): 143–155.

Burnham, John C. "Early References to Homosexual Communities in American Medical Writings." *Medical Aspects of Human Sexuality* 7(8) (1973): 34–49.

Burr, Chandler. *A Separate Creation: The Search for the Biological Origins of Sexual Orientation.* New York: Hyperion, 1996.

Casper, Johann Ludwig. "Über Nothzucht und Päderastie und deren Ermittlung seitens des Gerichtsarztes." *Vierteljahrsschrift für gerichtliche und öffentliche Medizin* 1 (1852): 21–78.

Chevalier, Julien. *Inversion sexuelle.* Paris: Masson, 1893.

Copeland, Peter, and Dean H. Hamer. *The Science of Desire: The Search for the Gay Gene and the Biology of Behavior.* New York: Simon & Schuster, 1994.

Crompton, Louis. *Homosexuality and the Sickness Theory.* Albany-Trust, 1969.

Ellis, Havelock, and John Addington Symonds. *Sexual Inversion.* New York: Arno Press, 1975.

Futuyma, Douglas J., and Stephen J. Risch. "Sexual Orientation, Sociobiology, and Evolution." *Journal of Homosexuality* 9 (1984): 157–68.

Green, Richard. *The "Sissy Boy Syndrome" and the Development of Homosexuality.* New Haven, Conn.: Yale University Press, 1987.

Hamer, Dean. *Living with Our Genes: Why They Matter More Than You Think.* New York: Doubleday, 1998.

Hansen, Bert. "American Physicians' Earliest Writings about Homosexuals, 1800–1900." *Milbank Quarterly* 67 (1989).

Hare, E. H. "Masturbatory Insanity: The History of an Idea"*Journal of Mental Science* 108 (452) (January, 1962).

Isay, Richard A. *Being Homosexual: Gay Men and Their Development.* New York: Avon Books, 1990.

Katz, Jonathan Ned. *The Invention of Heterosexuality.* New York: Dutton, 1995.

Kennedy, Hubert. "The Third Sex Theory of Karl Heinrich Ulrichs." *Journal of Homosexuality* 6 (winter 1981): 106.

Koertge, Noretta, ed. *The Nature and Causes of Homosexuality: A Philosophic and Scientific Inquiry.* New York: Haworth Press, 1981.

Krafft-Ebing, Richard von. *Psychopathia Sexualis.* Trans. Franklin S. Klaf. New York: Stein and Day, 1978.

Lanteri-Laura, Georges. *Lecture des perversions: Histoire de leur appropriation médicale.* Paris: Masson, 1979.

LeVay, Simon. *Queer Science: The Use and Abuse of Research on Homosexuality*. Cambridge, Mass.: MIT Press, 1996.

MacDonald, Robert H. "The Frightful Consequences of Onanism: Notes on the History of a Delusion," *Journal of the History of Ideas* 27 (3) (July–September 1967).

Moll, Dr. Albert. *Die konträre Sexualempfindung*. Berlin: Fischer, 1891.

Mondimore, Francis Mark. *A Natural History of Homosexuality*. Baltimore/London: Johns Hopkins University Press, 1996.

Money, John. *Gay, Straight, and In-Between: The Sexology of Erotic Orientation*. New York: Oxford University Press, 1988.

Paul, William et al., eds. *Homosexuality: Social, Psychological, and Biological Issues*. Beverly Hills, Calif.: Sage Publications, 1982.

Putterbaugh, Geoff, ed. *Twins and Homosexuality: A Casebook*. New York: Garland, 1990.

Rosario, Vernon A., ed. *Science and Homosexualities*. New York: Routledge, 1997.

Schmidt, Gunter. "Allies and Persecuters: Science and Medicine in the Homosexuality Issue." *Journal of Homosexuality* 10 (1984): 127–40.

Szaz, Thomas. *The Myth of Mental Illness*. New York: Delta, 1961.

———. *The Manufacture of Madness*. New York: Delta, 1970.

Tamassia, A. "Sull'inversione dell'istinto sesuale." *Rivista sperimentale freniatria e medicina legale* 4 (1878): 97–117.

Westphal, Karl Friedrich Otto. "Die konträre Sexualempfindung. Symptom eines neuropathischen (psychopathischen) Zustandes." *Archiv für Psychiatrie und Nervenkrankheiten* 2 (1) (1869): 73–108.

11. History

General References

Adam, Barry D. *The Rise of a Gay and Lesbian Liberation Movement*. New York: Twayne Publishers, 1995.

Ariès, Philippe. "Réflections sur l'histoire de l'homosexualité." *Communications* 35 (1982): 56–67.

Ariès, Philippe, and André Béjin, eds. *Sexualités Occidentales*. (Western Sexuality) Trans. Anthony Forster. Oxford, New York: B. Blackwell, 1985.

Blasius, Mark, and Shane Phelan, eds. *We Are Everywhere: A Historical Sourcebook in Gay and Lesbian Politics*. New York: Routledge, 1997.

Bleibtreu-Ehrenberg, Gisela. *Homosexualität: Die Geschichte eines Vorurteils.* Franfurt: Fischer, 1981.

Bullough, Vern. *Sexual Variance in Society and History.* New York: Wiley, 1976.

———. *Homosexuality: A History.* New York: New American Library, 1979.

Bullough, Vern, ed. *Sex, Society, and History.* New York: Science History Publications, 1976.

Cant, Bob, and Susan Hemmings, eds. *Radical Records: Thirty Years of Lesbian and Gay History.* London: Routledge, 1988.

Chauncey, George Jr., Martin Duberman, and Martha Vicinus eds. *Hidden from History: Reclaiming the Gay and Lesbian Past.* New York: New American Library Books, 1989.

Copley, A. R. H. *Sexual Moralities in France, 1780–1980: New Ideas on the Family, Divorce, and Homosexuality: An Essay on Moral Change.* London; New York: Routledge, 1989.

Cowan, Thomas Dale. *Gay Men and Women Who Enriched the World.* Boston: Alyson, 1992.

Cruikshank, Margaret. *The Gay and Lesbian Liberation Movement.* New York: Routledge, 1992.

Davenport-Hines, Richard. *Sex, Death, and Punishment.* London: Collins, 1990.

D'Emilio, John. *Making Trouble: Essays on Gay History, Politics, and the University.* New York: Routledge, 1992.

D'Emillio, John, and Estelle B. Freedman. *Intimate Matters: A History of Sexuality in America.* New York: Perennial Library, 1988.

Donaldson, Stephen, and Wayne R. Dynes, eds. *History of Homosexuality in Europe and America.* New York: Garland, 1992.

———. *Homosexuality and Government, Politics, and Prisons.* New York: Garland, 1992.

Duberman, Martin B. *About Time: Exploring the Gay Past.* New York: Meridian, 1991.

Garde, Noel I. *Jonathan to Gide: The Homosexual in History.* New York: Vantage, 1964.

Goldberg, Jonathan, ed. *Reclaiming Sodom.* New York: Routledge, 1994.

Hahn, Pierre. *Français, encore un, l'homosexualité et sa repression. Choix de textes recueillis et présentés par Pierre Hahn.* Paris: J. Martineau, 1970.

Halperin, David. *One Hundred Years of Homosexuality and Other Essays on Greek Love.* New York: Routledge, 1990.

Hardman, Paul D. *Homoaffectionalism: Male Bonding from Gilgamesh to the Present.* San Francisco: NF Division, GLB Publishers, 1993.

Hekma, Gert, Harry Oosterhuis, and James Steakley, eds. *Gay Men and the History of the Political Left.* New York, London: Haworth Press, 1995.

Hinsch, Bret. *Passions of the Cut Sleeve: The Male Homosexual Tradition in China.* Berkeley and Los Angeles: University of California Press, 1990.

Hohmann, Joachim S., ed. *Der unterdrückte Sexus: Historische Texte und Kommentäre zur Homosexualität.* Berlin: Andreas Achenbach Lollar, 1977.

(HOSI) Auslandsgruppe. *Rosa Liebe unterm roten Stern.* Hamburg: Frühlings Erwachen, 1984.

Hyde, H. Montgomery. *The Other Love: An Historical and Contemporary Survey of Homosexuality in Britain.* London: Heinemann, 1970.

Iwata, Jun'ichi, and Tsuneo Watanabe. *Love of the Samurai: A Thousand Years of Japanese Homosexuality.* London: Gay Men's Press, 1989.

Karlen, Arno. *Sexuality and Homosexuality: A New View.* New York: W. W. Norton, 1971.

Katz, Jonathan Ned. *Gay American History: Lesbians and Gay Men in the U.S.A.* New York: Thomas Y. Crowell Co., 1976.

———. *Gay/Lesbian Almanac: A New Documentary.* New York: Harper and Row, 1983.

Kepner, Jim. *Becoming A People: A 4,000-Year Gay and Lesbian Chronology.* Los Angeles: The National Gay Archives, 1983.

Kinsman, Gary. *The Regulation of Desire: Sexuality in Canada.* Montreal: Black Rose Books, 1987.

Kon, Igor S. *The Sexual Revolution in Russia.* Trans. James Riordan. New York: The Free Press, 1995.

Lever, Maurice. *Les bûchers de Sodome: Histoire des "infâmes."* Paris: Fayard, 1985.

Licata, Salvatore J. "The Homosexual Rights Movement in the United States: A Traditionally Overlooked Area of American History." *Journal of Homosexuality* 6 (1980/81): 161–90.

Licata, Salvatore J., and Robert P. Peterson, eds. *Historical Perspectives on Homosexuality.* New York; Haworth Press and Stein and Day, 1981.

———. *The Gay Past: A Collection of Historical Essays.* New York: Harrington Park Press, 1985.

Marcus, Eric. *Making History: The Struggle for Gay and Lesbian Equal Rights, 1945–1990: An Oral History.* New York: HarperCollins Publishers, 1992.

Miller, Neil. *Out of the Past: Gay and Lesbian History from 1869 to the Present.* New York: Vintage Books, 1995.

Peiss, Kathy, and Christina Simmons, eds. *Passion and Power: Sexuality and History.* Philadelphia: Temple University Press, 1989.

Rowse, Alfred Leslie. *Homosexuals in History: A Study of Ambivalence in Society, Literature, and the Arts*. New York: Dorset Press, 1983.

Spencer, Colin. *Homosexuality in History*. New York: Harcourt Brace, 1995.

Stryker, Susan, and Jim Van Buskirk. *Gay by the Bay: A History of Queer Culture in San Francisco*. San Francisco: Chronicle, 1996.

Thompson Mark, ed. *Long Road to Freedom: The Advocate History of the Gay and Lesbian Movement*. New York: St. Martin's Press, 1994.

Tielman, Rob. *Homoseksualiteit in Nederland: Studie van een emancipatienbeweging*. Amsterdam: Boom, Meppel, 1982.

Weeks, Jeffrey. *Coming Out; Homosexual Politics in Britain, from the Nineteenth Century to the Present*. London: Quartet Books, 1977.

———. *Sex, Politics,and Society: The Regulation of Sexuality since 1800*. London: Longman, 1981.

Young, Allen. *Gays under the Cuban Revolution*. San Francisco: Grey Fox, 1981.

Ancient/Medieval/Early Modern

Bailey, Derrick Sherwin, *Homosexuality and the Western Christian Tradition*. Hamden, Conn.: Archon Books, 1975.

Boswell, John. *Christianity, Social Tolerance, and Homosexuality: Gay People in Western Europe from the Beginning of the Christian Era to the Fourteenth Century*. Chicago: University of Chicago Press, 1980.

———. *Rediscovering Gay History*. London: Gay Christian Movement, 1982.

———. *Same-Sex Unions in Premodern Europe*. New York: Villard Books, 1994.

Bray, Alan. *Homosexuality in Renaissance England*. London: Gay Men's Press, 1982.

Brundage, James A. *Law, Sex, and Christian Society in Medieval Europe*. Chicago: University of Chicago Press, 1987.

Burg, B. R. *Sodomy and the Pirate Tradition: English Sea Rovers in the Seventeenth-Century Caribbean*. New York: New York University Press, 1984.

Carrasco, Rafael. *Inquisición y Represion Sexual en Valencia: Historia de los Sodomitas (1565–1785)*. Barcelona, Spain: Laertes, 1985.

Coward, D. A. "Attitudes to Homosexuality in Eighteenth-Century France." *Journal of European Studies* 10 (1980): 236.

Crompton, Louis. "Homosexuals and the Death Penality in Colonial America." *Journal of Homosexuality* 1(3) (1976): 277.

Daniel, Marc. *Hommes du grand siècle: Études sur l'homosexualité sous les règnes de Louis XIII et de Louis XIV.* Paris: Arcadie, 1957.

Deakin, Terence J. "Evidence for Homosexuality in Ancient Egypt." *International Journal of Greek Love* 1 (1966): 31–38.

Delon, Michel. "The Priest, the Philosopher, and Homosexuality in Enlightenment France." *Eighteenth-Century Life* 9 (n.s.) (1985): 122–31.

Dover, K. J. *Greek Homosexuality.* New York: Vintage, 1978.

Dowling, Linda C. *Hellenism and Homosexuality in Victorian Oxford.* Ithica, N.Y.: Cornell University Press, 1994.

Gay Academic Union, ed. *Homosexuality, Intolerance, and Christianity: A Critical Examination of John Boswell's Work.* 2d ed. New York: Gay Academic Union, 1985.

Gerard, Kent, and Gert Hekma, eds. *The Pursuit of Sodomy: Male Homosexuality in Renaissance and Enlightment Europe.* New York: Harrington Park Press, 1989.

Gilbert, A. N. "The Africaine Court Martial," *Journal of Homosexuality* 1, (1) (fall 1974), 111–122.

———. "Buggery and the British Navy, 1700–1861." *Journal of Social History* 10, (1) (fall 1976).

Goldberg, Jonathan, ed. *Queering the Renaissance.* Durham, N.C: Duke University Press, 1994.

Goodrich, Michael. *The Unmentionable Vice: Homosexuality in the Later Medieval Period.* Santa Barbara, Calif.: Ross-Erikson, 1979.

Hahn, Pierre. *Nos ancêtres les pervers: La vie des homosexuels sous le Second Empire.* Paris: Oliver Orban, 1979.

Hillard, David. "Unenglish and Unmanly: Anglo-Catholicism and Homosexuality." *Victorian Studies* 25 (1982): 181–210.

Hössli, Heinrich. *Eros. Die Männerliebe der Griechen, ihre Beziehungen zur Geschichte, Literatur und Gesetzgebung aller Zeiten. Oder, Forschungen über platonische Liebe ihre Wurdigung und Entwurdigung fur Sitten- und Natur- und Völkerkund.* 2d Munster: i.d. Schweiz, Beim, Herausgeher, 1892.

Lautmann, Rüdiger, and Angela Taeger, eds. *Männerliebe im alten Deutschland.* Verlag Rosa Winkel, 1992.

Leupp, Gary. *Male Colors: The Construction of Homosexuality in Tokugawa, Japan (1503–1868).* Berkeley: University of California Press, 1995.

Lilja, Saara. *Homosexuality in Republican and Augustan Rome.* Helsinki, Finland: Societas Scientiarum Fennica, 1983.

Meer, Theo van der. *De Wesentlijke Sonde van Sodomie en Andere Vuyligheeden: Sodomietenvervolgingen in Amsterdam, 1730–1811.* Amsterdam: Tabula, 1984.

———. "The Persecutions of Sodomites in Eighteenth Century Amsterdam: Changing Perceptions of Sodomy." *Journal of Homosexuality* 15 (1988): 245–85.

Monter, E. William. "La sodomie à l'époque moderne en Suisse romande."*Annales E.S.C.* 29 (1974): 1023–33.

———. "Sodomy and Heresy in Early Modern Switzerland." *Journal of Homosexuality* 6 (winter 1981): 41.

Morand, Paul. "Venise, Sodome de l'Adriatique." *Arcadie* 288 (1977): 629–35.

Norton, Rictor. *Mother Clap's Molly House: The Gay Subculture in England, 1700–1830.* London, East Haven, Conn.: GMP, Distributed in North America by InBook, 1992.

Rey, Michel. "Police et sodomie à Paris au XVIII siècle." *Revue d'Histoire Moderne et Contemporain* 29 (1982): 116.

———. "Parisian Homosexuals Create a Lifestyle, 1700–1750." *Eighteenth-Century Life* 9(3) (1985): 116.

Rocke, Michael. *Forbidden Friendships: Homosexuality and Male Culture in Renaissance Florence.* London: Oxford University Press, 1996.

Römer, von, L. S. A. M. *Uranism in the Netherlands Till the Nineteenth Century.* Trans. Michael A. Lombardi. Los Angeles: Urania Manuscripts, 1978.

Rousseau, G. S. "The Pursuit of Homosexuality in the Eighteenth Century: 'Utterly Confused Category' and/or Rich Depository?" *Eighteenth Century Life* 9 (1985): 132–68.

Ruggiero, Guido. *The Boundaries of Eros: Sex, Crime, and Sexuality in Rennaissance Venice.* New York: Oxford University Press, 1985.

Trumbach, Randolph. "London Sodomites: Homosexual Behavior and Western Culture in the Eighteenth Century." *Journal of Social History* 11(1) (1977): 1–33.

———. "Sodomitical Subcultures, Sodomitical Roles, and the Gender Revolution of the Eighteenth Century: The Recent Historiography." *Eighteenth-Century Life* 9 (1984): 109–21.

Valk, Emanuel. *Emanuel Valk: The Trial of a Gay Preacher in Eighteenth-Century Holland.* Trans. Michael Lombardi. Los Angeles: Urania Manuscripts, 1984.

The Early Homosexual Rights Movement (1864–1935)

Baktis, Dr. Grigorii von. *Die Sexualrevolution in Russland.* Berlin: Verlag der Syndikalist. Reprint. Osnabruck: Archiv Antiautoritäre Erziehung, 1925.

Barbedette, Gilles, and Michel Carassou. *Paris Gay 1925.* Paris: Presses de la Renaissance, 1981.

Berlin Museum, ed. *Eldorado: Homosexuelle Frauen und Männer in*

Berlin 1850–1950, Geschichte, Alltag und Kultur. Berlin: Frölich and Kaufmann, 1984.

British Society for the Study of Sex Psychology. *A Homosexual Emancipation Miscellany, c. 1835–1952.* New York: Arno, 1975.

Burton, Richard. "Terminal Essay." In *The Book of the Thousand Nights and a Night,* vol. 10, edited by Richard Burton, pp. 63–302. New York: Burton Club, 1886.

Carpenter, Edward. *Towards Democracy.* London: GMP Publishers, 1985.

Carpenter, Edward, ed. *Iolaus. An Anthology of Friendship.* New York: Pagan Press, 1982.

Chauncey, George. *Gay New York: Gender, Urban Culture, and the Making of the Gay Male World, 1890–1940.* New York: Basic Books, 1994.

Chester, Lewis, David Leitch, and Colin Simpson. *The Cleveland Street Affair.* Boston: Little Brown, 1976.

Ellis, Havelock, and John Addington Symonds. *Sexual Inversion.* New York: Arno Press, 1975.

Fout, John. "Sexual Politics in Wilhelmine Germany: The Male Gender Crisis, Moral Purity, and Homophobia." *Journal of the History of Sexuality* 2 (1992), 388–421.

Friedländer, Benedict. *Die Liebe Platons im Lichte der modernen Biologie.* Treptow bei Berlin: Bernhard Zack, 1909.

———. *Renaissance des Eros Uranios: Die physiologische Freundschaft, ein normaler Grundtrieb des Menschen und eine Frage der männlichen Gesellungsfreiheit.* New York: Arno Press, 1975.

Gallo, Max. *The Night of the Long Knives.* New York: Harper & Row, 1972.

Grau, Gunter, ed. *Hidden Holocaust? Gay and Lesbian Persecution in Germany, 1933–45.* Trans. Patrick Camiller. London; New York: Cassell, 1995.

Heger, Heinz. *The Men with the Pink Triangles.* Boston: Alyson, 1980.

Herzer, Manfred. "Kertbeny and the Nameless Love." *Journal of Homosexuality* 12 (1985): 1–26.

———. "Nazis, Psychiatrists, and Gays." *Cabirion* 12 (spring–summer, 1985): 1.

Hiller, Kurt. *An Appeal to the Second International Congress for Sexual Reform on the Behalf of an Oppressed Variety of Human Being.* Trans. John Lauritsen. New York: Red Butterfly, 1970.

Hirschfeld, Magnus. *Berlins Drittes Geschlecht.* Berlin: H. Seeman Nachfolger, 1904.

———. *Die Homosexualität des Mannes und des Weibes.* Berlin: Louis Marcus, 1914.

———. *The Restoration of the Good Name of Homosexual Men and*

Women and Other Writings. Trans. Michael Lombardi-Nash. Jacksonville, Fla.: Urania Manuscripts, 1992.

Hyde, H. Montgomery. *The Trial of Sir Roger Casement*. London: William Hodge, 1964.

————. *The Cleveland Street Scandal*. London: W. H. Allen, 1976.

Hyde, H. Montgomery, ed. *The Trials of Oscar Wilde*. London: William Hodge, 1948.

Kennedy, Hubert. "Before All Europe I Protest." *Body Politic* 42 (1978): 24.

————. "Gay Liberation 1864." *Body Politic* 41 (1978): 23.

————. *Ulrichs: The Life and Works of Karl Heinrich Ulrichs: Pioneer of the Modern Gay Movement*. Boston: Alyson Publications, 1988.

Kennedy, Hubert, and Harry Oosterhuis, eds. *Homosexuality and Male Bonding in Pre-Nazi Germany*. New York: Harrington Park Press, 1991.

Kertbeny, Karl Maria. *Das Gemeinschädliche des #143 des preussischen Strafgesetzbuches vom 14. April 1851 und daher seine nothwendige Tilgung als #152 im Entwurfe eines Strafgesetzbuches für den Norddeutschen Bund*. Leipzig: Serbe, 1869.

————. *#143 des preussischen Strafgesetzbuches vom 14. April 1851 und seine Aufrechterhaltung als #152 im Entwurfe eines Strafgesetzbuches für Norddeutschen Bund*. Leipzig: Serbe, 1869.

Lauritsen, John, and David Thorstad. *The Early Homosexual Rights Movement (1864–1935)*. New York: Times Change, 1974.

Lautmann, Rüdiger. "The Pink Triangle." *Journal of Homosexuality* 6, (1–2) (1980–1981): 146.

Lenz, Reimar. *The Wholesale Murder of Homosexuals in the Third Reich*. Los Angeles: Urania Manuscripts, 1979.

Mayne, Xavier. *The Intersexes: A History of Similisexualism As a Problem in Social Life*. New York: Arno, 1975.

Plant, Richard. *The Pink Triangle: The Nazi War against Homosexuals*. New York: Henry Holt, 1986.

Raile, A. L. *A Defense of Uranian Love*. London, 1928–1930.

Rector, Frank. *The Nazi Extermination of Homosexuals*. New York: Stein and Day, 1981.

Römer, von, L.S.A.M. "Vorläufige Mitteilung über die Darstellung eines Schemas der Geschlechtsdifferenzierung." *Jahrbuch für sexuelle Zwischenstufen* (6) (1904): 327–56.

Seel, Pierre. *Liberation Was for Others: Memoirs of a Gay Survivor of the Nazi Holocaust*. Trans. Joachim Neugroschel. New York: Da Capo Press, 1997.

Smith, F. B. "Labouchère's Amendment to the Criminal Law Amendment Bill," *Historical Studies* 17 (67) (October 1976).

Steakley, James. *The Homosexual Emancipation Movement in Germany*. New York: Arno, 1975.

Symonds, John Addington. *Male Love: A Problem in Greek Ethics and Other Writings*. New York: Pagan, 1983.

Tielman, Rob. *The Persecution of Homosexuals in the Netherlands during the Second World War*. Los Angeles: Urania Manuscripts, 1979.

Ulrichs, Karl Heinrich. *Forschungen über das Rätsel der Mannmännlichen Liebe* (c. 1898). *The Riddle of "Man-Manly" Love: The Pioneering Work on Male Homosexuality* (2 vols.). Trans. Michael A. Lombardi-Nash. Buffalo, N.Y.: Prometheus Books, 1994.

Young, Ian. *Gay Resistance: Homosexuals in the Anti-Nazi Underground*. Toronto: Stubblejumper Press, 1985.

The Modern Homosexual Rights Movement (1945–1969)

Abse, Leo. "The Sexual Offences Act." *British Journal of Criminology* (January, 1968).

Baudry, André, and Marc Daniel. *Les Homosexuels*. Paris, 1973.

Bérubé, Allan. *Coming Out Under Fire: The History of Gay Men and Women in World War Two*. New York: Free Press, 1990.

Champagne, Robert, ed. *Jim Egan, Canada's Pioneer Gay Activist*. Toronto: Canadian Lesbian and Gay History Network, 1987.

Cory, Donald Webster. *The Homosexual in America*. New York: Paperback Library, 1951.

Cory, Donald Webster, ed. *Homosexuality*. New York:: Julian Press, 1956.

Croft-Cooke, Rupert. *The Verdict of You All*. London: Secker & Warburg, 1955.

D'Emillo, John. *Sexual Politics, Sexual Communities: The Making of a Homosexual Minority in the United States, 1940–1970*. Chicago: University of Chicago Press, 1983.

Elmer, Martin. *Homofil—og hvad sa?* Kobenhavn: Vennen (D.B.K.), 1968.

Foster, Marion, and Kent Murray. *A Not So Gay World; Homosexuality in Canada*. Toronto: McClelland and Stewart, 1972.

Gerassi, John. *The Boys of Boise*. New York: Macmillan, 1966.

Grey, Antony. *The Citizen in the Street*. Albany Trust, 1969.

———. "Sexual Law Reform Society Working Party Report." *Criminal Law Review* (June, 1975).

———. *Quest for Justice: Towards Homosexual Emancipation*. London: Sinclair-Stevenson, 1992.

———. *Speaking Out: Sex, Law, Politics, and Society 1954–95*. London: Cassell, 1997.

Grey, Antony and D. J. West. "Homosexuals: New Law but No New Deal." *New Society* 27 (March 1969).

Guérin, Daniel. *Kinsey et la sexualité*. Paris, 1955.

———. "La Répression de l'homosexualité en France," *L'Express* (12) (December 1957).

———. *Essai sur la révolution sexuelle, après Reich et Kinsey*. Paris: P. Belfond, 1969.

———. *Homosexualité et Révolution*. Paris, 1983.

Hay, Harry. *Radically Gay: Gay Liberation in the Words of Its Founder*. Ed. Will Roscoe. Boston: Beacon Press, 1996.

Italiaander, Rolf, ed. *Weder Krankheit noch Verbrechen*. Hamburg: Gala Verlag, 1969.

Report of the Committee on Homosexual Offences and Prostitution. [Chair: Sir John Wolfenden] Cmnd. 247. London: HMSO, 1947.

Sagarin, Edward. *Structure and Ideology in an Association of Deviants*. New York: Arno Press, 1975.

Schiller, Greta, and Andrea Weiss. *Before Stonewall: The Making of Gay and Lesbian Community*. Tallahassee, Fla.: The Naiad Press, 1989.

Stümke, Hans-Georg, and Rudi Finkler. *Rosa Winkel, Rosa Listen: Homosexuelle und "gesunde Volksempfinden" von Auschwitz bis Heute*. Reinbeck bei Hamburg: Rowohlt, 1981.

Teal, Don. *The Gay Militants*. New York: Stein and Day, 1971.

Tobin, Kay, and Randy Wicker. *The Gay Crusaders*. New York: Arno Press, 1975.

Weltge, Ralph, ed. *The Same Sex*. Philadelphia: Pilgrim, 1969.

Wildeblood, Peter. *Against the Law*. London: Weidenfeld and Nicolson, 1955.

Wolfenden, Sir John, et al. *Report of the Committee on Homosexual Offenses and Prostitution*. Westport, Conn.: Greenwood Press, 1976.

The Contemporary Gay and Lesbian Liberation Movement (1969–)

Altman, Dennis. *Coming Out in the Seventies*. Sydney: Wild and Woolley, 1979.

———. *The Homosexualization of America, The Americanization of Homosexuality*. New York: St. Martin's Press, 1982.

Alwood, Edward. *Straight News: Gays, Lesbians, and the News Media*. New York: Columbia University Press, 1996.

Amnesty International. *Breaking the Silence: Human Rights Violations Based on Sexual Orientation*. New York: Amnesty International Publications, 1994.

Arguelles, Lourdes and B. Ruby Rich. "Homosexuality, Homophobia, and Revolution: Notes toward an Understanding of the Cuban Lesbian and Gay Male Experience, Pt. I." *Signs: Journal of Women in Culture and Society* 9 (1984): 683–99.

Asis, Enrique, and James Green. "Gays and Lesbians." *Report on the Americas* 26(4) (1993): 4–7.

Azmi Ramli, Wan. *Dilema mak nyah: suatu ilusi.* Kuala Lumpur, Malaysia: Utusan Publications and Distributors, 1991.

Bardakci, Murat. *Osmanli'da seks: sarayda gece dersleri.* Kadikoy, Istanbul: Gur Yayinlari, 1992.

Batista, Adriana, and Gina Fratti. *Liberación Homosexual.* Posada: Mexico, 1984.

Batselier, Steven de, and Laurence H. Ross, eds. *Les minorités homosexuelles.* Gembloux, Belgium: Editions Duculot, 1973.

Bawer, Bruce. *A Place at the Table: The Gay Individual in American Society.* New York: Poseidon Press, 1993.

Bell, Laurie. *On Our Own Terms.* Toronto: Coalition for Lesbian and Gay Rights in Ontario, 1991.

Bestuurscommissie Politiek N.V.I.H COC. *Homoseksualteit & asiel.* Amsterdam: Board Committee on Politics N.V.I.H COC, 1990.

Botero, Ebel. "Our Sisters and Brothers in Colombia." *Gay Community News* 8(25) (1981): 12.

Bull, Chris, and John Gallagher. *Perfect Enemies: The Religious Right, the Gay Movement, and the Politics of the 1990s.* New York: Crown, 1996.

Button, James W., Barbara A. Rienzo, and Kenneth D. Wald. *Private Lives, Public Conflicts: Battles over Gay Rights in American Communities.* Washington, D.C.: Congressional Quarterly Books, 1997.

Catalano, Donald, and Richard Steinman. "Eastern European Gay Groups Meet." *Gay Community News* 15(42) (1988): 4.

Chauvin, Lucien. "Organizing Gay Men and Lesbians in Peru." *Gay Community News* 19(6) (1991): 7.

Clapham, A., and C. Waaldijk, eds. *Homosexuality-A European Community Issue.* Dordrecht: Nijhoff, 1993.

Collier, Don, and John Ward. "Who Are the Radical Fairies?" *Gay Community News* 8(18) (1980): 8.

Consoli, Massimo. *Stonewall.* Rome: Napoleone, 1990.

Cunningham, Barry. *Gay Power: The Homosexual Revolt.* New York: Tower Publications, 1971.

Deitcher, David, ed. *Over the Rainbow: Lesbian and Gay Politics in America since Stonewall.* London: Boxtree, 1995.

Duberman, Martin B. *Stonewall.* New York: Dutton, 1993.

Elshtain, Jean Bethke. "Homosexual Politics." *Salmagundi* 58–59 (1982–83): 252.

Fahy, Una. *How to Make the World a Better Place for Gays and Lesbians*. New York: Warner Books, 1995.

Fernández, Alvaro, and Rubio M. Manuel. *Diagnostico sobre la realidad y necesidades de los grupos y organizaciones de homosexuales y lesbianas de América del sur*. Santiago de Chile: Comité de Servicio Chileno Cuáquero, 1992.

Fernbach, David. *The Rise and Fall of the GLF*. London: LSE Gay Culture Society, 1973.

Freeman, Mark, and Michael Ward. "Defending Gay Rights." *Radical America* 13(4) (1979): 11.

Front Homosexuel d'Action Révolutionnaire. *Rapport contre la normalité*. Paris: Editions Champ Libre, 1971.

Galloway, Bruce, ed. *Prejudice and Pride: Discrimination against Gay People in Modern Britain*. London; Boston: Routledge & Kegan Paul, 1983.

Gay, A. Nolder. *The View from the Closet: Essays on Gay Life and Liberation, 1973–1977*. Boston: Union Park Press, 1978.

Gay Left Collective, ed. *Homosexuality: Power and Politics*. London: Allison & Busby, 1980.

Gay Writers Group. *It Could Happen to You*. Boston: Alyson, 1983.

Gessen, Masha. *The Rights of Lesbians and Gay Men in the Russian Federation*. San Francisco: International Lesbian and Gay Human Rights Commission, 1994.

Ginsberg, Allen. *Gay Sunshine Interview with Allen Young*. Bolinas, Calif.: Grey Fox, 1974.

Girard, Jacques. *Le mouvement homosexuel en France, 1945–1980*. Paris: Editions Syros, 1981.

Goldsmith, Larry. "On the Hill and Out of the Closet." *Gay Community News* 11(6) (1983): 3.

Goodman, Gerre, et al. *No Turning Back: Lesbian and Gay Liberation for the 80s*. Philadelphia: New Society Publishers, 1983.

Gough, Jamie, and Mike MacNair. *Gay Liberation in the Eighties*. London: Pluto, 1985.

Grupo de Acción Gay. "Liberación sin Aqualane." *Sodoma* 2 (1985): 25.

Hannon, Gerald. "Taking It to the Streets." *Body Politic* 71 (1980): 9.

Hanscombe, Gillian E., and Lumsden, A. *Title Fight: The Battle for Gay News*. Brilliance Books, 1983.

Healey, Emma, and Angela Mason, eds. *Stonewall Twenty-five: The Making of the Lesbian and Gay Community in Britain*. London: Virago Press, 1994.

Hendriks, Aart, Rob Tielman, and Evert van der Veen, eds. *The Third Pink Book: A Global View of Lesbian and Gay Liberation and Oppression*. Buffalo, N.Y.: Prometheus Books, 1993.

———. *Rights of Passage: Struggles for Lesbian and Gay Legal Equality.* Toronto; Buffalo: University of Toronto Press, 1994.

Herman, Didi. *The AntiGay Agenda: Orthodox Vision and the Christian Right.* Chicago: University of Chicago Press, 1997.

Herman, Didi, and Carl Stychin, eds. *Legal Inversions: Lesbians, Gay Men, and the Politics of the Law.* Philadelphia: Temple University Press, 1996.

Hernández, Juan Jacobo, and Rafael Manrique. "10 Años del Movimiento Gay en Mexico." *La Guillotina* (16) (September 1988).

Hertzog, Mark. *The Lavender Vote: Lesbians, Gay Men, and Bisexuals in American Politics.* New York and London: New York University Press, 1996.

Hocquenghem, Guy. *Désir Homosexuel.* (Homosexual Desire), Trans. Daniella Dangoor. London: Allison & Busby, 1978.

———. *Race d'Ep!* Paris: Editions Libres/Hallier, 1979.

Hocquenghem, Guy, and Jean-Louis Bory. *Comment nous appelez-vous déjà? Ces hommes que l'on dit homosexuels.* Paris: Calmann-Levy, 1977.

International Association of Lesbians, Gay Women, and Gay Men, ed. *IGA Pink Book 1985.* Amsterdam: COC, 1985.

Irish Council for Civil Liberties. *Equality Now for Lesbians and Gay Men.* Dublin: ICCL, 1990.

Jackson, Ed, and Stan Persky, eds. *Flaunting It! A Decade of Journalism from the Body Politic: An Anthology.* Vancouver: New Star Books, Toronto: Pink Triangle Press, 1982.

Jeffrey-Poulter, Stephen. *Peers, Queers, and Commons: The Struggle for Gay Law Reform.* London: Routledge, 1991.

Johnston, Craig. "The Gay Movements." *Social Alternatives* 4 (1984): 18.

Kikel, Rudy. "Is Gay Good Enough?" *Gay Community News* 9(6) (1981): 12.

Kirk, Marshall, and Hunter Madsen. *After the Ball: How America Will Conquer Its Fear and Hatred of Gays in the 1990s.* New York: Doubleday, 1989.

Kleis, Per. "Homosexual Retrospect." *Pan International* (spring 1980): 4.

Kyper, John. "Organizing in Mexico." *Gay Community News* 7(8) (1979): 10.

Lemke, Jurgen. *Gay Voices from East Germany.* Edited by John Borneman. Trans. Steven Stoltenberg et al. Bloomington: Indiana University Press, 1991.

Lesbian and Gay Media Advocates. *Talk Back: The Gay Person's Guide to Media Action.* Boston: Alyson Publications, 1982.

Less than Gay: A Citizens Report on the Status of Homosexuality in India. New Delhi: AIDS Bhedbhav Virodhi Andolan, 1991.

Levin, James. *Reflections on the American Homosexual Rights Movement.* New York: Scholarship Committee, Gay Academic Union, 1983.

Lumsden, Ian. *Homosexuality, Society, and the State in Mexico.* Toronto: Canadian Gay Archives, 1991.

———. *Machos, Maricones, and Gays: Cuba and Homosexuality.* Philadelphia: Temple University Press, 1996.

Marotta, Toby. *The Politics of Homosexuality.* Boston: Houghton Mifflin, 1981.

Martin, Robert A. "Student Homophile League." *Gay Books Bulletin* 9 (1983): 30.

McCaskell, Tim. "Reich Replay." *Body Politic* 68 (1980): 20.

Merril, Michael. "Life after Dade." *Body Politic* 39 (1977–78): 11.

Mitchell, Pam, ed. *Pink Triangles: Radical Perspectives on Gay Liberation.* Boston: Alyson, 1980.

Moeller, Robert G. *Sex, Society, and the Law in the Postwar West Germany: Homosexuals and the Federal Constitutional Court.* Berkeley: Center for German and European Studies, University of California, 1993.

Monk, Jim. "License to Kill Gays." *Body Politic* 125 (1986): 16.

Mott, Luiz. "Report from Brazil." *Cabirion and Gay Books Bulletin* 11 (1984): 14.

Oraison, Marc. *La question homosexuelle.* Paris: Seuil, 1975.

Osborn, Torie. *Coming Home to America: A Roadmap to Gay and Lesbian Empowerment.* New York: St. Martin's Press, 1996.

Praunheim, Rosa Von. *Army of Lovers.* London: Gay Men's Press, 1980.

Rayside, David. "Gay Rights and Family Values. The Passage of Bill 7 in Ontario." *Studies in Political Economy* 26 (1988): 109–47.

———. *On the Fringe: Gays and Lesbians in Politics.* Ithaca, N.Y.: Cornell University Press, 1998.

Rose, Kieran. *Diverse Communities: The Evolution of Lesbian and Gay Politics in Ireland.* Cork: Cork University Press, 1994.

Schifter Sikora, Jacobo. *La Formación de una contracultura.* San José, Costa Rica: Ediciones Guayacán, 1989.

Severin, N. K. "Anatomy of a Gay Conservative." *Christopher Street* 72 (1983): 29.

Signorile, Michelangelo. *Queer in America: Sex, the Media, and the Closets of Power.* New York: Random House, 1993.

Smith, Anna Marie. *New Right Discourse on Race and Sexuality: Britain, 1968–1990.* Cambridge, England; New York: Cambridge University Press, 1994.

Sturgess, Bob. *No Offence: The Case for Homosexual Equality at Law.* CHE/SMG/USFI, 1975.

Sullivan, Andrew. *Virtually Normal: An Argument About Homosexuality.* New York: Alfred A. Knopf, 1995.

Sylvestre, Paul François. *Propos pour une libération (homo)sexuelle.* Montreal: Editions de l'Aurore, 1976.

———. *Les homosexuels s'organisent.* Ottawa: Editions Homeureux, 1979.

———. *Bougrerie en Nouvelle-France.* Hull, Quebec: Editions Asticou, 1983.

Tatchell, Peter. *The Battle for Bermondsey.* London: Heretic Books, 1983.

———. *Out in Europe.* London and Glasgow: Channel Four Television Publications, 1990.

———. *Europe in the Pink.* London: GMP, 1992.

Thompson, Denise. *Flaws in the Social Fabric: Homosexuals and Society in Sydney.* Sydney, Boston: G. Allen and Unwin, 1985.

Vaid, Urvashi. *Virtual Equality: The Mainstreaming of Gay and Lesbian Liberation.* New York: Doubleday, 1995.

Vassilas, Yanni. "Greek Gay Life under Socialists." *Gay Community News* 11(32) (1984): 15.

Vries, Sonja de. "Homosexuality, Socialism, and the Cuban Revolution." *Cuba Update* 15 (2) (March–May 1994).

Walderhaug, Arne. "The Emerging Gay Movement in Southeast Asia." *Outlines* 5(1) (1991): 16.

Wallis, Mick, and Simon Shepherd, eds. *Coming on Strong.* London; Boston: Unwin Hyman, 1989.

Walter, Aubrey, ed. *Come Together: The Years of Gay Liberation 1970–1973.* London: Gay Men's Press, 1980.

Winkler, Rudi, and Hans-George Stümke. *Rosa Winkel, Rosa Listen: Homosexuelle und "gesunde Volksempfinden" von Auschwitz bis Heute.* Reinbeck bei Hamburg: Rowohlt, 1981.

Yüzgün, Arslan. *Turkiyede escinsellik: (dun bugun).* Istanbul: Hur-Yuz, 1986.

12. Law

American Association of Law Libraries. Social Responsibilities Special Interest Section. Standing Committee on Lesbian and Gay Issues. "Sexual Orientation and the Law: A Selective Bibliography on Homosexuality and the Law, 1969–1993." *Law Library Journal* 86 (1) (winter 1994).

Ashman, P. et al., eds. *Homosexuality: A Community Issue: Essays on*

Why and How to Incorporate Lesbian and Gay Rights in the Law and Politics of the European Community. Dordrecht and Boston: Martinus Nijhoff, 1993.

Australasian Gay and Lesbian Law Journal. Annandale, N.S.W.: The Federation Press, 1993– .

Berrill, Kevin T., and Gregory M. Herek, eds. *Hate Crimes: Confronting Violence against Lesbians and Gay Men*. Newbury Park, Calif.: Sage Publications, 1992.

Botha, Kevan, and Edwin Cameron. "Sexual Privacy and the Law." In *South African Human Rights Handbook*, edited by Neil B. Boister, vol. 3. Durban: Centre for Socio-Legal Studies, 1994: 219–27.

Clifford, Denis, Hayden Curry, and Robin Leonard. *A Legal Guide for Lesbian and Gay Couples*. Berkeley: Nolo Press, 1994.

Cooper, Davina, and Didi Herman. "Getting the Family 'Right': Legislating Heterosexuality in Britain, 1986–1990." *Canadian Journal of Family Law* 10 (1991).

Dalla, Danilo. *"Ubi venus mutatur": omosessualita e diritto nel mondo romano*. Milan: A. Giuffre, 1987.

Daniel, Marc. "Histoire de la législation pénale française concernant l'homosexualité." *Arcadie* 96 (1961): 618–27; 97 (1961): 10–29.

Dawidoff, Robert, and Michael Nava. *Created Equal: Why Gay Rights Matter to America*. New York: St. Martin's Press, 1994.

D'Emillio, John. "Making and Unmaking Minorities: The Tensions between Gay Politics and History." *New York University Review of Law and Social Change* 14 (1984): 915–922.

Donaldson, Steven, and Wayne R. Dynes, eds. *Homosexuality: Discrimination, Criminology, and the Law*. New York: Garland Publishing, 1992.

European Court of Human Rights. *Norris Case (6/1987/129/180): Judgement/European Court of Human Rights*. Strasbourg, Council of Europe, 1988.

Fine, Derrick. *Lesbian and Gay Rights*. Cape Town: Social Justice Resource Project/Legal Education Action Project, Institute of Criminology, University of Cape Town, 1992.

Girard, Phillip. "Sexual Orientation as a Human Rights Issue in Canada, 1969–1985." *Dalhousie Law Journal* 10 (1986).

———. "From Subversion to Liberation: Homosexuals and the Immigration Act, 1952–1977." *Canadian Journal of Law and Society* 2 (1987).

Gold, Ronald. "Gay Rights Is a First Amendment Issue." *Civil Liberties* (November 1982): 6–7.

———. "Misreading Sodomy: A Critique of the Classification of 'Homosexuals' in Federal Equal Protection Law." In *Body Guards: The*

Cultural Politics of Gender Ambiguity, edited by Julia Epstein and Kristina Straub, 351–357. London: Routledge, 1991.

Halley, Janet E. "The Politics of the Closet: Towards Equal Protection for Gay, Lesbian, and Bisexual Identity." *UCLA Law Review* 36 (1989).

Harvard Law Review. *Sexual Orientation and the Law.* Cambridge, Mass.: Harvard University Press, 1989.

Heinze, Eric. *Sexual Orientation: A Human Right: An Essay on International Human Rights Law.* Dordrecht; Boston: M. Nijhoff Publishers, 1995.

Hunter, Nan D., Sherryl E. Michaelson, and Thomas B. Stoddard. *The Rights of Lesbians and Gay Men: The Basic ACLU Guide to a Gay Person's Rights.* 3d ed. Carbondale, Southern Illinois University Press, 1992.

Hunter, Nan D., and William B. Rubenstein, eds. *AIDS Agenda: Emerging Issues in Civil Rights.* New York: New Press, 1992.

Lafitte, François. "Homosexuality and the Law," *British Journal of Delinquency* (9) (1958–59).

Lambda Legal Defense and Education Fund. *Negotiating for Equal Employment Benefits: A Resource Packet.* New York: The Fund, 1994.

Law Reform Commission of Hong Kong. *Report on the Laws Governing Homosexual Conduct.* Hong Kong: The Commission, 1983.

Leonard, Arthur. *Sexuality and the Law: An Encyclopedia of Major Legal Cases.* New York: Garland, 1993.

McCuen, Gary E., ed. *Homosexuality and Gay Rights.* Hudson, Wis.: G. E. McCuen Publications, 1994.

Martínez, Ernesto A. *Guía Legal del Homosexual Urbano.* Mexico: Edamex, 1985.

Mohr, Richard. *Gays/Justice: A Study of Ethics, Society, and Law.* New York: Columbia University Press, 1988.

———. *A More Perfect Union: Why Straight America Must Stand up for Gay Rights.* Boston: Beacon Press, 1994.

Newton, David E. *Gay and Lesbian Rights: A Reference Handbook.* Santa Barbara, Calif.: ABC-CLIO, 1994.

Richards, David A. J. *Women, Gays, and the Constitution: The Grounds for Feminism and Gay Rights and the Constitution.* Chicago: University of Chicago Press, 1998.

Rubenstein, William B., ed. *Lesbians, Gay Men, and the Law.* New York: The New Press, 1993.

Ryder, Bruce. "Equality Rights and Sexual Orientation: Confronting Heterosexual Family Privilege." *Canadian Journal of Family Law* 9(1) (1990): 39–97.

Senak, Mark S. *HIV, AIDS, and the Law: A Guide to Our Rights and Challenges*. New York: Insight Books, 1996.

Simpson, Ruth. *From the Closet to the Courts*. New York: Viking, 1977.

Stoddard, Thomas B. "Lesbian and Gay Rights Litigation before a Hostile Federal Judiciary." *Harvard Civil Rights-Civil Liberties Law Review* 27(2) (1992): 555–73.

Wintemute, Robert. *Sexual Orientation and Human Rights: The United States Constitution, The European Convention, and the Canadian Charter*. New York; Oxford: Oxford University Press/Clarendon Press, 1995.

13. Gay Culture

Cross-Cultural Perspectives

Aldrich, Robert, and Gary Wotherspoon, eds. *Gay Perspectives: Essays in Australian Gay Culture*. Sydney N.S.W., Australia: Department of Economic History, University of Sydney, 1992.

Arboleda, Manuel. "Gay Life in Lima." *Gay Sunshine* 42–43 (1980): 30.

Ary R. M. *Gay, Dunia Ganjil Kaum Homofil*. Jakarta, Indonesia: Grafiti Pers, 1987.

Babuscio, Jack. *We Speak for Ourselves: The Experiences of Gay Men and Lesbians*. London: SPCK, 1988.

Bech, Henning. *When Men Meet: Homosexuality and Modernity*. Trans. Teresa Mesquit and Tim Davies. Chicago: University of Chicago Press, 1997.

Bornoff, Nicholas. *Pink Samurai: Love, Marriage, and Sex in Contemporary Japan*. New York: Pocket Books, 1991.

Boykin, Keith. *One More River to Cross: Black and Gay in America*. New York: Anchor Books, 1996.

Brown, Howard. *Familiar Faces, Hidden Lives: The Story of Homosexual Men in America Today*. New York: Harcourt Brace Jovanovich, 1977.

Burston, Paul, and Colin Richardson, eds. *A Queer Romance: Lesbians, Gay Men, and Popular Culture*. London, New York: Routledge, 1995.

Busscher, de Pierre-Oliver, and Rommel Mendes-Leite, eds. *Gay Studies from the French Cultures: Voices from France, Belgium, Brazil, Canada, and the Netherlands*. New York: Haworth Press, 1993.

Cabral, John. "Gay Life in Mainland China: I Very Fear!" *Christopher Street* 6 (2) (1982): 27–32.

Cameron, Edwin, and Mark Gevisser, eds. *Defiant Desire: Gay and Lesbian Lives in South Africa*. New York: Routledge, 1994.

Cant, Bob. *Invented Identities: Lesbians and Gays Talk about Migration*. London: Cassell, 1996.

Chesebro, James, ed. *Gayspeak*. New York: Pilgrim, 1981.

Childs, Maggie. "Japan's Homosexual Heritage." *Gai Saber* 1 (1977): 41–45.

Coe, Rov M. *A Sense of Pride: The Story of Gay Games II*. San Francisco: Pride Publications, 1986.

Daniel, Marc. "Arab Civilization and Male Love." Trans. Winston Leyland. *Gay Sunshine* 32 (1977): 1–11, 27.

de la Pena, Terri. "A Tale of Two Mexicos," *Lambda Book Report* 3 (2) (1992): 22–23.

Del Pizzo, Nancy, and Joseph Itiel. *Pure Vida! Gay and Lesbian Costa Rica*. San Francisco: Orchid House, 1993.

Denneny, Michael, Charles Ortleb, and Thomas Steele, eds. *The Christopher Street Reader*. New York: Coward McCann, 1983.

Duberman, Martin, ed. *A Queer World: The Center for Lesbian and Gay Studies Reader*. New York: New York University Press, 1997.

Dynes, Wayne R., and Stephen Donaldson, eds. *Asian Homosexuality*. New York: Garland, 1992.

Fisher, Peter. *The Gay Mystique: The Myth and Reality of Male Homosexuality*. New York: Stein and Day, 1972.

Forgione, Steve. "Living in Exile." *Gay Community News* 9(30) (1982): 7.

Goff, Michael, and the staff of *Out Magazine*. *Out in America*. New York: Viking Studio Books, 1994.

Goodwin, Joseph P. *More Man Than You'll Ever Be: Gay Folklore and Acculturation in Middle America*. Bloomington: Indiana University Press, 1989.

Grahn, Judy. *Another Mother Tongue: Gay Words, Gay Worlds*. Boston: Beacon Press, 1984.

Greene, Beverly, ed. *Ethnic and Cultural Diversity among Lesbians and Gay Men*. Thousand Oaks, Calif.: Sage Publications, 1997.

Grubb, Page, and Theo Van Der Meer. "Gayness in a Small Country." *Body Politic* 53 (1979): 23.

Hamilton, Wallace. *Christopher and Gay: A Partisan's View of the Greenwich Village Homosexual Scene*. New York: Saturday Review Press, 1973.

Hanawa, Yukiko, ed. *Circuits of Desire*. Durham, N.C.: Duke University Press, 1994.

Harris, Daniel. *The Rise and Fall of Gay Culture*. New York: Hyperion, 1997.

Hemphill, Essex, ed. *Brother to Brother: New Writing by Black Gay Men.* Boston: Alyson, 1991.

Herdt, Gilbert, ed. *Gay Culture in America: Essays from the Field.* Boston: Beacon Press, 1991.

Herrick, Thaddeus. "A View of Venezuelan Homosexuality." *Habari-Daftari* 4 (1984): 26.

Hunt, Morton M. *What You Should Know about Homosexuality.* New York: Farrar, Strauss, Giroux, 1977.

Issacs, Gordon, and Brian McKendrick. *Male Homosexuality in South Africa: Identity Formation, Culture, and Crisis.* New York: Oxford University Press, 1992.

Jackson, Peter. *Male Homosexuality in Thailand.* Elmhurst, N.Y.: Global Academic, 1989.

Jauregui, Carlos. *La Homosexualidad en la Argentina.* Buenos Aires: Tarso, 1987.

Jay, Karla, and Allen Young. *The Gay Report.* New York: Summit Books, 1979.

Jay, Karla, and Allen Young, eds. *Out of the Closets.* New York: Douglas/Links, 1972.

———. *Lavender Culture.* New York: New York University Press, 1994.

Kaiser, Charles. *The Gay Metropolis: 1940–1996.* Boston: Houghton Mifflin, 1997.

Kala, Arvind. *Invisible Minority: The Unknown World of the Indian Homosexual.* New Delhi: Dynamic Books, 1991.

Kleinberg, Seymour. *Alienated Affections: Being Gay in America.* New York: St. Martin's Press, 1980.

Lacey, E. A. "Latin America." *Gay Sunshine* 40–41 (1979): 22.

Lancaster, Roger N. *Life Is Hard: Machismo, Danger, and the Intimacy of Power in Nicaragua.* Berkeley: University of California Press, 1992.

Leinen, Stephen H. *Gay Cops.* New Brunswick, N.J.: Rutgers University Press, 1993.

Leong, Russel, ed. *Asian American Sexualities: Dimensions of the Gay and Lesbian Experience.* New York: Routledge, 1996.

Leyland, Winston, ed. *Gay Roots: Twenty Years of "Gay Sunshine."* San Francisco: Gay Sunshine Press, 1991.

Likosky, Stephan, ed. *Coming Out: An Anthology of International Gay and Lesbian Writings.* New York: Pantheon, 1992.

Luczak, Raymond, ed. *Eyes of Desire: A Deaf Gay and Lesbian Reader.* Boston: Alyson Publications, 1993.

Marcus, Eric. *Is It a Choice?: Answers to Three Hundred of the Most Frequently Asked Questions about Gays and Lesbians.* San Francisco: HarperSanFrancisco, 1993.

Miller, Merle. *On Being Different: What It Means to Be Homosexual.* New York: Random House, 1971.

Miller, Neil. *In Search of Gay America: Women and Men in a Time of Change.* New York: Atlantic Monthly Press, 1989.

———. *Out in the World: Gay and Lesbian Life from Buenos Aires to Bangkok.* New York: Random House, 1992.

Mirabet I Mullol, Antoni. *Homosexualidad Hoy.* Barcelona, Spain: Editorial Herder, 1985.

Murray, Stephen O. *Oceanic Homosexualities.* New York: Garland, 1992.

———. *American Gay.* Chicago: University of Chicago Press, 1996.

Murray, Stephen O., ed. *Cultural Diversity and Homosexualities.* New York: Irvington, 1987.

———. *Male Homosexuality in Central and South America.* San Francisco: Instituto Obregon, 1987.

———. *Latin American Male Homosexualities.* Albuquerque: University of New Mexico Press, 1995.

Murray, Stephen O., and Will Roscoe, eds. *Islamic Homosexualities: Culture, History, and Literature.* New York: New York University Press, 1997.

National Lesbian and Gay Survey. *Proust, Cole Porter, Michelangelo, Marc Almond, and Me: Writings by Gay Men on Their Lives and Lifestyles from the Archives of the National Lesbian and Gay Survey.* London; New York: Routledge, 1993.

Newton, Esther. *Cherry Grove, Fire Island: Sixty Years in America's First Gay and Lesbian Town.* Boston: Beacon Press, 1993.

Noguera, Gary, and Len Richmond, eds. *The Gay Liberation Book.* San Francisco: Ramparts Press, 1973.

———. *The New Gay Liberation Book: Writings and Photographs about Gay (Men's) Liberation.* Palo Alto, Calif.: Ramparts Press, 1979.

O'Carrol, Ide, and Eoin Collins, eds. *Lesbian and Gay Visions of Ireland: Towards the 21st Century.* London: Cassells, 1995.

Parker, R. "Youth, Identity, and Homosexuality: The Changing Shape of Sexual Life in Contemporary Brazil." *Journal of Homosexuality* 17 (3–4) (1989): 269–89.

———. *Bodies, Pleasures, and Passions: Sexual Culture in Contemporary Brazil.* Boston: Beacon Press, 1991.

Pettiway, Leon E. *Honey, Honey, Miss Thang: Being Black, Gay, and on the Streets.* Philadelphia: Temple University Press, 1996.

Plummer, Douglas. *Queer People.* New York: Citadel Press, 1965.

Preston, John, ed. *The Big Gay Book: A Man's Survival Guide for the Nineties.* New York: Plume, 1991.

Prieur, Annick. *Mema's House, Mexico City: On Transvestites, Queens, and Machos.* Chicago: University of Chicago Press, 1998.

Pronger, Brian. *The Arena of Masculinity: Sports, Homosexuality, and the Meaning of Sex.* New York: St. Martin's Press, 1990.

Ratti, Rakesh, ed. *A Lotus of Another Color: An Unfolding of the South Asian Gay and Lesbian Experience.* Boston: Alyson Publications, 1993.

Rist, Darrell Yates. *Heartlands: A Gay Man's Odyssey across America.* New York: Dutton, 1992.

Roscoe, Will, ed. *Living the Spirit: A Gay American Indian Anthology.* New York: St. Martin's Press, 1988.

Schuvaloff, George. "Gay Life in Russia." *Christopher Street* 1(3) (1976): 14–22.

Sears, James T. *Growing up Gay in the South: Race, Gender, and Journeys of the Spirit.* New York: Haworth Press, 1991.

Thompson, Mark, ed. *Gay Spirit: Myth and Meaning.* New York: St. Martin's Press, 1987.

Translation Group. *Gays in Indonesia.* Fitzroy, Australia: Sybylla Press, 1984.

Trevisan, João Silvério. *Perverts in Paradise.* Trans. Martin Foreman. London: G.M.P., 1986.

Tuller, David. *Cracks in the Iron Closet: Travels in Gay and Lesbian Russia.* Chicago: University of Chicago Press, 1996.

Van Naerssen, A. X., ed. *Gay Life in Dutch Society.* Binghamton, N.Y.: Harrington Park Press, 1987.

Warren, Carol A. B. *Identity and Community in the Gay World.* New York: Wiley, 1974.

White, Edmund. *States of Desire: Travels in Gay America.* New York: Dutton, 1980.

Gay Relationships

Beam, Joseph, ed. *In the Life: A Black Gay Anthology.* Boston, Mass.: Alyson Publications, 1986.

Berzon, Betty. *Permanent Partners: Building Gay and Lesbian Relationships That Last.* New York: Plume, 1988.

Berzon, Betty, and Robert Leighton, eds. *Positively Gay.* Millbrae, Calif.: Celestial Arts, 1979.

———. *Positively Gay: New Approaches to Gay and Lesbian Life.* Berkeley: Celestial Arts, 1992.

Clark, Donald H. *Loving Someone Gay.* Berkeley: Celestial Arts, 1987.

Eskridge, William N. Jr. *The Case for Same-Sex Marriage: From Sexual Liberty to Civilized Commitment.* New York: Free Press, 1996.

Gearhart, Sally, and William Johnson. *Loving Women/Loving Men*. San Francisco: Glide Publications, 1974.

Island, David, and Patrick Letellier. *Men Who Beat the Men Who Love Them: Battered Gay Men and Domestic Violence*. New York: Haworth Press, 1991.

Lee, John Alan, ed. *Gay Midlife and Maturity*. New York: Haworth Press, 1991.

Maddox, Brenda. *The Marrying Kind: Homosexuality and Marriage*. New York: Granada, 1982.

McWhirter, David P., and Andrew M. Mattison. *The Male Couple: How Relationships Develop*. Englewood Cliffs, N.J.: Prentice-Hall, 1984.

Nahas, Rebecca, and Myra Turley. *The New Couple: Women and Gay Men*. New York: Seaview Books, 1979.

Sherman, Suzanne, ed. *Lesbian and Gay Marriage: Private Commitments, Public Ceremonies*. Philadelphia: Temple University Press, 1992.

Silverstein, Charles. *Man to Man: Gay Couples in America*. New York: Morrow, 1981.

Smith, Mike, ed. *Black Men/White Men*. San Francisco: Gay Sunshine, 1982.

Uhrig, Larry J. *The Two of Us: Affirming, Celebrating, and Symbolizing Gay and Lesbian Relationships*. Boston: Alyson Publications, 1984.

Vida, Ginny, ed. *Our Right to Love*. Englewood Cliffs, N.J.: Prentice-Hall, 1978.

Vining, Donald. *How Can You Come Out if You've Never Been In? Essays on Gay Life and Relationships*. Trumansburg, N.Y.: Crossing Press, 1986.

Walker, Mitch. *Men Loving Men: A Gay Sex Guide and Consciousness Book*. San Francisco: Gay Sunshine Press, 1977.

Walker, Mitch, et al. *Visionary Love: A Spirit Book of Gay Mythology and Trans-Mutational Faerie*. San Francisco: Treeroots Press, 1980.

Whitney, Catherine. *Uncommon Lives: Gay Men and Straight Women*. New York: New American Library, 1991.

Gay Families

Barret, Robert L., and Brian E. Robinson. *Gay Fathers*. Lexington, Mass.: Lexington Books, 1990.

Benkov, Laura. *Reinventing the Family: The Emerging Story of Lesbian and Gay Parents*. New York: Crown Publishers, 1994.

Bosche, Susanne. *Jenny Lives with Eric and Martin*. London: Gay Men's Press, 1983.

Bozett, Fredrick W., ed. *Gay and Lesbian Parents*. New York: Praeger, 1987.

Bozett, Fredrick W., and Marvin Susman, eds. *Homosexuality and Family Relations*. New York: Harrington Park Press, 1990.

Corley, Andre Rip. *The Last Closet: A Gay Parent's Guide for Coming Out to Your Children*. Pompano Beach, Fla.: Exposition Press of Florida, 1987.

Gantz, Joe. *Whose Child Cries: Children of Gay Parents Talk about Their Lives*. Rolling Hills Estates, Calif.: Jalmar Press, 1983.

MacPike, Loralee, ed. *There's Something I've Been Meaning to Tell You*. Tallahassee, Fla.: Naiad Press, 1989.

Muller, Ann. *Parents Matter: Parents' Relationships with Lesbian Daughters and Gay Sons*. Tallahassee, Fla.: Naiad Press, 1987.

Preston, John, ed. *A Member of the Family: Gay Men Write about Their Families*. New York: Dutton, 1992.

Signorile, Michelangelo. *Outing Yourself: How to Come Out as Lesbian or Gay to Family, Friends, and Coworkers*. New York: Random House, 1995.

Weston, Kath. *Families We Choose: Lesbians, Gays, Kinship*. New York: Columbia University Press, 1991.

Gay Youth

Alyson, Sasha. *Young, Gay, and Proud*. Boston: Alyson Publications, 1981.

Boxer, Andrew, and Gilbert Herdt. *Children of Horizons: How Gay and Lesbian Teens Are Leading a New Way Out of the Closet*. Boston: Beacon Press, 1993.

Cunningham, John, and Frances Hanckel. *A Way of Love. A Way of Life: A Young Person's Introduction to What It Means to Be Gay*. New York: Lothrop, Lee and Shepard Books, 1979.

DeCrescenzo, Teresa, ed. *Helping Gay and Lesbian Youth: New Policies, New Programs, New Practice*. New York: Haworth Press, 1994.

Herdt, Gilbert, ed. *Gay and Lesbian Youth*. New York: Haworth Press, 1989.

Heron, Ann, ed. *Two Teenagers in Twenty: Writings by Gay and Lesbian Youth*. Boston: Alyson Publications, 1994.

Kantrowitz, Arnie. *Under the Rainbow: Growing Up Gay*. New York: Morrow, 1977.

Rench, Janice E. *Understanding Sexual Identity: A Book for Gay Teens and Their Friends*. Minneapolis, Minn.: Lerner Publications, 1990.

Rhodes, Robert A. *Coming Out in College: The Struggle for a Queer Identity*. Westport, Conn.: Bergin and Garvey, 1994.

Savin-Williams, Ritch C. *Gay and Lesbian Youth: Expressions of Identity*. New York: Hemisphere, 1990.

Walling, Donovan R. *Gay Teens at Risk*. Bloomington, Ind.: Phi Delta Kappa Educational Foundation, 1993.

Whitlock, Katherine. *Bridges of Respect: Creating Support for Lesbian and Gay Youth*. Philadelphia: American Friends Service Committee, 1988.

Bisexuality

Atkins, Dawn, ed. *Looking Queer: Body Image and Identity in Lesbian, Bisexual, Gay, and Transgendered Communities*. Binghamton, N.Y.: Haworth Press, 1997.

Beemyn, Brett, ed. *Creating a Place for Ourselves; Lesbian, Gay, and Bisexual Community Histories*. New York: Routledge, 1997.

Geller, Thomas, ed. *Bisexuality: A Reader and Sourcebook*. Ojai, Calif.: Times Change Press, 1990.

Gerber, Majorie B. *Vice Versa: Bisexuality and the Eroticism of Everyday Life*. New York: Simon and Schuster, 1995.

Hall, Donald E., and Maria Pramaggiore, eds. *Representing Bisexualities: Subjects and Cultures of Fluid Desire*. New York: New York University Press, 1996.

Hutchins, Loraine, and Lani Kaahumanu, eds. *Bi Any Other Name: Bisexual People Speak Out*. Boston: Alyson Publications, 1991.

Ilhan, Attila. *Yanlis Kadinlar Yanlis Erkekler*. Istanbul: Ozgur Yayin-Dagitim, 1985.

Klein, F., and T. Wolfe, eds. *Bisexualities: Theory and Practice*. New York: Haworth Press, 1985.

Murphy, Timothy F. "Freud Reconsidered: Bisexuality, Homosexuality, and Moral Judgement." *Journal of Homosexuality* 9 (1983/84): 65–77.

Rose, Sharon, and Chris Stevens, et al., eds. *Bisexual Horizons: Politics, Histories, Lives*. London: Lawrence & Wishart, 1996.

Tucker, Naomi, ed. *Bisexual Politics: Theories, Queries and Visions*. New York: Haworth Press, 1995.

Vorhaus, Martin Grossman. *Adam's Rib: An Analysis of Normal Bisexuality in Each of Us*. New York: Horizon Press, 1959.

Wolff, Charlotte. *Bisexuality: A Study*. London: Quartet, 1979.

Transgender

Benjamin, Harry. *The Transsexual Phenomenon*. New York: Julian Press, 1966.

Brown, Mildred L., and Chloe Ann Rounsley. *True Selves: Understanding Transsexualism: for Families, Friends, Coworkers, and Helping Professionals.* San Francisco: Jossey-Bass Publishers, 1996.

Bullough, Bonnie, Vern Bullough, and James Elias, eds. *Gender Blending.* Amherst, Mass.: Prometheus Books, 1997.

Cameron, Loren. *Body Alchemy: Transsexual Portraits.* Pittsburg: Cleis Press, 1996.

Council of Europe: Colloquy on European Law (Twenty-Third: 1993: Amsterdam, Netherlands). *Transsexualism, Medicine and Law: Proceedings, Twenty-Third Colloquy on European Law.* Strasbourg: Council of Europe, 1995.

Ekins, Richard. *Male Femaling: A Grounded Theory Approach to Cross-Dressing and Sex-Changing.* London; New York: Routledge, 1997.

Ekins, Richard, and Dave King, eds. *Blending Genders: Social Aspects of Cross-Dressing and Sex-Changing.* London/New York: Routledge, 1996.

Feinberg, Leslie. *Transgender Warriors: Making History from Joan of Arc to RuPaul.* Boston: Beacon Press, 1996.

Kirk, Shelia, M.D., and Martine Rothblatt. *Medical, Legal, and Workplace Issues for the Transsexual: A Guide for Successful Transformation: Male to Female, Female to Male.* Watertown, Mass: Together Lifeworks, 1995.

Lewins, Frank W. *Transsexualism in Society: A Sociology of Male-to-female Transsexuals.* South Melbourne, Australia: Macmillan Education, 1995.

MacKenzie, Gordene Olga. *Transgender Nation.* Bowling Green, Ohio: Bowling Green State University Popular Press, 1994.

Millot, Catherine. *Horsexe: Essay on Transexuality.* Trans. Kenneth Hylton. Brooklyn, N.Y.: Autonomedia, 1990.

Ramet, Sabrina Petra, ed. *Gender Reversals and Gender Cultures: Anthropoligical and Historical Perspectives.* London/New York: Routledge, 1996.

Ramsey, Gerald. *Transsexuals: Candid Answers to Private Questions.* Freedom, Calif: Crossing Press, 1996.

Rothblatt, Martine. *The Apartheid of Sex: A Manifesto on the Freedom of Gender.* New York: Crown Publishers, 1995.

Werther, Ralph a.k.a. Earl Lind. *The Female Impersonators.* New York: Arno Press, 1975.

Leathersex/SM

Baldwin, Guv. *Ties That Bind: The SM/Leather/Fetish Erotic Style: Issues, Commentaries and Advice.* Edited by Joseph Bean. Los Angeles: Daedalus, 1993.

Mains, Geoff. *Urban Aboriginals. A Celebration of Leathersexuality.* San Francisco: Gay Sunshine Press, 1984.

Thompson, Mark. *Leatherfolk: Radical Sex, People, Politics, and Practice.* Boston: Alyson, 1991.

Townsend, Larry. *The Leatherman's Handbook II.* New York: Carlyle Communications, 1989.

14. Contemporary Issues

AIDS

Altman, Dennis. *AIDS in the Mind of America.* Garden City, N.Y.: Doubleday, 1986.

Bayer, Ronald, and David Kirp, eds. *AIDS in the Industrialized Democracies: Passions, Politics, and Policies.* New Brunswick, N.J.: Rutgers University Press, 1992.

Berridge, Virginia, and Philip Strong, eds. *AIDS and Contemporary History.* Cambridge, England; New York: Cambridge University Press, 1993.

Carballo, Manuel, Aart Hendricks, and Rob Tielman, eds. *Bisexuality and HIV/AIDS: A Global Perspective.* Buffalo, N.Y.: Prometheus Books, 1991.

Dangerous Bedfellows, ed. *Policing Public Sex: Queer Politics and the Future of AIDS Activism.* Boston: South End Press, 1996.

Daniel, Herbert, and Richard Parker. *Sexuality, Politics, and AIDS in Brazil: In Another World?* London; Washington, D.C.: Falmer Press, 1993.

Derlaga, Valerian J., and Anita P. Barbee, eds. *HIV and Social Interaction.* Thousand Oaks, Calif.: Sage Publications, 1998.

Epstein, Steven. "Moral Contagion and the Medicalization of Gay Identity: AIDS in Historical Perspective." *Research in Law, Deviance, and Social Control* 9 (1988): 3–36.

Gagnon, John H., Peter M. Nardi, and Martin P. Levine, eds. *In Changing Times: Gay Men and Lesbians Encounter HIV/AIDS.* Chicago: University of Chicago Press, 1997.

Hallett, Michael A., guest editor. *Activism and Marginalization in the AIDS Crisis.* New York: Haworth Press, 1997.

Hirsch, Emmanuel. *AIDES solidaires.* Paris: Editions du Cerf, 1991.

Kayal, Philip M. *Bearing Witness: Gay Men's Health Crisis and the Politics of AIDS.* Boulder, Colo.: Westview Press, 1993.

Kramer, Larry. *Reports from the Holocaust: The Making of an AIDS Activist.* New York: St. Martin's Press, 1995.

Land, Helen, ed. *AIDS: A Complete Guide to Psychosocial Intervention*. Milwaukee: Family Service America, 1992.

Leiner, Marvin. *Sexual Politics in Cuba: Machismo, Homosexuality and AIDS*. Boulder, Colo.: Westview Press, 1994.

Mass, Lawrence D. *'We Must Love One Another or Die': The Life and Legacies of Larry Kramer*. New York: St. Martin's Press, 1997.

Padug, Robert. "More Than the Story of a Virus: Gay History, Gay Communities, and AIDS." *Radical America* 21 (2–3) 1987: 39–40.

Patton, Cindy. *Sex and Germs: The Politics of AIDS*. Boston: South End, 1985.

———. *Inventing AIDS*. New York: Routledge, 1990.

Shilts, Randy. *And the Band Played On: Politics, People, and the AIDS Epidemic*. New York: St. Martin's Press, 1987.

Watney, Simon. *Policing Desire: Pornography, AIDS, and the Media*. London: Cassell, 1997.

Education

Epstein, Debbie, ed. *Challenging Lesbian and Gay Inequalities in Education*. Buckingham, Philadelphia: Open University Press, 1994.

Gay Teachers' Group. *School's Out: Lesbian and Gay Rights in Education*. London: The Gay Teachers' Group, 1987.

Harbeck, Karen M., ed. *Coming Out of the Classroom Closet: Gay and Lesbian Students, Teachers, and Curricula*. New York: Haworth Press, 1992.

Harris, Simon. *Lesbian and Gay Issues in the English Classroom: The Importance of Being Honest*. Milton Keynes, England; Philadelphia: Open University Press, 1990.

Legg, W. Dorr, ed. *Homophile Studies in Theory and Practice*/Written and edited by W. Dorr Legg, et. al. Los Angeles: ONE Institute Press; San Francisco: GLB Publishers, 1994.

Marotta, Toby. *Sons of Harvard: Gay Men From the Class of 1967*. New York: Morrow, 1982.

McNaron, Toni A. H. *Poisoned Ivy: Lesbian and Gay Academics Confronting Homophobia*. Philadelphia: Temple University Press, 1996.

Rofes, Eric E. *Socrates, Plato, and Guys Like Me: Confessions of a Gay Schoolteacher*. Boston: Alyson Publications, 1985.

———. "Opening Up the Classroom Closet: Responding to the Education Needs of Gay and Lesbian Youth," *Harvard Educational Review* 59(4) (1989), 444–453.

Rutgers University. President's Select Committee for Lesbian and Gay Concerns. *In Every Classroom: The Report of the President's Select Committee for Lesbian and Gay Concerns*. New Brunswick, N.J.:

Office of Student Life Policy and Services, The State University of New Jersey, Rutgers, 1989.

Gays in the Military

Carey, John J., ed. *The Christian Argument for Gays and Lesbians in the Military: Essays by Mainline Church Leaders.* Lewiston, N.Y.: Mellen University Press, 1993.

Citizen Soldier. *The Khaki Closet: What You Need to Know about the U.S. Military If You're Gay, Lesbian, or Have Tested Positive on the HIV Test.* New York: Citizen Soldier, 1992.

Gibson, Edward Lawrence. *Get off My Ship: Ensign Berg vs. the U.S. Navy.* New York: Avon, 1978.

Herek, Gregory, Jared B. Jobe, and Ralph M. Carney, eds. *Out in Force: Sexual Orientation and the Military.* Chicago: University of Chicago Press, 1996.

Homosexuality in the Military: A Sourcebook of Official Uncensored U.S. Government Documents. Diane Publishing, 1991–1993.

Humphrey, Mary Ann. *My Country, My Right to Serve: Experiences of Gay Men and Women in the Military, World War II to the Present.* New York: HarperCollins, 1990.

Murphy, Lawrence. *Perverts by Official Order: The Campaign Against Homosexuals by the U.S. Navy.* New York: Haworth, 1988.

Rimmerman, Craig A., ed. *Gay Rights, Military Wrongs: Political Perspectives on Lesbians and Gays in the Military.* Hamden, Conn.: Garland, 1996.

Scott, Wilbur J., and Carson Stanley, eds. *Gays and Lesbians in the Military: Issues, Concerns, and Contrasts.* New York: Aldine de Gruyter, 1994.

Shawver, Lois. *And the Flag Was Still There: Straight People, Gay People, and Sexuality in the U.S. Military.* New York: Haworth Press, 1995.

Shilts, Randy. *Conduct Unbecoming: Lesbians and Gays in the U.S. Military: Vietnam to the Persian Gulf.* New York: St. Martin's Press, 1993.

Steffan, Joseph. *Gays in the Military: Joseph Steffan Versus the United States.* Ed. Marc Wolinsky and Kenneth Sherrill. Princeton, N.J.: Princeton University Press, 1993.

Tatchell, Peter. *We Don't Want to March Straight: Masculinity, Queers, and the Military.* London; New York: Cassell, 1995.

United States. General Accounting Office: *Homosexuals in the Military: Policies and Practices of Foreign Countries.* Report to the Honorable John W. Warner, U.S. Senate/United States General Accounting Office. Washington, D.C.: The Office.

Weinberg, Martin S., and Colin J. Williams. *Homosexuals and the Military: A Study of Less Than Honorable Discharge.* New York: Harper and Row, 1971.

Zeeland, Steven. *Barrack Buddies and Soldier Lovers: Dialogues with Gay Young Men in the U.S. Military.* New York: Harrington Park Press, 1993.

———. *Sailors and Sexual Identity: Crossing the Line Between "Straight" and "Gay" in the U.S. Navy.* New York: Haworth Press, 1995.

Zuniga, Jose. *Soldier of the Year? Jose Zuniga.* New York: Pocket Books, 1994.

Ethics

Champagne, John. *The Ethics of Marginality: A New Approach to Gay Studies.* Minneapolis: University of Minnesota Press, 1995.

Gross, Larry P. *Contested Closets: The Politics and Ethics of Outing.* Minneapolis: University of Minnesota Press, 1993.

Johansson, Warren, and William A. Percy. *Outing: Shattering the Conspiracy of Silence.* New York: Haworth Press, 1994.

Jung, Patricia Beattie, and Ralph F. Smith. *Heterosexism: An Ethical Challenge.* Albany: State University of New York Press, 1993.

Mohr, Richard. *Gay Ideas: Outing and Other Controversies.* Boston: Beacon Press, 1992.

Murphy, Timothy F., ed. *Gay Ethics: Controversies in Outing, Civil Rights, and Sexual Science.* New York: Haworth Press, 1994.

O'Carroll, Tom. *Paedophilia: The Radical Case.* London: Peter Owen, 1980.

Rossman, Parker. *Sexual Experience between Men and Boys: Exploring the Pederast Underground.* New York: Association Press, 1976.

Ruse, Michael. *Homosexuality.* Oxford: Basil Blackwell, 1988.

Tsang, Dan, ed. *The Age Taboo: Gay Male Sexuality, Power, and Consent.* Boston: Alyson, 1981.

Homosexuality and Religion

Balka, Christie, and Andy Rose, eds. *Twice Blessed: On Being Lesbian, Gay and Jewish.* Boston: Beacon Press, 1989.

Beck, A. and Hunt, R., eds. *Speaking Love's Name. Homosexuality-Some Catholic and Socialist Reflections.* Jubilee Group, 1988.

Bouldrey, Brian, ed. *Wrestling with the Angel: Faith and Religion in the Lives of Gay Men.* New York: Riverhead Books, 1996.

Boyd, Malcolm. *Gay Priest: An Inner Journey.* New York: St. Martin's Press, 1986.

Carey, John Jesse, ed. *The Sexuality Debate in North American Churches, 1988–1995: Controversies, Unresolved Issues, Future Prospects*. Lewiston, N.Y.: E. Mellen Press, 1995.

Clark, J. Michael. *A Defiant Celebration: Theological Ethics and Gay Sexuality*. Garland, Tex.: Tangelwuld Press, 1990.

————. *Beyond Our Ghettos: Gay Theology in Ecological Perspective*. Cleveland: Pilgrim Press, 1993.

Clark, J. Michael, and Michael L. Stemmeler, eds. *Homophobia and the Judaeo-Christian Tradition: Essays by J. Michael Clark et al.* Dallas: Monument Press; Distributed by Publishers Associates, 1990.

Coleman, Gerald. *Homosexuality: Catholic Teaching and Pastoral Practice*. New York: Paulist Press, 1995.

Coleman, Peter. *Christian Attitudes to Homosexuality*. London: SPCK, 1980.

Comstock, David, and Susan E. Henking, eds. *Que(e)ring Religion: A Critical Anthology*. New York: Continuum, 1997.

Conner, Randy P. *Blossom of Bone: Reclaiming the Connections between Homoeroticism and the Sacred*. San Francisco: Harper San Francisco, 1993.

DiMaria-Kuiper, Johannes W. *Hot under the Collar: Self-Portrait of a Gay Pastor*. Columbia, Mo.: Mercury Press, 1983.

Donaldson, Stephen, and Wayne R. Dynes, eds. *Homosexuality and Religion and Philosophy*. New York: Garland, 1992.

Edwards, George, R. *Gay/Lesbian Liberation: A Biblical Perspective*. New York: Pilgrim Press, 1984.

Enroth, Ronald M., and Gerald E. Jamison. *The Gay Church*. Grand Rapids, Mich.: Eerdmans, 1974.

Evans, Arthur. *Witchcraft and the Gay Counterculture: A Radical View of Western Civilization and Some of the People It Has Tried to Destroy*. Boston: Fag Rag Books, 1978.

————. *The God of Ecstasy: Sex Roles and the Madness of Dionysis*. New York: St. Martin's Press, 1988.

Fortunato, John E. *Embracing the Exile: Healing Journeys of Gay Christians*. New York: Seabury Press, 1982.

Gramick, Jeannine, ed. *Homosexuality in the Priesthood and the Religious Life*. New York: Crossroad, 1989.

Hartman, Keith. *Congregations in Conflict: The Battle over Homosexuality*. New Brunswick, N.J.: Rutgers University Press, 1996.

Hasbany, Richard, ed. *Homosexuality and Religion*. New York: Haworth Press, 1989.

Helminiak, Daniel A. *What the Bible Really Says about Homosexuality*. San Francisco: Alamo Square Press, 1994.

Hilton, Bruce. *Can Homophobia Be Cured?: Wrestling with Questions That Challenge the Church.* Nashville, Tenn.: Abingdon Press, 1992.

Holtz, Raymond C. *Listen to the Stories: Gay and Lesbian Catholics Talk about Their Lives and the Church.* New York: Garland, 1991.

Ide, Arthur Frederick. *The City of Sodom and Homosexuality in Western Religious Thought to 630 C.E..* Dallas: Monument, 1985.

James, Eric. *Homosexuality and a Pastoral Church.* Christian Action, 1988.

Jordon, Mark D. *The Invention of Sodomy in Christian Theology.* Chicago: University of Chicago Press, 1997.

Macourt, Malcolm, ed. *Toward a Theology of Gay Liberation.* London: SCM Press, 1977.

Mass, Lawrence. *Confessions of a Jewish Wagnerite: Being Gay and Jewish in America.* London: Cassell, 1994.

McNaught, Brian. *A Disturbed Peace: Selected Writings of an Irish Catholic Homosexual.* Washington, D.C.: Dignity, 1981.

———. *On Being Gay.* New York: St. Martin's Press, 1988.

McNeill, John J. *The Church and the Homosexual.* Boston: Beacon Press, 1993.

Melton, J. Gordon. *The Churches Speak on Homosexuality; Official Statements from Religious Bodies and Ecumenical Organizations.* Detroit: Gale Research, 1991.

Mollenkott, Virginia Ramsey, and Letha Scanzoni. *Is the Homosexual My Neighbor?* New York: Harper and Row, 1980.

Oberholtzer, Dwight, ed. *Is Gay Good? Ethics, Theology, and Homosexuality.* Philadelphia: Westminster Press, 1971.

Perry, Troy. *The Lord Is My Shepherd and He Knows I'm Gay.* New York: Bantam, 1973.

Pittenger, Norman. *Time for Consent: A Christian's Approach to Homosexuality.* London: SCM Press, 1976.

Raynes, Marybeth, Ron Schow, and Wayne Schow, eds. *Peculiar People: Mormons and Same-Sex Orientation.* Salt Lake City: Signature Books, 1991.

Scroggs, Robin. *The New Testament and Homosexuality: Contextual Background for Contemporary Debate.* Philadelphia: Fortress Press, 1983.

Shokeid, Moshe. *A Gay Synagogue in New York.* New York: Columbia University Press, 1995.

Swidler, Arlene, ed. *Homosexuality and World Religions.* Philadelphia: Trinity Press International, 1993.

White, Mel. *Stranger at the Gate: To Be Gay and Christian in America.* New York: Simon and Schuster, 1994.

Williams, Bruce. "Homosexuality and Christianity: A Review Discussion." *Thomist* 46 (1982): 609–25.

Wilson, Angelia R. *Below the Belt: Religion, Sexuality and Politics in the Rural South*. London: Cassell, 1998.

Wolf, James G., ed. *Gay Priests*. New York: Harper and Row, 1989.

Gays in the Workplace

Diamant, Louis, ed. *Homosexual Issues in the Workplace*. Washington, D.C.: Taylor and Francis, 1993.

Ellis, Allan, and Bob Powers. *A Manager's Guide to Sexual Orientation in the Workplace*. New York: Routledge, 1995.

Ellis, Allan L., and Ellen D. B. Riggle, eds. *Sexual Identity on the Job: Issues and Services*. New York; London: Harrington Park Press, 1996.

Ferejohn, John, and Barbara Fried et al. *Domestic Partner Benefits: A Case Study*. Washington, D.C.: College and University Personnel Association, 1994.

Friskopp, Annette, and Sharon Silverstein. *Straight Jobs, Gay Lives: Gay and Lesbian Professionals, the Harvard Business School, and the American Workplace*. New York: Scribner, 1995.

Lucas, Jay H., and James D. Woods. *The Corporate Closet: The Professional Lives of Gay Men in America*. New York: The Free Press, 1993.

McNaught, Brian. *Gay Issues in the Workplace*. New York: St. Martin's Press, 1993.

Miller, Gerald V. *The Gay Male's Odyssey in the Corporate World*. New York: Haworth Press, 1995.

Rasi, Richard A., and Lourdes Rodriguez-Nogues, eds. *Out in the Workplace: The Pleasures and Perils of Coming Out on the Job*. Los Angeles: Alyson Publications, 1995.

Spielman, Susan, and Liz Winfeld. *Straight Talk about Gays in the Workplace: Creating an Inclusive, Productive Environment for Everyone in Your Organization*. New York: AMACOM, 1995.

Zuckerman, Amy J., and George F. Simons. *Sexual Orientation in the Workplace: Gay Men, Lesbians, Bisexuals and Heterosexuals Working Together*. Thousand Oaks, Calif.: Sage Publications, 1996.

About The Author

Ronald J. Hunt (B.A., M.A., Ph.D. Ohio State University) is associate professor of Political Science at Ohio University in Athens, Ohio. Dr. Hunt has taught "Gay and Lesbian Politics" at Ohio University for over 15 years, during which time he accumulated much of the information presented in this volume. He has been active in the Lesbian, Gay, and Bisexual Caucus of the American Political Science Association since its inception, and there he has presented papers on the subject of gay politics. During 1997 and 1998, he served as chair of the caucus. He has also been active in a wide range of local and statewide gay rights initiatives. Hunt is currently working on a volume concerning the science and politics of the medical model of homosexuality.